# Fun with the Family™ Tennessee

Praise for the *Fun with the Family™* series

"Enables parents to turn family travel into an exploration "
—Alexandra Kennedy, Editor, *Family Fun*

"Bound to lead you and your kids to fun-filled days,
those times that help compose the
memories of childhood."
—Dorothy Jordon, *Family Travel Times*

# Help Us Keep This Guide Up to Date

Every effort has been made by the author and editors to make this guide as accurate and useful as possible. However, many changes can occur after a guide is published —establishments close, phone numbers change, hiking trails are rerouted, facilities come under new management, etc.

We would love to hear from you concerning your experiences with this guide and how you feel it could be improved and be kept up to date. While we may not be able to respond to all comments and suggestions, we'll take them to heart, and we'll make certain to share them with the author. Please send your comments and suggestions to the following address:

The Globe Pequot Press
Reader Response/Editorial Department
P.O. Box 480
Guilford, CT 06437

Or you may e-mail us at: editorial@GlobePequot.com

Thanks for your input, and happy travels!

INSIDERS'GUIDE®

FUN WITH THE FAMILY™ SERIES

# fun WITH the Family™

## TENNESSEE

HUNDREDS OF IDEAS FOR DAY TRIPS WITH THE KIDS

T. JENSEN LACEY

FOURTH EDITION

INSIDERS'GUIDE®

GUILFORD, CONNECTICUT
AN IMPRINT OF THE GLOBE PEQUOT PRESS

The prices, rates, and hours listed in this guidebook
were confirmed at press time. We recommend, however, that you
call establishments to obtain current information before traveling.

**INSIDERS'GUIDE**®

Text design by Nancy Freeborn and Linda Loiewski
Maps by Rusty Nelson © The Globe Pequot Press
Spot photography throughout © Photodisc

ISSN 1537-3525
ISBN 0-7627-2832-9


Manufactured in the United States of America
Fourth Edition/First Printing

To all Tennesseans—whether this is your residence or
if you're just visiting, while you're here, you're home.

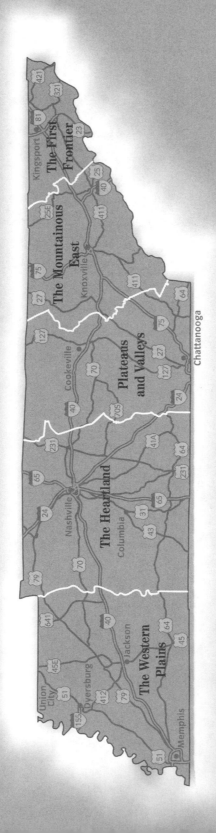

The First Frontier

Kingsport

The Mountainous East

Knoxville

Plateaus and Valleys

Chattanooga

Cookeville

The Heartland

Nashville

Columbia

The Western Plains

Jackson

Dyersburg

Union City

Memphis

# Contents

# Acknowledgments

Thanks to all the kind people of Tennessee who took the time to help make this fourth edition of *Fun with the Family Tennessee* as great as the previous three. From tourism offices to museum guides and folks at the many unexpected roadside attractions, the one thing everyone had in common (besides a love of the Volunteer State) was southern hospitality at its best. Take the time to see even a few of the venues mentioned in this book, and you will agree: Tennessee is a place of endless beauty, fascination, surprises, and charm.

# Introduction

**Kids, in the backseat:** Are we there yet?

**You:** Yes.

**Kids:** Where?

**You:** In Tennessee.

**Kids:** We know that. But *where* are we?

**You:** We're in the beautiful state of Tennessee, the sixteenth state to join the United States. Although no one knows what the name Tennessee means, it is of Cherokee origin. It's called the Volunteer State because of its remarkable record of furnishing volunteers in the War of 1812 and in the Mexican War. It covers 42,146 square miles and is . . .

**Kids:** Please! Cut it out with the history lesson. What are we going to do here? Are you going to bore us again with another state tour? Are we going to have fun?

**You:** There's nothing boring in Tennessee, kids. There are a zillion fun things for us to do as a family.

**Kids, as they giggle:** Yeah, name them.

Well, I may not list a zillion things to do in this book, but there are probably a zillion things to look at if you visit each site I point out as we travel from border to border. I thought I knew the state until I loaded the kids in the car and took off to research the book you are now holding. Along the way I discovered that Tennessee is virtually bulging at the seams with fun things for families to do together.

It's an easy state to get around. At its greatest distance from east to west, it's 480 miles, and from north to south, 115 miles. There are ninety-five counties and six telephone area codes; about half of it lies in the eastern time zone and half in the central zone.

It's also a very beautiful state. The eastern mountainous portion is bordered by the magnificent Appalachian range, and the western delta area is bordered by the mighty Mississippi

## **Welcome** Center

The Tennessee Department of Tourist Development operates fourteen Welcome Centers along Tennessee's interstates. Each has a toll-free telephone system that lets you make hotel, motel, and campground reservations anywhere in the state.

River. In between there is just about everything you can geographically imagine, from plateaus, valleys, majestic waterfalls, and gorges to cypress swamps, hardwood forests, and gently rolling hills and farmland.

There are twenty-nine major lakes and reservoirs, 19,000 miles of rivers and streams, and nearly 3,000 discovered caves, many of which are open to the public. There are more varieties of freshwater fish here than anywhere else in America, and there are more endangered plant and animal species in Tennessee than in any other inland state. In fact, the state's complex geology and mild climate contribute to a habitat of more than 2,700 different kinds of plants.

There are pilgrimages into the woods each spring from one end of the state to another to view some of the more than 400 species of native wildflowers. Each year during April and May, there are more than one hundred events that celebrate flowers and spring.

No matter where you are, you are always within an hour's drive of one of the fifty-three state parks. In those parks there are more than 2,900 developed camping sites and seven luxury resort inns, plus numerous other amenities and activities. In addition, there are four national parks.

Throughout Tennessee the national, state, and local governments have created parks, preserves, and refuges to protect and maintain the scenic and natural wonders of the state. Those same governments also have created laws and policies to protect the early architecture and man-made historic beauties within the state. As a result, there is an abundance of both natural and man-made wonders for families to visit and enjoy.

As you venture from area to area, I suggest you take the Tennessee Scenic Parkway System as often as you can. Specified highways, primarily two-lane roads, stretch 2,944 miles across the state, connecting most of the state parks, major lakes, historical sites, and recreational and entertainment attractions. The parkways are marked with a sign featuring a mockingbird, the state bird. The signs are mounted directly above the state highway designation numbers along the roads at key intersections.

In addition to the fun things you'll discover when traveling the Volunteer State, you'll find that southern hospitality is certainly no myth. It's alive and well in Tennessee. Everywhere you'll go, you'll find people who are friendly and courteous. In fact, they are almost *too* nice!

The state is full of crossroad communities and small town squares. During the warmer

## Tennessee **Highways**

Tennessee has 88,287 miles of highway, including 1,073 miles of interstate. The state maintains 13,797 miles of state routes, representing 16 percent of the total highway miles within Tennessee, which carry 71 percent of the traffic. The interstate system makes up a little more than 1 percent of the total highway mileage but carries 28 percent of all the traffic. I–40 is the main east-west route, linking the major cities of Memphis, Nashville, and Knoxville. North-south interstates are I–24 and I–65, both of which cross in Nashville, and I–75, which travels through Knoxville.

# Tennessee **Highway Patrol**

Here are the numbers of the Tennessee Highway Patrol throughout the state:

Chattanooga (423) 634–6890

Cookeville (931) 526–6143

Jackson (731) 423–5035

Kingsport (Fall Branch District) (423) 348–6144

Knoxville (865) 594–5800

Lawrenceburg (931) 766–1464

Memphis (901) 543–6281

Nashville (615) 741–3181

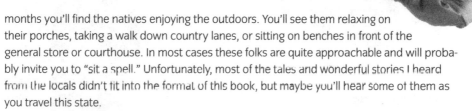

months you'll find the natives enjoying the outdoors. You'll see them relaxing on their porches, taking a walk down country lanes, or sitting on benches in front of the general store or courthouse. In most cases these folks are quite approachable and will proba- bly invite you to "sit a spell." Unfortunately, most of the tales and wonderful stories I heard from the locals didn't fit into the format of this book, but maybe you'll hear some of them as you travel this state.

For the sake of organization, I have divided the state into five areas: the First Frontier, the Mountainous East, Plateaus and Valleys, the Heartland, and the Western Plains. Each is distinct in its geography and in its offerings to visitors. I have devoted a chapter to each region and have given a brief description of the region and a synopsis of its activities and attractions at the beginning of each chapter.

There's a mixture of activities here that most families will be able to enjoy together. In some cases your kids may be too young or too old to participate in everything at each location, but there is something for everyone at practically every stop. Everything is listed by the city or town in which it is located. Where there are only one or two things to do in a town, I've listed two or three towns together. If you can't find the city or town you're inter- ested in, check the index at the back of the book. I have not provided a tour of the state and have not planned out an itinerary for you; I have simply listed the cities and towns throughout the state where you will find fun activities.

Before traveling any great distance to visit any one of my suggestions, you may want to call first to make sure it is open. Many of the smaller facilities are run by volunteers and may shut down for the day if things are slow or if enough volunteers can't be found to operate it. Also, many of the attractions listed are small family-run businesses, and if the family is busy doing other things, the attraction may open late or not open at all on a given day, especially during the winter months.

Although care has been taken to ensure accuracy in all listings, things may change. Admission rates are indicated with a symbol (see Rates for Attractions), but these may have changed by the time you visit. Hours and season of operation also may fluctuate.

# Interstate **Construction**

You've probably been in this situation: You and the family are cruising down the interstate, headed toward a fun place, when you notice orange and white barrels, flashing lights, or signs indicating road work ahead. Before you know it, traffic is at a standstill and you're in the middle of a big traffic jam.

To avoid interstate delays, you might want to call the Tennessee Department of Transportation Interstate Construction Hotline before you head out so you can plan an alternate route if necessary. The toll-free number is (800) 858–6349.

### Rates for Restaurants

| | |
|---|---|
| $ | most entrees less than $10 |
| $$ | most $10 to $15 |
| $$$ | most $16 to $20 |
| $$$$ | most more than $20 |

### Rates for Lodging

| | |
|---|---|
| $ | up to $50 |
| $$ | $51 to $75 |
| $$$ | $76 to $99 |
| $$$$ | $100 and up |

### Rates for Attractions

| | |
|---|---|
| $ | up to $5.00 per person |
| $$ | $5.01 to $10.00 per person |
| $$$ | $10.01 to $15.00 per person |
| $$$$ | $15.01 and up per person |

*Note: Admission rate symbols include prices for children and adults.*

You may want to contact the state tourism department for a colorful and informative vacation guide and map of the state. In the guide you will find a list of local tourism bureaus that will be able to provide even more specific information. Write to the Tennessee Department of Tourist Development, 320 Sixth Avenue North, fifth floor, Rachel Jackson Building, Nashville, TN 37243, or call (615) 741–7994 or (800) GO2–TENN. You can also order the vacation guide online at www.TNvacation.com.

Be careful, wear sunblock, and buckle up. Happy trails!

# Attractions Key

The following is a key to the icons found throughout the text.

| | | | |
|---|---|---|---|
| **SWIMMING** | | **FOOD** | |
| **BOATING / BOAT TOUR** | | **LODGING** | |
| **HISTORIC SITE** | | **CAMPING** | |
| **HIKING / WALKING** | | **MUSEUMS** | |
| **FISHING** | | **PERFORMING ARTS** | |
| **BIKING** | | **SPORTS/ATHLETICS** | |
| **AMUSEMENT PARK** | | **PICNICKING** | |
| **HORSEBACK RIDING** | | **PLAYGROUND** | |
| **SKIING/WINTER SPORTS** | | **SHOPPING** | |
| **PARK** | | **PLANTS/GARDENS/NATURE TRAILS** | |
| **ANIMAL VIEWING** | | **FARMS** | |

# the First Frontier

L egendary explorer Daniel Boone was seen a great deal around here more than 200 years ago, when this part of the state was considered America's new frontier. He was among the many adventurers who blazed the trails across the Appalachian Mountains that eventually led the way to the creation of some of the earliest settlements outside the original thirteen colonies.

Today, as the easternmost part of the state, the area is a harmonious and beautiful blend of old and new. Dense forests still cover much of the area, with the southern and eastern boundaries set by the Appalachian Mountains.

Jonesborough, the state's oldest city, is located here, and nearby Limestone is the birthplace of the icon of the American frontier, Davy Crockett. If you like visiting places associated with historic and legendary figures, you'll have a great deal to do around here.

In addition to Boone and Crockett, you'll be exploring the same streets on which U.S. presidents Andrew Jackson and Andrew Johnson took their daily walks. You'll also visit sites dedicated to famous people ranging from Maybelle Carter, the matriarch of the famous singing Carter family, to Archie Campbell, the funny barber on the long-running television show *Hee Haw*.

If legendary figures don't fit into your plans, how about a water park, a miniature golf course, a hands-on museum, a nature trail, or a wildlife park? The area has it all.

But enough promises. Let's begin our trek across the First Frontier so you can enjoy it for yourselves.

## Amazing Tennessee Facts

There is some debate about the origin of the name Tennessee. One theory is that the name originated from the old Yuchi Indian word *tana-see*, which means "old town." In the 1700s, white settlers who were traveling in the area associated the word with the name of a Cherokee Indian village and the name of a river in the Cherokee territory.

# THE FIRST FRONTIER

# Bulls Gap

Named for local gun maker John Bull, who settled here in the mid-1790s, this natural gap in Bays Mountain became a strategic location when the railroad was completed here in 1858. During the Civil War both the North and the South wanted to control the railroad through the mountains; as a result, Bulls Gap was the site of several skirmishes. If you're traveling in the Greeneville, Jonesborough, Limestone, or Rogersville areas, you might want to make a detour to Bulls Gap.

### Archie Campbell Tourism Complex (ages 10 and up)
**139 South Main Street; (423) 235–5216 (City Hall). Call in advance. Free.**

Even though the area has more than 200 years of history and architecture going for it, the event that put it on the map more than anything else was the birth of comedian Archie Campbell, who went on to become a member of the Grand Ole Opry in Nashville and to star in the long-running television variety show *Hee Haw*. He died in 1987.

Today, a reconstruction of his birthplace is in the town park, next to City Hall, alongside the Caboose Museum and the Quillen Store building. The house is not open on a regular basis, so if you want to tour the home, call first, and someone from City Hall will unlock it for you. A fun time to visit is over Labor Day weekend, when Archie Campbell Days take place.

### Bulls Gap Historic District (ages 8 and up)
**Downtown Old Bulls Gap; (423) 235–2186. Walking tour is free.**

Take a trip back in time with a stroll down Bulls Gap's 1800s Main Street. The street features more than two dozen historic structures, ranging from a country store to Gilley's Hotel. If you're out this way the first Sunday in December, you'll get to see an old-fashioned Christmas parade.

### Volunteer Speedway (ages 10 and up)
**14095 Andrew Johnson Highway; (423) 235–5020. Gates open 4:00 P.M. Web site: www .volunteerspeedway.com. $$–$$$.**

Race fans young and old alike will enjoy watching races held every Saturday on what is called the "world's fastest ⅜-mile, high-banked dirt track." Races include hobby stock, four-cylinder, super and limited model, and UMP modified cars.

## Where to Stay

**Comfort Inn,** 50 Speedway Lane; (423) 235–9111 or (800) 228–5150. Located off I–81 at exit 23; a pool and laundry facilities, free HBO, and a free continental breakfast. Expect rates to be higher during the Bristol Motor Speedway's spring and fall races. $$

## For More Information

**Rogersville/Hawkins County Chamber of Commerce,** 107 East Main Street, Suite 100, Rogersville, TN 37857; (423) 272–2186; www.hawkinscounty.org. Open 9:00 A.M. to 4:00 P.M., Monday through Friday.

# Greeneville

There are probably hundreds of towns and cities across the country named Greenville, but this is the only one that has that middle *e* in its name.

The sixteen counties that now make up the eastern part of Tennessee tried to form their own state between the years 1785 and 1788. They chose to call it Franklin; Greeneville was its capital. Leaders met and created a bill of rights and requested that North Carolina officials allow the new state. North Carolina refused, but under the leadership of John Sevier, Franklin operated like a state with its own assembly, administered its own justice, and forged its own treaties with local tribes. Today, the downtown area of Greeneville offers a walking tour of more than twenty-five historic structures. The entire historic district is on the National Register of Historic Places.

## Greeneville, with an *E*

Greeneville is named for Revolutionary War hero Gen. Nathanael Greene.

### Andrew Johnson National Historic Site (ages 10 and up)

**College and Depot Streets; (423) 638–3551. All attractions open daily except Thanksgiving, Christmas, and New Year's. Admission to visitor center and homestead are both free.**

The city's favorite son, Andrew Johnson, came to the area in 1826 when he was eighteen years old to establish himself as a tailor. A few years later, Johnson left Greeneville to become the seventeenth president of the United States. He didn't forget his roots, however, and he kept a residence and lived here with his family throughout his life.

The Andrew Johnson National Historic Site in the downtown area highlights Johnson's Greeneville years. His small tailor shop is preserved inside the site's visitor center. Across the street is the brick home in which he lived from 1831 to 1851. Over on Main Street, the house where he lived while he was president has also been preserved. The cemetery where he and his family are buried is a few miles away at the edge of town.

The visitor center and one of the homes have a great deal of Johnson memorabilia on display.

### Andrew Johnson Library and Museum (ages 10 and up)

**At Tusculum College just off State Route 107; (423) 636–7348. Open 9:00 A.M. to 5:00 P.M. Monday through Friday. Admission: $ (young children admitted free). (If you plan to visit the college's Doak House Museum, you can get a special rate.)**

If you want to find out more about Andrew Johnson, the city's Tusculum College, founded in 1794—making it the oldest college south of the Ohio River and west of the Allegheny Mountains—should be your next stop. The college's Andrew Johnson Library and Museum is the state's largest presidential library and houses a huge collection of the former president's papers, books, and memorabilia.

### Doak House Museum (ages 6 and up)

**At Tusculum College just off State Route 107; (423) 638–1111 or (423) 636–8554. Open 9:00 A.M. to 5:00 P.M. Monday through Friday. Admission: $. (If you're also visiting the college's Andrew Johnson Library and Museum, you can get a special rate.)**

A good place to learn about the history of religion and education in east Tennessee, the home of Tusculum College cofounder Samuel Doak features numerous Doak family artifacts from the mid-1800s, educational and religious artifacts, and documents from northeast Tennessee. Doak House offers a good example of the building materials and techniques of the time. The museum is a popular place for school group tours.

## Other Things to See and Do

**Dickson-Williams Mansion** (ages 8 and up), 108 North Irish Street; (423) 787–7746 or (423) 638–4111 (Greene County Partnership). Built in 1815, this home was called the Showplace of East Tennessee. Davy Crockett, Andrew Johnson, James K. Polk, and the Marquis de Lafayette were among its distinguished guests. During the Civil War the house served as headquarters for both Union and Confederate officers. Open by appointment only. Admission: $

**Historic Greeneville District** (all ages), Main Street; (423) 638–4111 (Greene County Partnership). There are more than twenty-five buildings in the Historic Greeneville District, including a replica of the capitol of the "Lost State of Franklin." Guided tours are available.

**Nathanael Greene Museum** (all ages), 101 West McKee Street; (423) 636–1558. Open 10:00 A.M. to 4:00 P.M. Tuesday through Saturday. **Free,** but donations are accepted. Learn about the first one hundred years of Greeneville/Greene County history at the city and county heritage museum. There's a special gallery with "touchable" exhibits for children. Located on the corner opposite the Andrew Johnson Homestead.

**Appalachian Trail** (ages 5 and up), 4900 Asheville Highway; (423) 638–4109. A stretch of the Appalachian Trail known as the longest footpath in the world begins at the Waterville exit off I-40 in Cocke County and follows the Tennessee/North Carolina state line. There are a number of places where you can arrange a pickup if you have more than one car, as this particular stretch is 25 miles long. The hike is **free** but you may want to call the Ranger Station (423–638–4109) to check on trail conditions before you go.

## Where to Eat

**Stan's Bar-B-Q,** 2620 East Andrew Johnson Highway; (423) 787–0017. Dine inside or pick up an order to go at the drive-through. Located about a mile from Tusculum College, Stan's serves barbecue ribs, sandwiches, and plates, as well as steaks. There's a children's menu. $–$$

**Tannery Downtown,** 117 East Depot Street; (423) 638–2772. Gourmet sandwiches, soups, and salads are on the menu at Tannery Downtown, open for lunch Monday through Friday. There's a children's menu, too. The restaurant is housed in the Tannery Building, one of downtown Greeneville's historic structures. $

## Where to Stay

**General Morgan Inn and Conference Center,** 111 North Main Street; (423) 787–1000 or (800) 223–2679. Located in historic downtown Greeneville, this hotel was created from four interconnected railroad hotels dating from the late 1800s. Inside, the hotel appears much as it did then. The fifty-two guest rooms are traditionally appointed, and there are plenty of modern amenities, including room service, cable TV, and workout privileges at a local facility. Brumley's, the hotel's fine-dining restaurant, serves continental and southern cuisine for breakfast, lunch, and dinner. $$$–$$$$

**Comfort Inn,** 1790 East Andrew Johnson Highway; (423) 639–4185. This two-story, ninety-room property offers rooms with either an exterior or an interior entrance.

Outdoor pool, fitness facilitiy, breakfast included in rate. $–$$

**Kinser Park,** 650 Kinser Park Lane (off Highway 70 S and East Allen's Bridge Road); (423) 639–5912. Open 7:00 A.M. to 11:00 P.M. April through October; closed November through March. Admission is **free.**

One of the nicest places in which to park your RV while staying in the area is Kinser Park, a 250-acre, city-and-county-owned facility that offers more than one hundred campsites overlooking the Nolichucky River. Its central location and its facilities make the park a great family place to spend a few days while you explore the First Frontier.

This place is almost a one-stop resort by itself. You'll find a swimming pool, miniature golf course, large playground, water slide, tennis courts, golf course, driving range, and boat ramp access to the river.

## For More Information

**Greene County Partnership,** 115 Academy Street, Greeneville, TN 37743; (423) 638–4111; www.GreenCountyPartnership .com. Open 8:00 A.M. to 5:00 P.M. Monday through Friday.

# Erwin

### Erwin National Fish Hatchery (all ages)
520 Federal Hatchery Road; (423) 743–4712. Public pavilion and grounds open daily until dark; visitor center open 7:00 A.M. to 3:30 P.M. Monday through Friday. **Free.**

Be sure to visit the fish hatchery; it's quite an operation. Established in 1894, the hatchery raises four strains of rainbow trout, which annually produce eighteen million eggs that are shipped to hatcheries across the country.

### Unicoi County Heritage Museum (all ages)
1715 Old Johnson City Highway (Highway 107); (423) 743–9449. Open daily May through October, weekends November and December; closed January through March. **Free,** but donations are welcome.

The Unicoi County Heritage Museum, located on the grounds of the National Fish Hatchery, is loaded with local and county artifacts and memorabilia, including newspaper accounts of Murderous Mary, an elephant that was tried for murder in 1916, found guilty, and hanged.

## Unicoi County Apple Festival (all ages)

**Downtown Erwin; (423) 743–3000 (Chamber of Commerce). First Friday and Saturday in October. Free.**

A fun event to catch in Erwin each fall is the Unicoi County Apple Festival. For nearly thirty years, this crafts and entertainment festival has drawn more than 90,000 people to Erwin. It has been consistently named one of the Southeastern Tourism Society's "Top 20 Events of the Southeast" and is a two-time winner of the NETA Pinnacle Award. The festival includes continuous music and dancing, handmade crafts, the Blue Ridge Pottery Club Show and Sale, various local items, and a sanctioned 4-mile foot race.

The area around Erwin and Unicoi County is apple-growing country at its finest, and during apple season you'll find a great variety of the wonderful fruit on sale throughout the region. Many orchards have small fruit stands along the highway, and some will allow you to walk through the trees to pick your own. To find specific orchard locations and where you can pick your own as a family adventure, call the University Agricultural Extension Service at (423) 743-9584.

## Nolichucky River White-Water Rafting (ages 5 and up)

**(423) 743–3000 (Chamber of Commerce).**

If it's true family adventure you're looking for, you'll probably be interested in doing a bit of white-water rafting while you're in this part of the state. Several rivers in eastern Tennessee are ranked quite highly by white-water aficionados. The Nolichucky offers a mix of adventures from wild to calm. Many companies offer various trips down the rivers, and most limit the minimum age of participants. For safety purposes, it just makes sense.

Cherokee Adventures, located on Highway 81 (2000 Jonesborough Road) on the Nolichucky River, offers a wide variety of rafting opportunity. The company offers a selection of river trips for ages five and over. Water conditions range from class IV rapids down to a gentle drift. There are also hayrides for the younger kids, mountain biking opportunities, camping for customers, and a restaurant.

A brochure explains all the offerings. Reservations are recommended. "Most of our trips are full, so it's best to reserve a time," one of the guides told me. He added that there are times when walk-ins can be accommodated. "But don't count on it," he noted. Other companies that raft the Nolichucky River include USA Raft (423–743–7111), Nantahala Outdoor Center (828–488–2175), and High Mountain Expeditions (828–295–4200).

# Amazing Tennessee Facts

Erwin is Tennessee's largest valley town. It began as a railroad village some one hundred years ago. Today Erwin is still a railroad town. You can see the CSX rail yards in full operation, linking the Great Lakes to the southern coast of the United States.

## Other Things to See and Do

Antiquing is a popular pastime in Erwin. The following are some popular shops. Most feature collectible Blue Ridge pottery, which was made from about 1920 to 1957:

**Main Street Mall,** 105 South Main Avenue; (423) 743–7810.

**Stegall's Pottery,** 200 Nolichucky Avenue; (423) 743–3227.

**Valley Beautiful Antique Mall,** 109 South Main Avenue; (423) 743–4136.

## Where to Eat

**Rivers Edge Smoke House,** 2000 Jonesborough Road; (423) 743–3713. Overlooking the beautiful Nolichucky River and a huge cliff known as the Devil's Looking Glass, you can get barbecue and pizza, salads and charbroiled burgers. They also have a children's menu. It's a very relaxed atmosphere, and you can eat at picnic tables outside if you like. $

**Park Place Restaurant,** 1201 Rock Creek Road; (423) 743–2074. Home cooking is the specialty at Park Place Restaurant. The hearty breakfasts and daily lunch specials are filling and affordable. Youngsters can order from their own menu. $

## Where to Stay

**Best Southern Motel,** 1315 Asheville Highway; (423) 743–6438. Lots of budget-minded families stay at this fifteen-room motel at the edge of downtown Erwin. $

**Family Inns of America—Buffalo Mountain Resort,** Route 2, 100 Country Club Drive, Unicoi; (423) 743–9181. About a five-minute drive from both Erwin and Johnson City and about twenty minutes from Jonesborough. Rooms have views of Buffalo Mountain and the Cherokee National Forest. Amenities include the "largest swimming pool in Tennessee" (Olympic-size plus 10 inches), free continental breakfast, free HBO, an on-site family-style restaurant. $

**Holiday Inn Express,** 2002 Temple Hill Road; (423) 743–4100 or (800) HOLIDAY. Some of the sixty-one rooms at this hotel overlook the Nolichucky River, popular with white-water rafters. Free continental breakfast, in-room movies, guest laundry facilities, hot tub. Located a half mile from an Appalachian Trail trailhead. $$–$$$

**Super 8 Motel,** 1101 Buffalo Street; (423) 743–0200 or (800) 800–8000. Relatively new, with large deluxe rooms, free continental breakfast, micro-fridge, cable TV, free HBO, free local calls. Rates vary depending on season. $–$$$$

## For More Information

**Unicoi County Chamber of Commerce,**
P.O. Box 713, 100 South Main Avenue, Erwin,
TN 37650; (423) 743–3000, www.unicoi

county.org. Open 8:00 A.M. to 5:00 P.M. Monday through Friday, 9:00 A.M. to 1:00 P.M. Saturday.

# Limestone

### Davy Crockett Birthplace State Park (all ages)
**1245 Davy Crockett Park Road, 3 miles off Highway 11 East; (423) 257–2167. Park open daily 8:00 A.M. to 9:30 P.M., 8:00 A.M. to dusk Memorial Day through Labor Day. Office and museum open 8:00 A.M. to 4:30 P.M. Monday through Friday remainder of year. Free.**

Most of us grew up believing that Davy Crockett was born on a mountaintop in Tennessee and killed him a bear when he was only three. Walt Disney's representation of the legend of Davy Crockett made the native Tennessean one of the best-known historic figures of all times.

First of all, no, he wasn't born on a mountaintop. He was born in a little log cabin along the banks of the Nolichucky River, near the mouth of Limestone Creek. The bear-killing story is probably also legend, so you can believe it if you want to.

Today, in the Davy Crockett Birthplace State Park, an accurate historical reproduction of that tiny log cabin sits where the original structure once stood. A cornerstone from the original cabin is on display. The site honors the August 17, 1786, birth of David Crockett, who went on to become "the King of the Wild Frontier."

Though it all started here for David (he never signed his name Davy), several areas of the state claim him as their legendary own. He was born here in the east, ran a gristmill in the center of the state, and was elected to Congress from western Tennessee.

The park offers a campground, picnic area, swimming pool, and visitor center.

Before heading into the park, you might want to visit the little village of Limestone and buy a few picnic supplies at the convenience market at the corner of Bridge Street and Opie Arnold Road. There you'll find gas, groceries, an amusement center, and a video rental store. (However, they didn't have what we *really* wanted before going into the park—coonskin caps!)

## A Natural Choice

The town of Limestone was first known as Freedom. Later it was called Kleppers Depot in honor of Jacob Klepper, who donated land for a train depot on the East Tennessee, Virginia, and Georgia Railroad line.

During the Civil War, the name Limestone came into use, possibly because of Limestone Creek, which runs through the area, and from the abundance of natural limestone rock in the area.

## Where to Stay

**Davy Crockett Birthplace State Park Campground,** 1245 Davy Crockett Park Road; (423) 257–2167. This campground on the banks of the Nolichucky River is inside the park. It offers seventy-three campsites, some with full RV hookups, water, and electricity. It also has a bathhouse and a playground, and if you hold a current fishing license, you can fish from the riverbank. Open year-round. $

## For More Information

**Greene County Partnership,** 115 Academy Street, Greeneville, TN 37743; (423) 638–4111; www.GreeneCountyPartnership. com. Open 8:00 A.M. to 5:00 P.M. Monday through Friday.

# Jonesborough

Six miles south of Johnson City, just off Highway 11 East, is the historic town of Jonesborough. What a beautiful place this is. If you want to know what the "good old days" really looked like, all you need to do is drive through the center of town on Main Street, originally called the Great Stage Road. Founded in 1779, Jonesborough is Tennessee's oldest incorporated town, and the restored downtown area offers a rare glimpse into a town of a century ago.

By the 1960s the downtown area looked like a ghost town, with businesses and customers having gone off to nearby malls. The city leaders began an aggressive, multimillion-dollar historic renovation program that brought the area back to life with style and dignity. As a result, Jonesborough became the first town in Tennessee to be added to the National Register of Historic Places.

The historic district now has a fun mix of shops, historic homesteads, and restaurants. There's something in the district to please everyone.

### Historic Jonesborough Visitors Center (all ages)

117 Boone Street; (423) 753–1010. **Open 8:00 A.M. to 5:00 P.M. Monday through Friday, 10:00 A.M. to 5:00 P.M. Saturday and Sunday. Free.**

A good place to start your Jonesborough journey is at the visitor center. There is an on-site gift shop filled with items made in the area. The folks there can set you up with a walking-tour guide map as well as an architectural primer pamphlet, *An Introduction to Building Watching*.

### Times & Tales or Strolling Stories Tours (ages 10 and up)

P.O. Box 765; (423) 753–9882. **Tours are by reservation for groups of six or more. A meeting place for the tour is determined when reservations are made for the Times and Tales Tour. Admission: $–$$.**

If you would like a personal tour of the area, you can sign up for the Strolling Stories tour or the Times & Tales tours, which will give you a look inside historic homes and buildings. The guides are wonderful storytellers, and through their stories and anecdotes, history seems to come alive. While these tours are more suitable for adults than for children, kid-friendly tours are available at the Jonesborough-Washington County History Museum. The Strolling Stories tour leaves the visitor center Tuesday through Saurday at 10:00 A.M. No reservations are needed.

# Building Tennessee's **First Town**

The town of Jonesborough was authorized by the North Carolina Assembly in 1779, seventeen years before Tennessee became a state. As the seat of Washington County, which at the time encompassed all of what is now Tennessee, Jonesborough was the first town seat west of the Appalachian Mountains.

The town was named for Willie Jones of North Carolina, described as a patriot, statesman, and friend of the westward-bound pioneers.

From the very beginning, building restrictions were placed on the town to ensure that Jonesborough would not become a disorganized group of ramshackle cabins and huts. The original hundred acres were to be laid out in regular streets and one-acre lots, each of which sold for $75. One lot was set aside for the courthouse and public square.

Within three years of purchasing a lot, each property owner was required to build a brick, stone, or frame house, 20 feet long and 16 feet wide, with a brick or stone chimney.

Today Jonesborough appears much as it did in its early years. One Hollywood director called the town's Main Street the most perfect nineteenth-century business district façade in America. Strolling along Jonesborough's brick sidewalks under antique lighting, among the historic buildings, you can imagine what the town was like back then.

### Jonesborough-Washington County History Museum (all ages)
**117 Boone Street; (423) 753–1015. Open 8:00 A.M. to 5:00 P.M. Monday through Friday, 10:00 A.M. to 5:00 P.M. Saturday and Sunday. Admission: $.**

The county's history museum is located in the visitor center. The museum features artifacts, photographs, and changing exhibits that take visitors from pioneer times through the twenty-first century. You can tour the restored 1886 Oak Hill School, which served grades one through eight until 1954. The school won the Tennessee Association of Museums' Award of Excellence in 2000.

Guided tours of the museum and a wetlands preserve, offered through the museum, are more suited for younger children than are the Times & Tales tours.

## Historic Jonesborough Carriage Tours (all ages)

**Carriages depart in front of the Chester Inn on Main Street; (423) 543–2511. Open 11:00 A.M. to 6:00 P.M. Tuesday through Sunday from April through December. Reservations required during other months and before or after regular hours. Rates: $–$$.**

If you'd like to see the historic area without walking it, carriage tours are available from Historic Jonesborough Carriage Tours. You'll be carried through town in an antique carriage drawn by Belgian draft horses.

## Chester Inn (all ages)

**116 West Main Street, (423) 753–2171**

The Chester Inn, a facility that dates to 1797, has hosted presidents, authors, and other famous people through the years. The young Andrew Jackson stayed here in 1788 while working on his law degree. The building is now owned by the state, and it houses the National Association for the Preservation and Perpetuation of Storytelling. The Chester Inn is currently used only for administrative offices but is a visual and historical point of interest, and you can walk the grounds around it.

## Amazing Tennessee Facts

The world's first periodicals devoted to the abolition of slavery were published in Jonesborough. In 1819 the *Manumission Intelligencer* was published, followed the next year by the *Emancipator*.

## National Storytelling Festival (all ages)

**(423) 753–2171 or (800) 952–8392; www.storytellingfestival.net. Three day admission $$$$; call for information on single-day rates.**

Since 1973 people from all over have visited Jonesborough during the first full weekend of October to attend the National Storytelling Festival. Today the town is recognized as the birthplace of the storytelling renaissance in America. While children especially are enchanted by storytelling, a trip to this festival will win over just about any adult as well. The three-day festival showcases the best storytellers, stories, and traditions from across the world. Some 10,000 people attend each year.

## Wetlands Water Park (all ages)

**1521 Persimmon Ridge Road; (423) 753–1553 or (888) 662–1885. Open daily from Memorial Day through Labor Day. Call for rates.**

The best way to cool off in this part of the state is at the Wetlands Water Park, just

outside of town. The park features water slides, flumes, and a lazy river where you can float the day away while sunning atop an inner tube. Boardwalk-style nature trails go out over the adjacent natural wetlands area. Turn the kids loose, get yourself a nice cool drink, and then sit back and relax.

## The International Storytelling Center (all ages)

116 Main Street; (800) 952–8392. Open daily 8:00 A.M. to 5:00 P.M. **Free.**

Located right next to the Chester Inn, this newly built center is the international home to storytelling, with an interpretive center where visitors can enjoy storytelling, a small theater with live performances at various times, and a storytelling gift shop. There are two huge meeting rooms with beautiful patios and gardens.

## Teller-in-Residence Concerts (all ages)

116 West Main Street; (423) 753–2171. Performances daily June through October at 2:00 P.M. $.

The International Storytelling Center features daily performances by nationally renowned storytellers, who come here from across the country to share their tales both tall and true.

## Other Things to See and Do

Many of the restored historic structures in town house various shops. An old saloon building on Courthouse Square now houses The Crafty Peddler, a country store offering local crafts. The Old Town Hall at 144 East Main Street has more than thirty shops inside. In addition, there are quilt shops, antiques shops, and the Cherry Tree Craft Shop at 111 East Main Street, which carries the work of 200 regional craftspersons. Jonesborough Art Glass on 101 East Main Street and another gallery called Acorns and Ivy on 100 North Cherokee Street are new art galleries featuring fine art from regional artists.

## Where to Eat

**Bistro 105,** 105 East Main Street; (423) 753–9009. You'll find salads, quiche, and burgers on the menu here. Open daily for lunch and dinner. $

**Main Street Cafe,** 117½ West Main Street; (423) 753–2460. Housed in the old 1920s post office building, Main Street Cafe has been a favorite since it opened in 1982. The menu features fresh grilled items, sandwiches, salads, and homemade desserts. The children's menu offers such kid-pleasers as the Main Street Dog and a variety of peanut butter concoctions. Open Monday through Saturday. $

**Old Sweet Shop,** 129 East Main Street; (423) 753–8851. Open daily 11:30 A.M. to 5:00 P.M. Old-fashioned ice cream parlor with old-time malts, sundaes, and ice cream. Limited lunch menu with soups and salads. The decor brings in the children, and the food keeps them coming back. $

**The Cranberry Thistle,** 103 East Main Street; (423) 753–0090. This place is one of the locals' favorites, and with good reason. It's reasonable and has daily specials, especially for dinner. Try one of the gourmet coffees after a good meal, while the kids enjoy homemade dessert. $

**Harmony Grocery Restaurant,** 1121 Painter Road; (423) 348—8000. This unique dining establishment is housed in an original nineteenth–century general store and features classic New Orleans–style cuisine. $–$$

## Where to Stay

**Blaire-Moore House,** 201 West Main Street; (423) 753–0044 or (888) 453–0044. Built in 1832 and listed on the National Register of Historic Places, this bed-and-breakfast offers two guest bedrooms and one guest suite. Each room has a private bath and porch. A gourmet breakfast is served each morning. $$$–$$$$

**Eureka Hotel,** 127 West Main Street; (877) 734–6100. Recently renovated to accentuate the character of this 200-year-old inn, Eureka has sixteen rooms uniquely decorated with modern amenities but late-1870s decor and charm. Continental breakfast. $$$$

**Franklin House Bed and Breakfast,** 116 Franklin Avenue; (423) 753–3819. Restored 1840s home, with three guest rooms, private baths, and a guest apartment available. Full country breakfast. $$$–$$$$

**Hawley House Bed & Breakfast,** 114 East Woodrow Avenue; (423) 753– 8002. Jonesborough doesn't have any motels or hotels, but there are several bed-and-breakfast inns. One is the Hawley House. This log,

stone, and frame house is the oldest house in Jonesborough. Built in 1793, the house offers three bedrooms, private baths, and a full breakfast. Enjoy antique furnishings and a wraparound porch. $$$–$$$$

**May-Ledbetter House Bed and Breakfast,** 130 West Main Street; (423) 753–7568. A lovingly restored 1904 Victorian house, with two guest rooms with private baths. Full country breakfast, patio, gardens, and a wraparound porch overlooking historic Main Street. $$$–$$$$

**Cherokee Mountain Llama Bed and Breakfast,** 201 Charlie Hicks Road; (423) 913–2781. This pet-friendly bed-and-breakfast is on twenty acres of mountain ridge, with fantastic valley views, hiking trails, and gardens. Five miles outside Jonesborough proper, it offers family-size suites, some with sitting rooms and all with private baths and a guest lounge. Rock a while on the porch or go visit the five curious llamas. Enjoy gourmet breakfasts and afternoon snacks. Cribs are available for your little ones. $$$–$$$$

## For More Information

**Historic Jonesborough Tourism Cooperative,** 111 West Main Street, Suite 202, Jonesborough, TN 37659; (877) 913–1612; www.historicjonesborough.com. Open 8:30 A.M. to 5:00 P.M. Monday through Friday.

# Johnson City

The largest of northeast Tennessee's Tri-Cities, which include Bristol and Kingsport, Johnson City offers several attractions for families traveling the First Frontier. Its location—7 miles from Jonesborough, 7 miles from Elizabethton, and 24 miles from Bristol—makes it a convenient destination.

Johnson City is surrounded by thousands of acres of forested mountain land and offers quite a few recreational opportunities.

### Hands On! Regional Museum (all ages)

315 East Main Street; (423) 434–HAND. Open 9:00 A.M. to 5:00 P.M. Tuesday through Friday, 10:00 A.M. to 5:00 P.M. Saturday, 1:00 to 5:00 P.M. Sunday, 9:00 A.M. to 5:00 P.M. Monday, June through August; closed Monday, September through May. $; free for children under 3.

Please touch. You're not told to do that in too many museums, but it's encouraged here. Unlike most touchy-feely museums, this one is not totally dedicated to the sciences, nor is it only for kids. I think I had more fun here than did all the other kids combined.

Simply put, this is an interactive museum of the arts, humanities, and science all in a fun and colorful environment. It's a place that stimulates discovery, thought, and understanding. Visitors can make a project with recycled materials to take with them when they leave, or they can take apart the life-size models of the human body and put them back together to see how everything fits.

In the Kid's Bank, the little ones can withdraw Hands On! money from an account or do their banking at an automated teller machine. Or the entire family can climb aboard the Ark and meet animals from around the world, visit the Kindermart to buy groceries, or take an imaginary flight in a real Cessna airplane. In all, there are more than two hours' worth of activities to educate and entertain the entire family.

In addition to its own displays, traveling exhibits are presented here throughout the year and special seasonal events are held, all in the name of fun and education.

## Amazing
# Tennessee Facts

Johnson City has long been a center for higher education. The state's first school, Washington Academy, was established in Johnson City in 1780, and today Johnson City is home to East Tennessee State University, the ETSU James H. Quillen College of Medicine, Milligan College, and the Emmanuel School of Religion.

### Tipton-Haynes State Historic Site (ages 8 and up)

2620 South Roan Street; (423) 926–3631. Open daily April through October; 10:00 A.M. to 5:00 P.M. Monday through Saturday, 2:00 to 5:00 P.M. Sunday. November through March, open 10:00 A.M. to 4:00 P.M. Monday through Friday. Closed Thanksgiving, day after Thanksgiving, and December 21 to January 8. $.

Johnson City resident John Tipton was a member of the 1776 constitutional convention, and today, the home he built in 1784 is a significant piece of restored history. Through the years the original house and the farm complex surrounding it were home to Tipton, his son John Tipton Jr., and Confederate senator Landon Carter Haynes, whose lives represent the history of this part of the state from 1783 to 1870.

A cave and a spring are located on the property, which made it a perfect resting and hiding place for native hunters. The first white explorers in the area followed a buffalo trail through the property, and it is believed that Daniel Boone set up a hunting camp near the spring.

Tipton did not agree with some of the other local landowners and did not endorse the idea of making Franklin a state. That point alone created quite a problem between him and John Sevier, the main proponent of Franklin's statehood. The Battle of the Lost State of Franklin took place on the property during the winter of 1788.

Known today as the Tipton-Haynes State Historic Site, the property has ten original and restored buildings. Additionally, the cave can still be visited and an herb garden and a nature trail are open for strolling. Spinning demonstrations take place in the loom house.

Other buildings include a double corncrib barn, a smokehouse, a law office, and the original "necessary" house.

# Brick by **Brick**

While exploring the Johnson City area, you may notice many beautiful brick sculptures. These are produced by Johnny Hagerman, a brick sculptor for General Shale Brick. General Shale, headquartered in Johnson City, is the nation's leading brick manufacturer.

The company dates to 1928, when the merger of two area brick plants created General Shale Products Corporation, a small company that manufactured fifty-five million bricks in its first year of operation. In 1997 General Shale's brick production capacity was one billion bricks per year. The company has plants throughout the South and Midwest and manufactures bricks in 300 different colors and textures.

## Buffalo Mountain Park (all ages)
**High Ridge Road (off University Parkway in south Johnson City); (423) 283–5815. Open year-round, but closes during rainy and snowy conditions. Free.**

The Johnson City Parks and Recreation Department operates two very diverse parks in its district, Buffalo Mountain Park and Winged Deer Park. Buffalo Mountain Park is a 650-acre nature preserve featuring 14 miles of hiking trails, scenic overlooks, and easily accessible picnic areas. If you'd like a guide to go along and point out the various flora and fauna, you can make special arrangements with the rangers.

**Winged Deer Park** (all ages)
**Highway 11 E in north Johnson City; (423) 283–5815. Open daily. Free.**

Winged Deer Park, a city-owned recreational facility, is a 200-acre sports complex featuring softball and soccer fields. There's a concessions stand as well. The best thing this park has to offer to the traveling family is its 2 miles of paved and lighted woodland walking trails. It's an easy walk, and there's a lot to be seen from the path. This is an excellent birding area, too.

## Other Things to See and Do

**B. Carroll Reece Museum** (ages 10 and up), Gilbreath Circle, on the campus of East Tennessee State University; (423) 439–4392. Open 9:00 A.M. to 4:00 P.M. Monday through Wednesday and Friday, 9:00 A.M. to 7:00 P.M. Thursday, and 1:00 to 4:00 P.M. Saturday and Sunday. This art and history museum has three permanent galleries and three galleries that feature temporary exhibits. **Free.**

**The Mall at Johnson City,** 2011 North Roan Street; (423) 282–5312. Open 10:00 A.M. to 9:00 P.M. Monday through Saturday and 1:00 to 6:00 P.M. Sunday. With more than eighty stores, this mall is bound to have what you're looking for.

**Museum of Ancient Brick** (ages 10 and up), 3211 North Roan Street; (423) 282–4661. Open 8:00 A.M. to 5:00 P.M. Monday through Friday. Several displays of brick, some dating to biblical times, are featured at this museum, located in the office reception area of brick manufacturer General Shale Brick. **Free.**

**U.S. Flea Market Mall,** 3501 Bristol Highway; (423) 854–4860. Open 9:00 A.M. to 6:00 P.M. Friday through Sunday. Weekend shoppers will find plenty of bargains here.

## Where to Eat

**The Firehouse Restaurant,** 627 West Walnut Street; (423) 929–7377. A fun place to have lunch or dinner any day of the week, this restaurant opened in 1979 in old firehouse Station No. 2, built in 1930. Firefighting memorabilia, including an antique fire truck, fills the space. The Firehouse serves hickory-smoked barbecue, ribs, and great steaks and burgers. There's a nice children's menu. $–$$

## Where to Stay

**Comfort Inn 1900,** South Roan Street; (423) 928–9600. Relatively new hotel with forty-three rooms on two floors; several nearby restaurants. Banquet and meeting rooms available, fax machine on premises for guest use. Some rooms have an iron and ironing board and a refrigerator, and all rooms have a coffeemaker and a microwave oven. Outdoor pool, free continental breakfast. $–$$$$

**Doubletree Hotel Johnson City,** 211 Mockingbird Lane; (423) 929–2000. Comfortable hotel with 186 guest rooms, a sports-themed restaurant and lounge, a business center for working travelers, a concierge level, and a pool. Within walking distance to a shopping mall, restaurants, and a movie theater. $$$

**Hampton Inn,** 508 North State of Franklin Road; (423) 929–8000. Three-story hotel. Some rooms have a microwave, a refrigerator, a hot tub, and a desk. Free breakfast buffet, twenty-four-hour fruit and beverage service in the lobby, free HBO, and a pool. $$

## For More Information

**Johnson City Convention and Visitors Bureau,** P.O. Drawer 180, 603 East Market Street, Johnson City, TN 37605; (423) 461–8000 or (800) 852–3392; www.johnson citytnchamber.com. Open 8:00 A.M. to 5:00 P.M. Monday through Friday.

# Elizabethton

As the number of early settlers along the Watauga and the Nolichucky Rivers increased, so did their need for protection and their need to record life's transactions and daily business. In 1772 they gathered to organize their own government. Using the Virginia laws as a guide, the men formed the Watauga Association and created their own set of rules and regulations, which today is considered the first written constitution by men of American birth.

## Pronunciation

One sure way to let the locals know that you're a tourist is by mispronouncing the town names. Elizabethton is pronounced "E-liz-a-BETH-ton."

### Sycamore Shoals State Historic Area (all ages)
**U.S. Highway 321; (423) 543–5808. Open daily. Free.**

The first settlement of the area is where Sycamore Shoals State Historic Area and the town of Elizabethton are now located, and it was in this area that the Watauga Association built a fort to protect itself from native tribes, specifically, the Cherokees. The original fort is long gone, but state officials at Sycamore Shoals have reconstructed the fort about a mile from where the original one was located.

As the centerpiece of the sixty-one-acre state park, the fort is open to the public and usually has people on hand to interpret the early days of the Wataugans and the other significant historical events of the area. A visitor center at 1651 West Elk Avenue houses a museum and a theater that shows a film depicting the area's early history.

### *The Wataugans* Outdoor Drama (all ages)
**1651 West Elk Avenue; (423) 547–3852 or (888) 547–3852. Last three weekend evenings in July. Admission: $–$$.**

In July the Watauga Historical Association presents a two-act outdoor drama.

### Doe River Covered Bridge (all ages)
Off U.S. Highway 19 East; (423) 547–3850.

In downtown Elizabethton one of the state's oldest original covered bridges provides passage over the Doe River. Known locally by many as the "kissing bridge" because of the cover it provides for secretive bussing, the bridge is the focal point for the city's riverside park. There's plenty of space in the park for picnicking and for the kids to blow off a bit of energy.

The bridge was built in 1882 and is still in use today. The **free** annual Covered Bridge Celebration takes place the first week of June and features all kinds of fun for the entire family. Activities include concerts, a crafts show, an antique car show, bike races, and kids' games and contests.

## Gone **Fishin'**

If you like to fish, you'll find plenty of opportunities in northeast Tennessee. The area's lakes and rivers provide walleye, rainbow and brown trout, smallmouth bass, an occasional largemouth, white and black bass, crappie, and catfish.

Be sure to get a license if you're over age twelve. Three-day, nonresident fishing licenses (no trout) range in price from about $6.00 for ages thirteen to fifteen to $20.50 for an adult; ten-day passes are $15.50 and $30.50; annual passes are $26.00 and $51.00.

Licenses are available from most county court clerks, sporting goods stores, hardware stores, interested merchants, and all Tennessee Wildlife Resource Agency offices.

### Roan Mountain State Park (all ages)
Highway 143, Roan Mountain (about 20 miles south of Elizabethton); (423) 772–3303 or (800) 250–8620. Open year-round. Admission is **free.** (The gardens on Roan Mountain are open May through October; Admission: $.)

If you're here in June, you absolutely *must* visit Roan Mountain. In mid- to late June, when the rhododendrons are in bloom, you'll see a display of nature's flora like you've never seen before. Even the kids will gasp in disbelief at this one. Comprising 600 acres of spectacular blooms, this naturalist's paradise is the largest rhododendron garden in the United States. Officials said these are the Catawba variety, known for their colorful rose-purple blooms.

The best place to start your mountain adventure is at the Roan Mountain State Park visitor center, just off State Route 143. There you can pick up information about the park's seven different walking trails. The rangers also will point you in the right direction to get the best view of the rhododendron display. Roan Mountain straddles the North Carolina/Tennessee border, and its peak, at 6,285 feet, makes it one of the highest in the eastern United States.

As you drive the 10 miles from the visitor center to the top of the mountain, there are several convenient pull-offs providing wonderful views of the lush Cherokee National Forest, which surrounds the mountain. The park offers thirty rental cabins, eighty-seven campsites, a museum, a meeting facility, a large group cabin, and a swimming pool. You don't have to be staying here to enjoy the heated pool, but it will cost you $2.25 per person if you'd like to take a swim. The park is quite active during the wintertime as well, with three different designated trails for cross-country skiing. No equipment is provided, so you'll have to bring your own.

### Rhododendron Festival (all ages)
**Roan Mountain; (423) 725–2270, (423) 772–3303, or (800) 250–8620.**

To celebrate the blooming hillside, the annual Rhododendron Festival takes place the third weekend in June in the park. Put on by the Roan Mountain Citizens Club, the festival features native arts and crafts, mountain music and dancing, local food festivals, and wildlife tours.

## Other Things to See and Do

**The John and Landon Carter Mansion** (ages 8 and up), 1013 Broad Street; (423) 543 6140 or (423) 543 5808. Built between 1775 and 1780, this is the oldest frame house in the state. It is usually open from mid-May through mid-August, Wednesday through Sunday. **Free.**

**Watauga Dam** (all ages), Wilbur/Siam Roads; (423) 239–2000 (Tennessee Valley Authority). Completed in 1949, Watauga Dam is 950 feet long and rises 331 feet above its foundation. It impounds the Watauga River, which is about 16 miles long and has 106 miles of shoreline. **Free.**

**Wilbur Dam** (all ages), Wilbur/Siam Roads; (423) 239–2000 (Tennessee Valley Authority). Wilbur Dam, located about 1½ miles downstream from Watauga Dam, is 375 feet long and 77 feet high. It was built in 1912. The

Tennessee Valley Authority (TVA) purchased the dam and lake in 1945, rehabilitated the dam, and began using it to generate power in 1950, making it the second oldest dam in the TVA system (Norris Dam is the oldest). It's named for Jim Wilbur, who ran a successful logging operation in the area. **Free.**

## Where to Eat

**The Coffee Company,** 444 East Elk Avenue; (423) 542–3438. Gourmet coffee, sandwiches, soups, and desserts, plus live music on the first and third Thursday evenings of each month. Plenty of health-conscious fare here, plus kid-pleasers like toasted cheese and PBJ sandwiches. $

**Dino's Restaurant,** 420 Elk Avenue; (423) 542–5541. Dino's has been a local favorite for some forty years. Italian and American specialties and a kids' menu make this a nice place for a family meal. Most items are under $8.50. $

**Duck Duck Goose Cafe,** 515 East Elk Avenue; (423) 543–4212. Across from Duck Crossing Antique Mall; offers daily lunch specials and affordable children's favorites. $

**Southern Cafe,** 408 East Elk Avenue; (423) 542–5132. This eatery has a great hometown atmosphere with home-style cooking. Serving lunch and dinner, with a varied menu to please everybody. $

**City Market,** 449 E Street; (423) 543–1751. A favorite of the locals, City Market has an excellent lunch menu and plenty of homemade pies for the kids' sweet tooth (and your own). $

**Rustlers on the River,** 630 Broad Street; (423) 543–2727. Enjoy lunch on the dining deck, on the banks of the Watauga River, when weather permits. Barbecue is the house specialty, and the children's menu offers a variety to please your most finicky eater. $

## Where to Stay

**Bee Cliff Cabins,** 141 Steele Bridge Road; (423) 542–6033. Located on the banks of the Watauga River. Four fully furnished cabins sleep six. All have full kitchens and baths, one with wheelchair access. A separate lodge sleeps ten, and another two-story lodge with a recreation room sleeps fifteen. Dock on the river where you can fish or canoe. $$

**Comfort Inn,** 1515 Highway 19 East Bypass; (423) 542–4466 or (800) 228–5150. Located about 2 miles from the Doe River Covered Bridge; free continental breakfast, swimming pool, an exercise room, free HBO, and free apple cider and lemonade. $–$$

**Days Inn,** 505 West Elk Avenue, (423) 543–3344 or (800) 329–7466. Sixty-unit motel about 1 mile from Sycamore Shoals State Historic Area. Swimming pool, free HBO, laundry facilities, and free continental breakfast. $

**Meredith Valley Cabins,** 341 Sycamore Shoals Drive; (423) 542–4136. Two cabins located on the Watauga River. Each is completely furnished and sleeps six people. $$

**RiverRidge Campground,** 642 Smalling Road; (423) 542–6187. Open year-round. Offers convenient access to the Watauga River for trout fishing, tubing, or canoeing; hiking trails. Call for rates.

**Stoney Creek RV Park,** 108 Price Road; (423) 474–3505. Beautiful RV park with full hookups, and a dumping station. Near Bristol Speedway, shopping, and restaurants. $

## For More Information

**Elizabethton/Carter County Tourism Council,** 500 Veterans Memorial Parkway, P.O. Box 190, Elizabethton, TN 37643; (423) 547–3850. www.tourelizabethton.com. Open 8:00 A.M. to 5:00 P.M. Monday through Friday.

# Piney Flats

**Rocky Mount** (ages 6 and up)
200 Hyder Hill Road, 5½ miles from I–181, between Johnson City and Bristol; (423) 538–7396 or (888) 538–1791. Open year-round. Hours: 10:00 A.M. to 5:00 P.M. Monday through Saturday, 1:00 to 5:00 P.M. Sunday (March through mid-October); winter hours are usually 1:00 to 4:00 P.M. Monday through Saturday. $. Additional rates may apply.

Rocky Mount could possibly be the most historically significant structure still standing in the state. Built in 1770 by William Cobb, the two-story log cabin is the oldest original territorial capital in the United States and one of the oldest buildings in Tennessee.

Completely restored, the original cabin is now the centerpiece of a living-history museum. Interpreters in historic clothing greet you as you enter and invite you to become a member of the Cobb family in the year 1791 and experience the lifestyle of the frontier. As members of the "family" perform daily chores in the kitchen and weaving cabin, they demonstrate the skills of the typical pioneer family of the region.

### Overmountain Museum (all ages)
**Located in the visitor center at Rocky Mount; (423) 538–7396 or (888) 538–1791. $. Admission is included with admission to Rocky Mount.**

This large gallery features modern exhibits, many of which relate to the early life of the area.

## For More Information

**Johnson City Convention and Visitors Bureau,** 603 East Market Street, Johnson City, TN 37601; (423) 461–8000 or (800) 852–3392; www.johnsoncitytn.com. Open 8:00 A.M. to 5:00 P.M. Monday through Friday.

# Blountville

### Appalachian Caverns (all ages)
**420 Cave Hill Road (take exit 69 off I–81 and follow the signs); (423) 323–2337; www.appalachiancavern.org; e-mail: cavern@preferred.com. Open daily year-round except Thanksgiving and the week before Christmas to the second week of January. Admission: $–$$. Children under 4 admitted free.**

In Blountville, you can get a glimpse of what Tennessee looks like from the bottom up; that is, from far below ground. Appalachian Caverns were nearly 500 million years in the making and today are operated by a nonprofit organization that uses all profits to help clean up the environment.

For many years the great cavern lay mostly in silence, though occasionally it provided fun for the daring spelunker. It was a shelter for native tribes and a safe haven for the makers of moonshine. Now, however, there is nearly a mile of well-lit walkways where guides will lead you safely past deep crevices and colorful columns of manganese, iron, calcium, and copper.

The kids will especially get a kick out of the Great Room, where the cave ceilings reach a height of 135 feet. A special three-and-a-half-hour "wild tour" is offered for the more daring family members who want to crawl through tight spaces and are able to do some strenuous climbing.

### Blountville Historic District (ages 10 and up) 🏛️ 👫
State Highway 126; (423) 323–7437 or (423) 323–5686. Free.

If you still feel like walking, take time to visit the historic downtown area of Blountville. You can pick up a walking map at the Anderson Townhouse, located on the main street of town. The city fathers claim to have more original log houses still in use than any other town in the state. Whether that's true or not, there certainly are a lot of beautifully restored homes and storefronts along the city's main street.

Among them is the Old Deery Inn. Located next to the Sullivan County Courthouse, the inn was built sometime around 1785 and operated as such, off and on, until 1939. There are eighteen rooms inside and ten outbuildings on the property. The inn is now a private residence, but you can appreciate the architecture from the sidewalk. Being on a major stagecoach line, as Blountville was, the inn, as well as the entire town, hosted the biggest names of the day, including Andrew Jackson, Andrew Johnson, and James K. Polk, all three U.S. presidents who hailed from Tennessee.

The city was laid out in 1792 and was the seat of government for the county. It soon became the social and educational center of the area. Those sophisticated influences are reflected in the architecture (and the stories behind the structures) of the twenty buildings that are currently listed on the National Register of Historic Places.

### Cooper's Gem Mine (ages 6 and up)
1136 Big Hollow Road; (423) 323–5680. Open March through October. Hours: Monday through Friday, 11:00 A.M. to 5:00 P.M.; Saturday, noon to 5:00 P.M.; closed Sunday. $–$$ (based on buckets purchased).

At Cooper's Gem Mine, the kids have the rare opportunity to pan for precious gemstones. You can buy a bucket of ore and take it out back to a clear-running country stream, step up to the sluice, and wash away the dirt and sand. What you find you keep. Although no diamonds have been found yet, owner Barbara Lawson said that plenty of other stones, from rubies to amethysts, have been uncovered.

The flumes operate seasonally, but the inside gift shop, which specializes in hand-made crafts, and the rock shop are open year-round. Barbara went to school to learn jewelry making and can mount your "found" treasures into pieces of jewelry.

Brochures with a map to the gem mine are available throughout the area, or you can call Barbara at the aforementioned number.

## Other Things to See and Do

**Muddy Creek Raceway** (ages 4 and up), 313 Maple Lane; (423) 323– 5497; www.victory-sports.com. Family motorcycle racing and mud drag nationals on eight weekends from May through October. Racers as young as 4 can participate. $–$$

## Where to Eat

**Pardner's Bar-B-Que,** 5444 U.S. Highway 11E, Piney Flats; (423) 538–5539. Just a few miles south of Blountville, Pardner's has been a local favorite since the early 1980s. No children's menu, but the prices are very reasonable. $

**Ridgewood Restaurant,** 900 Elizabethton Highway (Old 19E), Bluff City; (423) 538–7543. Open since 1948, Ridgewood has a national reputation for its barbecue, having been featured in such magazines as *Southern Living, People, Metropolitan Home,* and *Food & Wine.* The restaurant is just south of Blountville; take Highway 37 to Elizabethton Highway. Closed Monday. $

## Where to Stay

**Rocky Top Campground,** 496 Pearl Lane; (423) 323–2535. Forty-five sites, open year-round. Pets are welcome. Amenities include cable TV.

**Smith Haven Bed & Breakfast,** 2357 State Route 37; (423) 323–0174 or (800) 606–4833, www.canjoe.com. This historic farmhouse offers three guest rooms, three baths, and a full breakfast. Owners John and Catharine Van Arsdall focus on the traditional music, foods, and lifestyle of east Tennessee. Music lovers will enjoy their live, old-time country music and bluegrass jam sessions. Children and pets are welcome. There's a twenty-seven-hole golf course across the street. For NASCAR fans, the Bristol Motor Speedway is 1½ miles away. Reservations are preferred. $$–$$$$

## For More Information

**Bristol Convention and Visitors Bureau,** 20 Volunteer Parkway, Bristol, TN 37620; (423) 989–4850; www.bristolchamber .org. Open 8:30 A.M. to 5:00 P.M. Monday through Friday.

**Kingsport Convention and Visitors Bureau,** P.O. Box 1403, 151 East Main Street, Kingsport, TN 37662; (423) 392–8820 or (800) 743–5282; www.kingsportchamber.org. Open 8:00 A.M. to 5:00 P.M. Monday through Friday.

# Bristol

This city is about as close to another state as you can get. In fact, the state line runs down the middle of the city's State Street, separating Bristol, Virginia, from Bristol, Tennessee. Small, brass state-line markers are embedded in the middle of the street between the double yellow lines.

A trip to Bristol isn't a family trip unless you give kids the opportunity to stand in the middle of the street and straddle the yellow lines, with one leg in each state. Caution: Since State Street is quite busy, you should do it at an intersection, with the stoplight in your favor. Also, don't be surprised at the "oh no, not another one" look from the locals as you snap that souvenir photo.

### Bristol Caverns (all ages)
**1157 Bristol Caverns Highway (State Highway 435), just off Highway 421 South; (423) 878–2011. Open 9:00 A.M. to 5:00 P.M. Monday through Saturday March 15 to October 31, 10:00 A.M. to 4:00 P.M. Monday through Saturday November 1 to March 14, 12:30 to 5:00 P.M. Sunday in summer, and 12:30 to 4:00 P.M. Sunday in winter; closed Thanksgiving, Christmas Eve, Christmas Day, and Easter. $–$$. Under 5 free.**

A great deal of history lies underground in the Bristol Caverns. It has a timeless beauty and is considered the largest cavern in the Smoky Mountain region. A walk along the well-groomed trails in the cave takes you past geological formations that have taken millions of years to create.

In frontier days, as Daniel Boone and his fellow explorers cleared the trails above ground, Native Americans were using the underground river in the cavern as an attack-and-escape route in their raids on the early settlers. The cavern was rediscovered by accident by a local landowner in 1863 and has been in commercial operation since 1944. Guided tours begin about every twenty minutes and take about an hour to complete.

The well-versed guides are great, and if you get one with a fun-loving personality, you and the kids will have an extra good time. Guides like to point out special formations without telling you what you are "supposed" to visualize. They then encourage the kids to use their creativity to identify what they see. "You can see just about anything you really want to see," one guide said.

One of the nicest areas in the cave is appropriately called Panorama Point, from which you can view all three levels.

# Bristol's **Country Music Heritage**

While Nashville is the city that most people associate with country music today, Bristol, Tennessee, about 300 miles east of Music City U.S.A., is widely known as the birthplace of country music. In 1927 Ralph Peer of the Victor Talking Machine Company established a recording studio in Bristol. That's where the Carter Family and Jimmie Rodgers recorded the first nationally distributed country music. Their 1927 recording sessions, known as the Bristol Sessions, laid the groundwork for what became the country music industry. What had been known as Appalachian folk music was transformed into a national sensation.

Bristol has been officially recognized by the commonwealth of Virginia and the state of Tennessee as the official "Birthplace of Country Music," with a monument paying tribute to this heritage; the monument is located off State Street, near the Randall Street Expressway, across from Twin City Federal Bank. There is also a marker and mural on State Street, near Eighth Street, recognizing the city's country music legacy. As part of its annual Folklife Festival in 2003, the Smithsonian Institution celebrated the seventy-fifth anniversary of Bristol's country music roots with a special program on Appalachian music.

The Birthplace of Country Music Alliance (BCMA), based in Bristol, was formed to recognize and promote Bristol's country music heritage. The organization has a museum and information center in the Bristol Mall, located off I–81 at exit 1. For more information contact the BCMA at (276) 645–0035.

# Spelunk, Spelunking, **Spelunked!**

*Spelunking*: It's a fun word to pronounce (it means "cave exploration"), and for many, it's a lot of fun.

Do you enjoy spelunking, or are you interested in learning more about it? The National Speleological Society is an excellent resource. The NSS was founded more than fifty years ago for the purpose of advancing the study, conservation, exploration, and knowledge of caves.

Nationwide, more than 12,000 members in 200 chapters, known as "grottos," conduct regular meetings to bring cavers together within their region and coordinate activities, which could include mapping, cleaning, and gating sensitive caves. There are more than a dozen grottos in Tennessee.

For more information contact the NSS at 2813 Cave Avenue, Huntsville, AL 35810; (256) 852–1300. You can also visit their Web site at www.caves.org.

## Bristol Motor Speedway (ages 8 and up) 

**2801 Highway 11E; (423) 764–1161. Ticket prices vary from event to event and by season.**

The noisiest place in Bristol on certain dates of the year is an attraction Bristonians are quite proud of, the Bristol Motor Speedway. Known as the world's fastest half-mile track, the raceway, with its high-banked curves, is home to six major NASCAR events and is the site of NASCAR's famous fall night race. Admission to the speedway is pricey, starting at $27 to as high as $110. There's also a NASCAR souvenir shop that has plenty of "toys" to keep all the race fans in your family happy.

## Steele Creek Park (all ages) 

**80 Lake Shore Drive (at the edge of Bristol); (423) 989–5616. Open daily 9:00 A.M. to 9:00 P.M. $.**

Before leaving town, pack a picnic and head out to beautiful Steele Creek Park, the state's third-largest city park. In the foothills of the Appalachians, the 2,000-acre, heavily forested park is a fun family place to while away a few hours. Among the offerings here are a scenic half-mile train ride, a cool mountain lake for paddleboating and fishing, a nature center, a golf course, and 25 miles of hiking trails. The nature center offers a variety of educational and fun programs for children and adults, which changes depending on the season. Most facilities are open year-round.

## Other Things to See and Do

**Bristol Sign** (all ages), State Street near Randall Street. This neon sign, listed on the National Register of Historic Places, proclaims BRISTOL IS A GOOD PLACE TO LIVE. It was erected in 1910 as a symbol of unity between Bristol, Tennessee, and Bristol, Virginia. It's located above the line dividing the two states.

**Historic Downtown Bristol** (ages 8 and up), (423) 989–4850 (Bristol Convention and Visitors Bureau). Bristol's revitalized downtown district features several historic buildings, specialty shops, restaurants, and more.

**Paramount Center for the Arts** (ages 10 and up), 518 State Street; (423) 274–8920.

Built in 1931, this theater is on the National Register of Historic Places. A $2.2 million renovation completed in 1991 restored it to its original, opulent Art Deco style. Originally known as the Paramount Theatre, the building now features plays, Wurlitzer organ performances, and other entertainment.

**Tennessee Ernie Ford Home** (ages 8 and up), Anderson Street; (423) 989–4850 (Bristol Chamber of Commerce). Call for hours and admission prices. On the outskirts of Bristol, the quaint birthplace of the beloved entertainer, best known for his 1955 hit single "Sixteen Tons," features memoirs of his career, including his induction to the Country Music Hall of Fame. It isn't open on a regular basis, so call for a schedule.

## A State **Divided**

During the Civil War, Tennesseans were divided over the issues of slavery, secession, and war. Two months before the outbreak of the war in 1861, voters had decided not to even hold a convention to consider seceding from the Union; the state saw no need to follow in the footsteps of other Southern states. However, public opinion shifted after President Lincoln ordered troops to subdue the rebelling states. Tennesseans saw the invasion of their homeland as a threat, and that became a reason for secession. Reluctantly, Tennessee voted to leave the Union and became the last state to join the Confederacy. Throughout the state, however, there remained much support for the Union. East Tennessee, in particular, was loyal to the Union.

## Where to Eat

**The Manna Bagel Company,** 654 State Street; (423) 652–2216. On the Tennessee side of State Street, this restaurant serves bagels, sandwiches (on a bagel, wheat bread, or croissant), pizza bagels, sweets, and coffee beverages. Kids can get a half sandwich, cookies, and chips. $

**KP Duty,** 520 State Street; (423) 764–3889. This gourmet cafe specializes in sandwiches, salads, homemade soups, and quiche. They'll cook up kid-friendly fare on request. $ lunch, $–$$$ dinner (dinner on Friday and Saturday only)

**The Vineyard Restaurant,** 603 Gate City Highway (off I–81, exit 1); (276) 466–4244. On the Virginia side, this restaurant serves traditional Italian cuisine in a romantic yet kid-friendly setting. It also serves American-style lunches. $$ lunch, $$$ dinner

**The Troutdale Dining Room,** 412 Sixth Street; (423) 968–9099. Located on the Tennessee side of Bristol, this upscale restaurant features imaginative American and multiethnic creations in a Victorian house setting. Open for dinner only. $$$

## Where to Stay

**Best Western,** 111 Holiday Drive; (423) 968–1101. Pool, small exercise room. On-grounds restaurant that serves everything from pizza to steaks. Free continental breakfast. $$

**Hampton Inn in Bristol,** 3299 West State Street; (423) 764–3600. This five-story, ninety-one room hotel was completely renovated in 2001. Free breakfast buffet, pool, and HBO. The hotel is about fifteen minutes from the Bristol Motor Speedway. $–$$$$

**Holiday Inn Hotel and Suites Convention Center,** 3005 Linden Drive, Bristol, Virginia; (276) 466–4100. This ten-story, 255-room hotel is about fifteen minutes from the Bristol Motor Speedway and about ten minutes from downtown Bristol. The Tinseltown megaplex is right across the street. Outdoor heated pool, Jacuzzi, workout facilities, laundry facilities, and a family-style restaurant. $$–$$$$

**Comfort Inn,** 2368 Lee Highway, Bristol, Virginia; (276) 466–3881. Off exit 5, I–81, this hotel is ten minutes from Bristol Motor Speedway. Amenities include complimentary continental breakfast, pet-friendly rooms, an outdoor pool, meeting rooms, and suites. $$–$$$

## For More Information

**Bristol Convention and Visitors Bureau,** 20 Volunteer Parkway, Bristol, TN 37620; (423) 989–4850; www.bristolchamber .org. Open 8:30 A.M. to 5:00 P.M. Monday through Friday.

# Kingsport

Originally chartered in 1822, then later in 1917, the city of Kingsport is named for William King's Port, a boatyard located along the Holston River. The boatyard became a strategic port for flatboats carrying loads of iron and salt south and was key to the further development of the city and to America's westward migration.

If you're traveling the First Frontier, Kingsport is 21 miles northwest of Johnson City, 25 miles west of Bristol, and 32 miles east of Rogersville.

### Bays Mountain Park (all ages)

**853 Bays Mountain Park Road, 3 miles off I–181; (423) 229–9447. Open year-round except for major holidays. Hours vary according to season. $. Additional fees for planetarium, nature programs, and barge rides.**

In 1917 a forty-four-acre lake was created to provide water to the city of Kingsport. Today that lake is the tranquil centerpiece of Bays Mountain Park, a 3,000-acre city-owned oasis of green beauty within the city limits. If there is a single, perfect place for a full day of family fun in the First Frontier, this is it. City leaders say this is the largest municipal park in the United States.

One of the primary missions of the park is environmental education and among its offerings are 22 miles of trails where you'll more than likely run into a few native animal species, including white-tailed deer, bobcats, and wild turkey. A waterfowl aviary gives you some great close-up views, and special habitats for the gray wolf, deer, and river otters help bring those species in closer for better viewing. A freshwater aquarium allows a close-up look at native fish and their surroundings.

The nature center houses an exhibit gallery filled with many interesting displays; you may get so interested in them you'll forget all about going outside to enjoy nature at its finest. Allow plenty of time to explore. You can pick up a trail map at the nature center before setting out on your adventure.

Another area you learn about at Bays Mountain Park is the one "way out there." The various wonders of the universe are projected inside the planetarium theater, and large telescopes are used to show close-ups of the sun, moon, and planets as well as stars and galaxies light-years distant. Various exhibits highlight the space sciences.

While you're here, be sure to take a barge ride on the lake. It's a lot of fun, and you'll see some beautiful sights along the way and get some great views of the aquatic life. Also, if your family enjoys learning about pioneer life, the park's Farmstead Museum features displays on pioneer tools and implements.

## Warriors' Path State Park (all ages)

**490 Hemlock Road, 2 miles south of Kingsport, off Highway 36; (423) 239–8531. Open year-round, 7:00 A.M. to 11:00 P.M. summer, 7:00 A.M. to 10:00 P.M. spring and fall, 7:00 A.M. to 9:00 P.M. winter. Free.**

The area is blessed with another fantastic public park, Warriors' Path State Park. Once a pathway for Cherokee Indians and early white settlers, the area is now a place for outdoor exploration and family fun.

The 950-acre park is situated on the shores of the Tennessee Valley Authority's Patrick Henry Reservoir on the Holston River. The most popular activities are centered around the lake itself, including pleasure boating, waterskiing, and fishing. Paddleboats and small fishing boats are available for rent, and boat launching ramps are available at no cost. *Warning:* Anyone in your family over thirteen years old who wants to fish must have a valid Tennessee fishing license. Otherwise, you may be taking your family on an unexpected tour of the county courthouse.

Other offerings at the park include a 135-site campground on an island; an Olympic-size swimming pool with a water slide; an eighteen-hole Frisbee-golf course; a par-seventy-two championship eighteen-hole golf course with a driving range, practice green, and pro shop; and a good selection of riding horses and ponies available for rent at the stables. Two miles of horse trails wind through the scenic woodlands.

## The Exchange Place (all ages)

**4812 Orebank Road; (423) 288–6071. Open May through October, 10:00 A.M. to 2:00 P.M. Thursday and Friday and 2:00 to 4:30 P.M. Saturday and Sunday. Free.**

The Exchange Place, one of the nicest farm homesteads in the Southeast, features eight buildings, six of them original to the site and dating from 1820 to 1850. At one time this complex was the center of a self-supporting plantation of more than 1,400 acres.

One of the restored original buildings was a stagecoach stop, where early travelers could exchange their Virginia currency for Tennessee currency and vice versa. The Main House was built in 1820 and restored in 1975. It was originally the main dwelling house of the farm and now contains furnishings typical of a well-to-do farm of the mid-1800s.

The entire complex is listed on the National Register of Historic Places and is open to the public as a living farm museum. Craft demonstrations almost always take place during the summer months and include spinning and weaving, quilting, and basketry. The former grainery is now a museum of farm equipment, and the old neighborhood store building is now a shop that sells local crafts.

Several special events take place on the grounds, including the Fall Folk Arts Festival in late September, an old-fashioned marbles tournament in late June, and the Spring Garden Fair in late April. Admission is charged only for special events.

## The Netherland Inn (ages 6 and up)

**2144 Netherland Inn Road; (423) 292–9649 or (423) 246–7986. Open 2:00 to 4:00 P.M. weekends May through October; open weekdays May through October for group tours by appointment only. Admission: $, under 6 free.**

Believe it or not, a nationally known boatyard was in operation in Kingsport along the Holston River in 1802. William King had a reputation as a master builder, and people came from as far away as New Orleans for a river vessel. Across the Stage Coach Road from the boatyards was the Netherland Inn, an always-busy inn and tavern where the likes of the state's three presidents whiled away hours visiting with their friends. This three-story Federal architectural gem has been completely restored and is filled with beautiful museum furnishings that depict an intimate study of a way of life in one of the South's most important American frontier settlements.

As you tour this magnificent house museum, step out onto one of the three great porches. From there you can view the site of the former boatyards, now called Boatyard Park. The riverside park features miles of footpaths, plenty of picnic tables, a wide array of playground equipment, a swinging bridge over the Holston River, gift shops, and fishing piers.

**Netherland Inn Log Cabin Children's Museum** (all ages)
2144 Netherland Inn Road; (423) 292–9649 or (423) 246–7986. Open 2:00 to 4:00 P.M. weekends May through October and on weekdays during scheduled group tours. Admission is included in the Netherland Inn admission price.

Adjacent to the Main House is the Netherland Inn Log Cabin Children's Museum. It's a log cabin that was moved here from Virginia. Daniel Boone was said to have lived in the cabin between 1773 and 1775. Today it's full of wondrous toys, games, and costumes of the eighteenth and nineteenth centuries. Various children's activities are held during the warmer months of the year.

## Other Things to See and Do

**Allandale Mansion** (ages 10 and up), 4444 West Stone Drive; (423) 229–9422. Tours by appointment only. A classic example of Georgian architecture, this mansion, known as Kingsport's White House, is filled with antiques from around the world. The twenty-five-acre estate also includes formal gardens, a barn that may be rented for parties, and a pond that's home to graceful swans.

**Downtown Kingsport** (all ages), West Main Street; (423) 246–6550 (Downtown Kingsport Association). Downtown Heritage Trail walking-tour brochures are available at the Downtown Kingsport Association office at 140 Main Street and at the Chamber of Commerce office at 151 East Main Street. **Free.** Restored historic buildings, plus a variety of shops, await visitors to Kingsport's downtown area. The annual arts and crafts festival is held here the weekend after Labor Day. On December 31, the First Night Celebration takes place here.

## Where to Eat

**Pratt's BBQ Barn,** 1225 East Stone Drive; (423) 246–5749. Open for lunch Monday through Friday, Pratt's is known for its affordable buffet. The buffet options change daily, but you can always count on real country cooking and, of course, barbecue. Don't pass up the brownies if they're available. $

**Skoby's,** 1001 Konnarock Road; (423) 245–2761. You can fill up on steaks, seafood, or pasta at Skoby's, and the kids can chow down on their favorites from the children's menu. Each room is unique, with a different decor and theme. Kids love the Clown Room. Popular with everyone from families to business travelers, Skoby's is open for dinner only, but the adjacent walk-up deli is open for lunch. $$

## Where to Stay

**Comfort Inn,** 100 Indian Center Court; (423) 378–4418 or (800) 228–5150. Free deluxe continental breakfast, free HBO, pool, dry sauna, and hot tub. Bristol Motor Speedway and historic Jonesborough are each about 20 miles away, and Bays Mountain Park is about 8 miles away. $$

**Holiday Inn Express,** 4234 Fort Henry Drive; (423) 239–3400 or (800) HOLIDAY. Free deluxe continental breakfast, HBO, and a guest laundry room. Warriors' Path State Park is just minutes away. $$

## For More Information

**Kingsport Convention and Visitors Bureau,** P.O. Box 1403, 151 East Main Street, Kingsport, TN 37662; (423) 392–8820 or (800) 743–5282; www.kcvb.org. Open 8:00 A.M. to 5:00 P.M. Monday through Friday.

# Rogersville

The tiny town of Rogersville has several interesting attractions for families interested in learning about the history of the First Frontier. Rogersville is about 60 miles northeast of Knoxville, 30 miles southwest of the Tri-Cities area, and about 45 miles from historic Jonesborough, making it an easy and interesting day trip from any of these areas.

### Tennessee Newspaper Printing Museum (all ages)

415 South Depot Street; (423) 272–1961. Open 10:00 A.M. to 4:00 P.M. Tuesday through Thursday. $.

A good place to start your visit to this little historic town is at this museum. It's a restored Southern Railway facility, built in 1890, and now houses the museum of Rogersville's printing history. The state's first newspaper was printed here in 1791.

### Rogersville Historic District (all ages)

Main Street; (423) 272–2186. Guided tours available for groups of thirty or more; call two weeks in advance to schedule appointment. **Free.**

The city's historic district includes many restored original structures that are now on the National Register of Historic Places. A walking tour brochure is available at most of the stores and offices in town, including the chamber of commerce office, located in back of U.S. Bank.

## Renaissance Faire

For the first two weekends in June, Rogersville becomes a medieval town, with knights and their ladies fair attired as they would have been in the days of old. Some of the festivities include a human chess match, storytelling, performances by the Shakespeare Ensemble from East Tennessee State University, period dancing and games of skill (sword-fighting and archery), puppet shows, and a dragon's-egg hunt. For more information, visit www.shakespeare andfriends.org.

One of the stops on the walking tour is the Hawkins County Courthouse, one of the most photographed buildings in the South. Built in 1836, this is the oldest original courthouse in the state. You're welcome to go on in and look around—for **free.**

### Ebbing and Flowing Spring (ages 4 and up)

840 Ebbing and Flowing Spring Road; (423) 272–2186. **Free.**

Just outside Rogersville is a fascinating natural phenomenon— the Ebbing and Flowing Spring. This is one of only two springs in the world known to flow and stop at regular intervals (this one does so at two-hour-and-forty-seven-minute intervals). This has been happening for at least the past 200 years. The nearby Ebbing and Flowing Spring School was built in the early 1800s. The Ebbing and Flowing Spring United Methodist Church met in the school from 1820 until a permanent church was built nearby in 1898. The church is still used regularly by the congregation.

## Other Things to See and Do

**Crockett Spring Park,** 200 Crockett Street; (423) 272–1961. **Free.** This is where Davy Crockett's grandparents lived and were massacred in 1777. Now a public park, the property includes a natural spring, a cemetery, and a native tree park.

**Rogersville City Park,** Park Boulevard; (423) 272–4545. **Free.** This thirty-eight-acre park has picnic pavilions, a playground, ball fields, basketball and tennis courts, a fishing pond, and a swimming pool.

## Where to Eat

**Charlie's Restaurant,** 4017 Highway 66, #9; (423) 272–2197. This family-style restaurant is best known for its barbecue, but also serves tasty chicken and catfish. Kids can choose from PBJ sandwiches, burgers, chicken tenders, and grilled cheese. $

**El Pueblito Authentic Mexican Restaurant,** 120 East Main Street; (423) 921–0057. This family-style restaurant is best known for its authentic Mexican cuisine. Its children's menu is a hit. $

**The Fisherman's Dock,** 315 Park View Boulevard; (423) 921–3702. This is the place to go for seafood of all kinds. There's a children's menu with such favorites as chicken fingers and popcorn shrimp. $

## Where to Stay

**Holiday Inn Express,** 7139 Highway 11 West; (423) 272–1842 or (800) HOLIDAY. This forty-three-room hotel opened in mid-1998. All rooms have coffeemakers, hair dryers, irons, and ironing boards, and some rooms have refrigerators and microwaves. There's a free deluxe continental breakfast each morning. $$

**Sandman Motel,** 4319 Highway 66 South; (423) 272–6800. You won't get many extras here, but this locally owned motel is a good choice for budget-conscious families. There are forty rooms, free cable, and a free continental breakfast. A couple of fast-food restaurants are right across the street. $

**Hale Springs Inn,** 110 West Main Street; (423) 272–5171. Located on the historic downtown square, this is Tennessee's oldest operating inn. Built in 1824, it has large antiques-filled rooms. The inn has hosted three presidents among its guests: Andrew Jackson, Andrew Johnson, and James K. Polk. Even if you don't stay there, you can take a self-guided tour. $$$$

# For More Information

**Rogersville/Hawkins County Chamber of Commerce Visitor Information Center,** 107 East Main Street, Suite 100, Rogersville, TN 37857; (423) 272–2186; www.rogersville.com. Open 9:00 A.M. to 4:00 P.M. Monday through Friday.

# the Mountainous East

T all smoky mountains, large cavernous river gorges, lush green forests, and tens of thousands of acres of beautiful lakes and rivers all combine to dominate the Mountainous East, the most rugged, natural area of the state.

This nature-oriented region is home to the 500,000-acre Great Smoky Mountains National Park, the most visited national park in the country, and the Big South Fork National River and Recreation Area. Both are among the most beautiful natural areas in the Southeast.

At the foothills of the Great Smokies, you'll find the tourist areas of Gatlinburg, Sevierville, and Pigeon Forge, each offering thousands of motel rooms, campgrounds, and the usual family attractions that have a tendency to pop up in these types of areas— miniature golf, go-cart tracks, and outlet shopping malls.

This region is also known for its early development of the atomic bomb in the "secret city" of Oak Ridge, its utopian society in the classy village of Rugby, and its World's Fair in Knoxville. Museums and living-history villages throughout the area have dedicated their collections and grounds to the preservation of mountain life, while many communities have preserved that lifestyle by their very existence.

This is a diverse area with myriad opportunities for unique family outings and activities. You'll find fun, ranging from riding a roller coaster at the Dollywood theme park in Pigeon Forge to gliding along in a glass-bottomed boat at the Lost Sea in Sweetwater, the world's largest underground lake.

## Amazing Tennessee Facts

Tennessee's state bird is the mockingbird.

# THE MOUNTAINOUS EAST

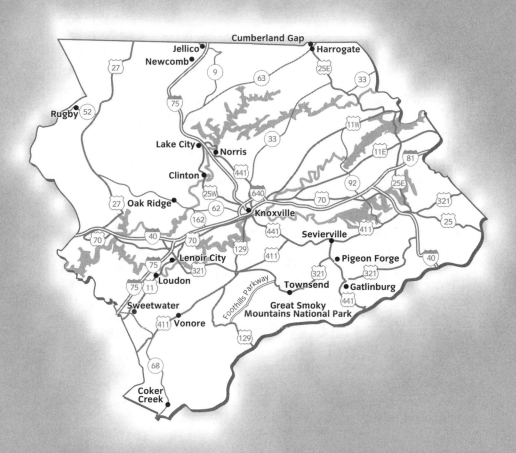

# Cumberland Gap/Harrogate

Cumberland Gap is probably the most historic natural passageway through the mountains. Much of the early westward movement of America came through this V-shaped gap in the Appalachians. Long before white settlers traversed this giant wall of stone known as the Appalachians, Native American tribes crossed the mountains, using trails marked by the buffalo.

Daniel Boone spent several years exploring this area in the early 1770s, and when the peace treaties with native tribes were signed, he and thirty men were called back to mark and stake out the Wilderness Trail from Long Island (now Kingsport) into Kentucky. Immigration began immediately, and by the end of the Revolutionary War, more than 12,000 persons had followed the Wilderness Trail through the gap into the new territory. Records show that by 1800, more than 300,000 people had crossed the gap moving west, including Abraham Lincoln's parents.

**Harrogate City Park** (all ages)

**Corner of Highway 25E and Highway 63; (423) 869–0211 (Harrogate City Hall). Open during daylight hours, seven days a week. Free.**

Here you'll find ball courts, a playground, a hiking trail, a mountain bike trail, a gazebo and picnic shelter, and a soccer field. The trails connect to Cumberland Gap National Historical Park.

## The Highland **Games (all ages)**

The Highland Games are held in Harrogate City Park the second weekend in October. During this event, the descendents of the Scottish settlers to the area celebrate their heritage. Featured activities include Scottish dancing, food, athletic competitions, and music. $, 12 and under admitted **free.**

**Cumberland Gap Historic District** (ages 8 and up)

**Colwyn Avenue; (423) 869–3860 (Town Hall) or (800) 332–8164 (Claiborne County Chamber of Commerce).**

Cumberland Gap's historic downtown area has a nice variety of restored homes and quaint shops. Among the historic places open to the public are the Towne Hall—the original schoolhouse—much as it was in the 1920s, and the Old Drugstore, a century-old pharmacy. There's also a historic iron furnace, built in the early 1820s and used to make iron that was shipped off to Chattanooga and to blacksmiths throughout the region. At its peak the furnace created more than thirty-five tons of pig iron a week.

## Cumberland Gap National Historical Park (all ages)

**Highway 25 East, just north of Harrogate and Cumberland Gap. Open daily 8:00 A.M. to dusk. The visitor center is located on Highway 25 East in Middlesboro, Kentucky; (606) 248–2817. The visitor center is open 8:00 A.M. to 5:00 P.M. (until 6:00 P.M. in the summer). Free.**

For a real family adventure, you'll want to visit Cumberland Gap National Historical Park, which runs along the top of Cumberland Mountain. The 20,000-acre park is located in Tennessee, Virginia, and Kentucky on the site where the original path crossed through the gap in the mountains. Today, you can get through the mountain via the four-lane Cumberland Gap Tunnel.

The park offers more than 50 miles of hiking trails, ranging from short, self-guided nature trails to longer, overnight treks. There is a 160-site campground in the Virginia part of the park. Be sure to go to the top of the mountain and check out the view.

## Hensley Settlement (all ages)

**Cumberland Gap National Historical Park; (606) 248–2817. Tours offered daily May 1 through October 31. Reservations recommended. $–$$.**

The idea of wanting to get away from it all is not a new one; just look what Sherman Hensley did in 1904. He and his relatives moved into the mountains a few miles from Cumberland Gap. The Hensleys and the Gibbons, related by marriage, forsook settled areas for the remote mountaintop. They became self-sufficient while the rest of America was learning to rely more on each other for basic needs. The last Hensley left the area in 1951, leaving the twelve scattered farmsteads abandoned.

Since 1965, the National Park Service has restored parts of the Hensley Settlement, including three houses, several barns, many fences, the schoolhouse, and the cemetery. Another means of getting to the settlement is on foot, following a 3½-mile path up the side of the mountain.

Amazing
**Tennessee Facts**

Tennessee became the sixteenth state of the Union on June 1, 1796.

## Abraham Lincoln Library and Museum (ages 6 and up)

**Highway 25 East, Harrogate; (423) 869–6235. Open daily. $, under 6 admitted free.**

The Lincoln Memorial Museum, on the campus of Lincoln Memorial University, is a living memorial to the sixteenth president of the United States. This place is a tremendous source of information about Lincoln. After you visit the campus and the museum, you'll never think of Honest Abe in the same way. The university itself is a direct outgrowth of the staunch patriotism of the eastern Tennessee mountain folk during the Civil War.

In 1863 Lincoln told Union general O. O. Howard, "General, if you come out of this horror and misery alive . . . I want you to do something for these people who have been shut out from the world all these years." In 1896 Howard founded the university and dedicated it as a living memorial to his former commander in chief. The charter was signed in 1897 on February 12, Lincoln's birthday.

The charter mandated the establishment of a museum to house memorabilia of Lincoln and the era. That collection now numbers more than 25,000 items and is still growing. One of the most popular items here is the ebony cane Lincoln carried to Ford's Theatre on the night he was assassinated.

## Other Things to See and Do

**Cudjo's Caverns** (all ages), Cumberland Gap National Historical Park; (606) 248–2817. Call for updated hours and admission prices. Located inside the mountain underneath the Wilderness Road, Cudjo's Caverns features many beautiful stalactite and stalagmite formations.

## Where to Eat

**Webb's Country Kitchen,** 602 Colwyn Avenue, downtown; (423) 869–5877. $

**Ye Olde Tea and Coffee Shop,** 527 Colwyn Avenue; (423) 869–4844 or (800) 899–4844. $ (lunch), $$–$$$ (dinner)

## Where to Stay

**Cumberland Gap Inn,** 630 Brooklyn Street; (423) 869–9172 or (888) 408– 0127. Fireplaces in some rooms. $$–$$$

**Ramada Inn of Cumberland Gap,** Highway 58; (423) 869–3631 or (800) 2–RAMADA. Family-style restaurant. $$

## For More Information

**Claiborne County Chamber of Commerce,** 3222 Highway 25E, Suite 1, Tazewell, TN 37879; (423) 626–4149 or (800) 332–8164; www.claibornecounty. com. Open 8:30 A.M. to 4:30 P.M. Monday through Friday.

# Jellico/Newcomb

One of the most scenic highways in this part of the state connects Jellico with Lafollette. Although it seems much longer, Highway 25 West curves and twists for 29 fun miles. If stomachs allow, alert the kids to count all the "roller coaster" bumps you'll be going over. The road follows Clear Fork Canyon through the mountains.

The highway is a great alternative to interstate driving, but you'll have to adjust your speed to the road conditions. Plus, you'll probably want to pull off a couple of times to enjoy the scenery and the canyons. Several bitter skirmishes were fought around here during the Civil War.

Amazing
# Tennessee Facts

Jellico, first settled in 1795, was incorporated in 1883. A trading center for the booming coal mine industry, the town was named for the seam of high-quality bituminous coal known as Jellico coal. Jellico coal got its name from the Angelica plant, which grows wild in the surrounding mountains. Early settlers were said to have used the plant to make an intoxicating drink called Jelco or Gelca.

## Fourth of July Celebration (all ages)

**Veterans Park, downtown Jellico; (423) 784–3275. The weekend closest to July 4. Free.**

The streets are full of crafts fairs, parties, and festivities for three days. There's a country music concert, usually starring a well-known entertainer, plus fireworks, parades, and ball games.

## Indian Mountain State Park (all ages)

**Off I–75, at the Jellico exit; (423) 784–7958. Open sunrise to sundown. Free. Fees charged for some activities and for camping.**

Indian Mountain, one of Tennessee's smallest state parks, is snuggled into the Cumberland Mountains within the city limits of Jellico and is an often-cited example of ideal land reclamation. This area of the mountains had tremendous sources of coal, which was mined for many years by stripping the land. By the early 1950s the strip mines were abandoned, leaving the scarred lands behind.

The city leaders hated the unsightly land and went after federal funds to help reclaim it. With the assistance of those funds, the area was made into a local park in the late 1960s. Several years later it was handed over to the state.

There's lots of good fishing here, ranging from bluegill and crappie to the twenty-plus-pound catfish that have been caught. This park is also popular with campers. This is mainly a day-use park, with a lot of locals coming in and enjoying the walking trails and the ponds. If you don't feel like walking, you can rent a paddleboat and take a family cruise.

## Old Fashion Fall Fest (all ages)

**Veterans Park, downtown Jellico; (423) 784–3275.**

The first weekend in October, Jellico turns back the clock to the days of its forefathers with a variety of events, including pie-eating contests; horseshoe pitching; soap-making, woodworking, basket-weaving, weaving, spinning, and molasses-making demonstrations; and all kinds of food and music.

### Crazy Quilt Friendship Center (all ages)

2967 Highway 297, Newcomb; (423) 784–6022. Open 9:00 A.M. to 4:30 P.M. Monday through Friday, 10:00 A.M. to 4:00 P.M. Saturday. Free.

About 4 miles down Highway 297 from Jellico, you'll find the Crazy Quilt Friendship Center. It's a nonprofit outlet for the crafts produced by locals. You'll find some great mountain treasures here, including quilts, cornhusk dolls, wooden toys, and just about anything else that can be made by the local folk artists.

## Other Things to See and Do

**Grace Moore monument,** Downtown Park. Free. Grace Moore was an internationally known opera and film star who grew up in Jellico. She died in a plane crash in 1947.

## Where to Eat

**Gregory's Family Tree Restaurant,** 1417 Fifth Street (in the Days Inn); (423) 784–4176. Good home cooking and daily lunch specials. $

## Where to Stay

**Best Western Holiday Plaza Motel,** Highway 25 West, off I–75 at exit 160, Jellico, TN; (423) 784–7241 or (800) 528–1234. $

**Indian Mountain State Park (camping),** off I–75, at exit 160; (423) 784–7958. Forty-nine campsites; grills, picnic tables, hookups, and bathhouse. $

## For More Information

**Jellico Tourism,** 104 North Main Street, Jellico, TN 37762; (423) 784–3275. Open 9:00 A.M. to 4:00 P.M. Monday through Friday.

# Rugby

### Historic Rugby

5517 Rugby Highway (Highway 52); (888) 214–3400. Guided tours available daily. $. Fees allow you access to four historic buildings and the visitor center museum. Other facilities, including an 1880s hiking trail and the Gentlemen's Swimming Hole, are free.

Throughout history, forward-thinking individuals have tried to create perfect societies based on their religious or philosophical beliefs. None of these "utopian" societies has lasted to the present. Of the three experiments in Tennessee during the late 1800s, Rugby was the largest and has left us with the most evidence of the dreamers' visions.

Famous British author, statesman, and social reformer Thomas Hughes launched his utopian idea at Rugby in 1880. It was to be a cooperative, class-free society where Britain's younger sons of gentry and artisans, tradesmen, and farming families could build a new community through agriculture, temperance, and high Christian principles.

The utopian dream lives on today in the beautiful, quaint village of Rugby. The modern residents, however, are the ones keeping the dreams alive, not the followers of Hughes. Ironically, living in Rugby today, with its architecture combining the best of British and Appalachian heritage, is about as close to living in utopia as one could get. At its peak in 1884, its population was about 350. Today, approximately eighty people reside in Rugby.

The area has been listed on the National Register of Historic Places since 1972. Little has been changed by modern technology. More than twenty of the original seventy buildings have been preserved or restored, and a few of them are open to the public.

A visit to town should start at the Schoolhouse Visitor Centre. There you'll find exhibits and artifacts that trace Rugby from its founding to today's renaissance movement.

Among the buildings open to the public is Christ Church Episcopal. Built in 1887, it still has the original hanging lamps and the 1849 rosewood organ. The Thomas Hughes Library with its 7,000 volumes of Victorian literature, stands today virtually unchanged from the days when the doors opened in 1882.

The guided tour allows access to the library, schoolhouse, church, and founder's home. There is also a museum shop, a print shop, and a crafts commissary, all in original buildings.

Historic Rugby sponsors year-round special events, crafts workshops, and outdoor workshops. Walking trails built in 1880, which have been maintained ever since, lead to the "Gentlemen's Swimming Hole" and what locals call the Meeting of the Waters, where the Clear Forks and White Oak Streams join.

## Where to Eat

**Harrow Road Cafe,** 5545 Highway 52; (423) 628–2350. British and Appalachian foods. $–$$

## Where to Stay

**Grey Gables Bed & Breakfast Inn,** Highway 52; (423) 628–5252. Eight-room country inn. Fireplace, TV, great food. $$

**Newbury House Bed & Breakfast,** P.O. Box 8; (888) 214–3400. The colony's first boardinghouse, Newbury House has six Victorian-furnished rooms with fireplaces. Ages 10 and up welcome. $$$$

**Pioneer Cottage,** Highway 52; (888) 214–3400. Five-room cottage built in 1880. Screened porch. No TV, radio, or phone. Pioneer Cottage welcomes children of all ages. $$$

## For More Information

**Historic Rugby,** P.O. Box 8, 5517 Rugby Highway, Rugby, TN 37733; (888) 214–3400; www.historicrugby.org. Open 9:00 A.M. to 5:30 P.M. daily.

# Norris/Clinton/Lake City

The Tennessee Valley Authority (TVA) brought recreational life to this area of the state in 1933, when President Franklin Roosevelt created the agency whose initial objectives were flood control, navigation, and electrical power. It wasn't long after construction began on Norris Dam, the first TVA project, that it became clear that scenic beauty and recreation would also be a major asset of the program. The three cities of Norris, Clinton, and Lake City are not to be missed while you're in East Tennessee.

The city of Norris, which TVA officials said would be a model city, was built nearby to house some of the 2,800 workers on the TVA project. Houses and dormitories were built, and the birth of the town began. It was laid out with large, green common areas and houses built at varying angles on small lots. There were at least a dozen styles of houses, all made of different materials so they would look different. Most houses were all electric. The schools and public offices faced a large common green.

In 1947 the TVA sold the town to a large corporation, which then resold the individual houses to current tenants or to the public on the open market. Today most of the style and sophistication of the small community has been preserved. It is still a good example of a planned community.

## Anderson County Welcome Center

**Off I–75 at exit 122; (800) 524–3602; www.yallcome.org. Open 9:00 A.M. to 5:00 P.M. Monday through Saturday. Free.**

You can pick up brochures and get other information about the area and its attractions here. Local musicians (fiddlers, banjo players, and other "pickers") entertain visitors every Thursday from 1:00 to 3:00 P.M.

## Norris Dam State Park (all ages)

**125 Village Green Circle, off Highway 441; (865) 426–7461. Open 8:00 A.M. to 10:00 P.M. Free.**

Norris Dam State Park is located on 4,000 acres on the shores of Norris Lake at the site of the dam. In addition to the natural wonders of the area, which include caves, streams, scenic valleys, and a virgin forest, there are sites such as an eighteenth-century gristmill, a threshing barn, and the Lenoir Museum.

This area has everything needed for a perfect family outing. The park itself has two different campgrounds, complete with bathhouses and dump stations, and nineteen rustic cabins and ten deluxe cabins. Picnic sites are located throughout the area.

The Village Green area features a swimming pool, a kiddie pool, modern bathhouses, and concession stands. Lifeguards are on duty. The recreation center in the Village Green offers archery, badminton, volleyball, shuffleboard, and many other activities. Equipment can be checked out at the ranger's station.

There are also many miles of woodland trails that meander throughout the park and the adjacent lands, which provide spectacular views of the lake and its surrounding hills and valleys. The dam has overlooks on both sides with picnic areas and rest rooms.

Norris Dam State Park also has programs during summer months for children of all ages, and all programs are **free.** Some examples are Snakes of Tennessee, Owl Prowl, and Hill Cave Tours. During October and November the park has fall color trips on Norris Lake, and other seasonally appropriate programs are offered throughout the year.

### Lenoir Museum (ages 8 and up)

**2121 Norris Freeway (Highway 441), 1 mile below Norris Dam; (865) 494–9688. Open year-round 9:00 A.M. to 5:00 P.M. Tuesday through Sunday. Closed Monday.** Free.

The Lenoir Museum, located within Norris Dam State Park, houses the immense collection that Will Lenoir and his wife, Helen, accumulated over sixty years. Both strongly desired that societal changes not wipe out an appreciation of the hard work and ingenuity that were a part of the everyday life they felt was disappearing.

Their collection is eclectic and unique, but it's the stories of the people behind the items that make this a fun place to visit. The stories were collected and preserved as dearly as the items themselves. Presented by docents, the stories bring life to history and create a fun environment for the entire family to learn about the past in this area of the state. It's probably the most unpretentious, hands-on museum you'll ever visit.

### Caleb Crosby Threshing Barn (all ages)

**Clear Creek Road; (865) 426–7461. Open year-round.** Free.

Located near the Lenoir Museum is the Caleb Crosby Threshing Barn. Built in the 1830s, the barn was dismantled when the TVA lake was to flood the area on which it stood. It was reconstructed here in 1978 and now houses much of its original machinery and many old farm tools made in the 1800s.

### Rice Grist Mill (all ages)

**Norris Dam State Park; (865) 494–0720. Open April 15 through November 30, 8:30 A.M. to 4:30 P.M. Wednesday through Sunday. Closed Monday and Tuesday.** Free.

The Rice Grist Mill, adjacent to the barn and the museum, was built in 1798 and was an active mill until 1935, when the TVA was set to flood its location. It was moved to its present location and today still grinds corn each summer for the public to view and learn about. The mill is also a gift and crafts shop.

### Museum of Appalachia (all ages)

**Highway 61, 1 mile east of I–75; (865) 494–0514 or (865) 494–7680. Open year-round. 8:00 A.M. to 5:00 P.M. or later (hours extended in the spring, summer, and fall). Admission: $–$$. Rates are different for special events such as the Fall Homecoming.**

John Rice Irwin created and still operates a sixty-five-acre collection known as the Museum of Appalachia. The idea to start a private museum came from his love and appreciation for the people of Appalachia and from his grandfather's wish that he would "start a little museum" with some of the authentic pioneer items that he gave the boy.

Today there are more than thirty authentic log cabins and buildings that Irwin has collected and moved onto his property. Within those buildings is a collection of more than 250,000 historical artifacts. The complex has a lived-in look that Rice preferred over the lifeless museum look. Each structure appears to be lived in and is authentically furnished for its period. The entire facility has a split rail fence around it, and costumed interpreters are on hand to give it a living-history feel. It has been called "the most authentic and complete replica of pioneer Appalachian life in the world."

Kids love this place. There is plenty of room for them to move around and a lot of action going on, from shingle making to a rifle-making display to spinning and weaving demonstrations. From spring plowing and planting to holiday celebrations, the complex traces the life of Appalachian pioneers. The annual Fall Homecoming held here on the second weekend in October is a wonderful event; if you want to come, be sure to make your hotel reservations early in the year.

## Appalachian Arts Craft Shop (all ages)

**Highway 61, across from the Museum of Appalachia; (865) 494–9854. Open 10:00 A.M. to 6:00 P.M. Monday through Saturday, 1:00 to 5:00 P.M. Sunday. Free.**

One of the country's oldest successful craft co-ops is located across Highway 61 from the museum. You'll find a full array of locally created crafts including pottery, baskets, quilts, toys, dolls, weaving, and wood items.

## Coal Creek Motor Discovery Trail (all ages)

**Anderson County Tourism Center, 115 Welcome Lane, Clinton; (865) 457–4547; www.coal creekaml.com. Open twenty-four hours a day.**

This self-guided driving tour meanders through the Lake City (formerly known as Coal Creek), Beech Grove, Fraterville, and Briceville communities and tells visitors the history of mining in this community and the impact it had on the history of mining in the United States. It was here in the early 1900s that two mining disasters killed hundreds of miners, which led to the improvement of working conditions in mines across the country. All historic points on the trail, including cemeteries, are marked with historical markers.

## Other Things to See and Do

**Coal Miners Museum of the Cumberland Mountains** (all ages), Lake City Community Center, 1 mile off I–75 at exit 128; (865) 457–4542 or (800) 524–3602. Call for hours. **Free.** This small but fascinating museum features articles that belonged to the miners who were killed in the Fratersville mine explosion in the early 1900s.

## Where to Eat

**Golden Girls Restaurant,** Off I–75 at exit 122; (865) 457–3302. Family-style restaurant with daily lunch and dinner specials. $

**Harrison's.** Off I–75 at exit 122; (865) 463–MENU. Steak, seafood, and pasta to please even the most finicky eater. Desserts are made fresh daily. Caters especially to kids. $

## Where to Stay

**Comfort Inn,** 120 Welcome Lane; (865) 457–2255 or (800) 228–5150. $$

**Holiday Inn Express,** 141 Buffalo Road; (865) 457–2233 or (800) HOLIDAY. $$

**Skunk Ridge Tree Farm and Bed & Breakfast,** 1203 Mountain View Drive; (865) 494–0214; www.skunkridge.com. This charming, family-owned combination Christmas-tree farm and bed-and-breakfast offers kids plenty of space to roam. You can even board your horses here, and there's a riding ring. The kids will enjoy the pool in the warm months. The two spacious bedrooms have private baths and cable TV. The breakfasts are wonderful. $$–$$$

## For More Information

**Anderson County Tourism Council,** 115 Welcome Lane, Clinton, TN 37716; (865) 457–4542 or (800) 524–3602; www.yallcome .com. Open 9:00 A.M. to 5:00 P.M. Monday through Saturday.

# Oak Ridge

The city of Oak Ridge was created more than sixty years ago as part of the federal government's Manhattan Project, the code name for the American effort to develop the atomic bomb. Beginning in 1942 the government came into this rural part of the state and started to create a military boomtown.

As you can imagine, security was quite tight, and only a handful of the thousands who worked here knew the true nature of the project. Each had his or her own work to do and knew nothing beyond that. It was not until the dropping of the first atomic bombs in 1945 that the inhabitants behind the fences learned they had been members of the Manhattan Project. Their city produced uranium 235 and plutonium 239, the fuel necessary for the atomic bomb.

The city, which grew to a population of more than 75,000 during the war, remained under direct governmental supervision, and a large barbed-wire fence surrounded most of the 60,000 acres. The fences came down in 1949, and the city was incorporated. Most of the "Secret City" still stands.

### Oak Ridge Driving Tour (all ages)

300 South Tulane Avenue; (865) 482–7821; www.oakridgevisitor.com. Tour guides available at both American Museum of Science and Energy and Oak Ridge Welcome Center. **Free.**

Visit historic Oak Ridge and get a unique view of the community, historic sites, and attractions with the guidance of a compact disc or cassette tape. This enables you to take a leisurely stop at the many highlighted attractions along your route.

### American Museum of Science and Energy (all ages)

300 South Tulane Avenue; (865) 576–3200; www.amse.org. Open Tuesday through Saturday 9:00 A.M. to 5:00 P.M. and Sunday 1:00 to 5:00 P.M. Closed Monday. $.

If you want the complete story, you'll find it at the U.S. Department of Energy's American Museum of Science and Energy, the world's largest and most comprehensive energy exhibition. You'll learn about science and energy through interactive exhibits, live demonstrations, computers, and audiovisual presentations. There's plenty of fun, interactive exhibits for the kids, and they'll be able to pick up some scientific games and toys in the gift shop.

### Children's Museum of Oak Ridge (all ages)

461 West Outer Drive; (865) 482–1074; www.newsite.com/cmor. Open 9:00 A.M. to 5:00 P.M. Monday through Friday, 1:30 to 4:30 P.M. Saturday and Sunday from September through May; June through August, Saturday hours are 11:00 A.M. to 4:00 P.M. Admission: $–$$, under 3 admitted **free.**

Based on the premise that "I hear and I forget, I see and I remember, I do and I understand," the Children's Museum of Oak Ridge is a wonderful hands-on learning center. I don't recall ever seeing so many smiles on faces as I did the day we visited here. This is a must-stop, whether you live in the state or are just passing through.

There are twelve exhibition areas where you can explore, experience, and discover. Kids can explore the past by becoming a pioneer living in an 1880s log cabin, or they can go underground to dig in a coal mine. They can learn about the World War II era and the part Oak Ridge played in it, and they can travel to Japan, Norway, Africa, and the North Pole to learn about faraway cultures. My kids especially liked the nature area, where they got to touch various works of Mother Nature. Don't miss the life-size dollhouse and the rain forest exhibit.

### Secret City Scenic Excursions Train (all ages)

Highway 58, west of Oak Ridge, exit 356 off I-40 West; (865) 241–2140; www.techscribes .com/sarm. Excursions on selected Saturdays and Sundays; call for a schedule. Rates: $–$$. Groups of up to ten (caboose), $125.00.

Take a trip aboard a 1940s-era railroad car through the once-secret part of Oak Ridge. The 12-mile round-trip excursion starts at the East Tennessee Technology Park, the former K-25

Manhattan Project site, and travels through rolling countryside and across a scenic bridge to historic Blair, Tennessee.

### Oak Ridge Facilities Public Bus Tour (ages 10 and up)
**The tour begins at American Museum of Science and Energy, 300 South Tulane Avenue; (865) 576–3200. Tour runs Tuesday through Friday, noon to 2:30 P.M., May through September. $, includes admission to AMSE.**

Take this unique tour highlighting the history of science and technology at the three Department of Energy Oak Ridge facilities and the American Museum of Science and Energy. Included in the tour are the Oak Ridge Nuclear Laboratory Graphite Reactor (a National Historic Landmark), the East Tennessee Technology Park, and a visitor overlook. This guided tour provides a close-up look at what was known as World War II's "Secret City."

## Other Things to See and Do

**Cedar Hill** (all ages), at the corner of West Outer Drive and Michigan Avenue. **Free.** This seven-acre city park has a great playground for the kids. It's surrounded by cedar trees and is a nice, cool place to picnic and play.

## Where to Eat

**Big Ed's Pizza,** 101 Broadway; (865) 482–4885. The best pizza in town. $–$$

**The Soup Kitchen,** 47 East Tennessee Avenue, in historic Jackson Square; (865) 482–3525. Chili and many types of soup. $

## Where to Stay

**Comfort Inn,** 433 South Rutgers Avenue; (865) 481–8200 or (800) 553–7830. $$–$$$

## For More Information

**Oak Ridge Convention and Visitors Bureau,** 302 South Tulane Avenue, Oak Ridge, TN 37830; (865) 482–7821 or (800) 887–3429; www.oakridgevisitor.com. Open 9:00 A.M. to 5:00 P.M. Monday through Friday, and 9:00 A.M. to 1:00 P.M. Saturday. (Closed on Saturday November through May.)

# Knoxville

### Gateway Regional Visitors Center and Volunteer Landing (all ages)
**900 Volunteer Landing Lane; (800) 727–8045. Open year-round 9:00 A.M. to 5:00 P.M. Monday through Saturday. April through October also open 1:00 to 5:00 P.M. Sunday. Free.**

Located along the riverfront, this visitor center is a good place to stop for information on the entire region. Exhibits concentrate on sites within a 100-mile radius of Knoxville and include portions of six states. Outside, a plaza area is surrounded by waterfalls and native plantings. There is a gift shop, too.

### Knoxville Zoo (all ages)
**3500 Knoxville Zoo Drive, 3 miles from downtown Knoxville, just off I–40 East; (865) 637–5331; www.knoxville-zoo.org. Open 10:00 A.M. to 4:30 P.M. daily. Admission: $–$$, under 3 admitted free.**

The 53-acre Knoxville Zoo, located in the 130-acre Chilhowee Park, has more than 1,000 creatures representing every continent. What makes this place so interesting is that you won't find animals in little cages. Most live in large re-created natural habitats that give a better idea of how the inhabitants would live in the wild. Chimp Ridge, for example, features a 240-foot-high waterfall, termite mounds, boulders, streambeds, and trees full of vines.

Step into the heart of the Great Smoky Mountains and come face to face with a black bear at the new entrance to the zoo, Black Bear Falls. This exhibit features a 40-foot-long tunnel designed as a huge hollow log, which provides people coming into the zoo with an up-close experience with the black bears. It also features four waterfalls, each with more than a 20-foot drop. Water misters create a foglike haze similar to what you would see in the Smokies.

The zoo has a reputation for its big cat collection. You'll find beautiful lions, tigers, leopards, cheetahs, and pumas, all living as they would in the wild. Be sure to spend some time watching Ravi, a magnificent white tiger. The hilly, well-landscaped zoo is a great place to take a leisurely stroll in the shade on a hot afternoon.

In addition to the animals and the nice petting zoo, there are camel rides and a train ride, each requiring an additional fee.

## Amazing Tennessee Facts

The first African elephant born in the Western Hemisphere was Little Diamond, born in March 1978 at the Knoxville Zoo.

### Knoxville Museum of Art (ages 8 and up)
**1050 World's Fair Park Drive; (865) 525–6101; www.knoxart.org. Open Tuesday and Wednesday noon to 8:00 P.M., Thursday and Friday noon to 9:00 P.M., and Saturday and Sunday 11:00 A.M. to 5:00 P.M. Admission: $, 17 and under free every Tuesday 5:00 to 8:00 P.M.**

The contemporary-looking Knoxville Museum of Art is located at World's Fair Park. Faced with Tennessee pink marble, the modular 53,200-square-foot structure houses a collection of Tennessee art as well as ever-changing traveling exhibits.

### Fort Kid (all ages)

**World's Fair Park. Open from sunrise to sunset. Free.**

Across the street from the art museum is Fort Kid, a playground built by volunteers as a community project. Run by the Parks and Recreation Department, the area has a rustic look with all types of swinging, climbing, and crawling activities.

### Ijams Nature Center (all ages)

**2915 Island Home Avenue; (865) 577–4717; www.ijams.org. Trails open daily from 8:00 A.M. until sunset. Visitor Center is open Monday through Friday, 9:00 A.M. to dusk, Saturday noon to 4:00 P.M., and Sunday 1:00 to 5:00 P.M. Free.**

Overlooking the Tennessee River, the eighty-acre Ijams Nature Center provides a piece of the wilds in downtown Knoxville. Developed as an environmental education center, it encompasses woods, meadows, and wildflower marshes, all connected by a series of trails. An active lecture and program schedule almost guarantees that something will be going on when you drop by.

### *Star of Knoxville* Riverboat (all ages)

**300 Neyland Drive; (865) 525–STAR; www.tnriverboat.com. Open daily April through December, weekdays January through March. Hours vary. $$–$$$ (varies as to time and type of cruise—sightseeing, lunch, or dinner).**

A sampling of river life can be had by taking a cruise on the *Star of Knoxville,* a genuine 325-passenger riverboat stern-wheeler. There are all kinds of special parties and dinner cruises set up, including daily sightseeing rides complete with a narrated guide. You'll cruise by the University of Tennessee, the downtown skyline, some of the oldest houses in the city, and sites that the Cherokees called home.

Amazing
# Tennessee Facts

Knoxville is the third largest city in the state, after Memphis and Nashville.

### Discovery Center (all ages)

**516 North Beaman Street, in Chilhowee Park, next to the zoo; (865) 594–1494. Open 9:00 A.M. to 5:00 P.M. Monday through Friday, and 10:00 A.M. to 5:00 P.M. Saturday. Admission: $.**

The Discovery Center, a museum of science and world cultures, offers a nice selection of mind-expanding exhibits and activities. The Cosmic Arcade presents hands-on activities relating to computers, lasers, holograms, plasma balls, lightning, microscopes, and stereograms, and the Akima Planetarium features a lineup of out-of-this-world programs. You'll also view ten aquariums, a living beehive, an insect zoo, butterflies, birds, and dinosaurs.

### James White Fort (all ages)

**205 East Hill Avenue; (865) 525–6514. Open 9:30 A.M. to 4:30 P.M. Monday through Saturday, March through December; 10:00 A.M. to 4:00 P.M. Monday through Friday, January and February. Admission: $, under 5 admitted free.**

Take a step back in time and visit the James White Fort, located on a bluff above the Tennessee River in downtown Knoxville. Built in 1786 by Gen. James White, the founder of the city, the complex consists of his home, three cabins, and the stockade walls used as protection against Native American attacks.

   Today those buildings have been restored, and several more have been added to house an extensive collection of authentic artifacts. The original houses, a museum, a loom house, a smokehouse, and a blacksmith's shop are all open to the public. Tour guides dressed in period clothing have a great deal of knowledge about the complex and the pioneer life of the area, and they have some great fun stories to tell.

### Women's Basketball Hall of Fame (ages 6 and up)

**700 Hall of Fame Drive, next to Volunteer Landing; (865) 633–9000; www.wbhof.com. Open 10:00 A.M. to 7:00 P.M. Monday through Saturday, 1:00 to 6:00 P.M. on Sunday. $–$$, under 5 admitted free.**

This 30,000-square-foot attraction opened in 1999 as a fun, interactive, hands-on experience. If you like basketball, you'll want to check it out. Exhibits focus on the past, present, and future of the sport. Pause for a moment at the main entrance and take in the panoramic view of the Tennessee River, Smoky Mountains, and downtown Knoxville.

### Dogwood Arts Festival (all ages)

**Call (865) 637–4561 for a listing and schedule of events; www.dogwoodarts.com. Most events are free.**

Knoxville has a reputation for having a fun celebration for any and all seasons. Probably the best known is the annual Dogwood Arts Festival held during the month of April, when the millions of dogwood trees in the city are in bloom. In addition to nature's great pink-and-white contribution, there are musical concerts ranging from bluegrass to jazz, dance programs, children's activities, crafts, and various cultural events. Six trails covering 50 miles of dogwood blooms have been developed. You can drive your own car on those routes, or you can take a free bus tour.

### Three Rivers Rambler (all ages)

**401 Henley Street; (865) 524–9411. Train runs March 31 through November 1. Departure times are 2:00 P.M. and 5:00 P.M. Saturday and Sunday. Admission: $$–$$$.**

All aboard! Take a scenic ninety-minute round-trip train ride from downtown Knoxville to the forks of the Tennessee River

aboard this historic train. Witness the beauty of East Tennessee in a unique way as you ride this train, complete with a 1925 steam engine *(Lindy)*, a 1925 Pullman car *(Resplendid)*, two 1932 coach cars, an open-air rail, and a luxury caboose *(Desire)*. The train steams out of Volunteer Landing for a one-of-a-kind experience.

## Other Things to See and Do

**Celebration Station** (all ages), 400 North Peters Road; (865) 539–2288. Open noon to 10:00 P.M. Sunday through Thursday, noon to 11:00 P.M. Friday and Saturday. **Free.** Activities are pay as you play. Miniature golf, bumper boats, go-carts, arcade games, children's rides, and a snack bar themed as a 1950s diner.

**East Tennessee Historical Society Museum** (all ages), 600 Market Street, (865) 215–8824; www.east-tennessee-history .org. Open 10:00 A.M. to 4:00 P.M. Monday through Saturday, 1:00 to 5:00 P.M. Sunday. **Free.** This museum offers lots of hands-on exhibits and a children's area called Davy's Attic. The small log cabin is kid-size and contains clothing like Davy Crockett wore, books for children, and puppets so kids can create their own shows. There are boxes throughout the permanent exhibits containing items children can pick up and examine that relate to the period.

**Frank H. McClung Museum** (all ages), 1327 Circle Park Drive on the University of Tennessee campus; (865) 974–2144; www.mcclungmuseum.utk.edu. Open 9:00 A.M. to 5:00 P.M. Monday through Saturday. **Free.** This museum contains exhibits that pertain to the archaeology and native peoples of Tennessee, along with some exhibits that relate to ancient Egypt. There are lots of interesting artifacts—including a real mummy and a dinosaur footprint.

**Haley Heritage Square** (all ages), 1600 Dandridge Avenue, in Morningside Park, less than 1 mile east of downtown; (865) 523–7263 or (800) 727–8045. Open daily sunrise to sunset. **Free.** A 13-foot bronze statue of Alex Haley, the Pulitzer Prize–winning author of Roots, is the centerpiece of this attraction. Haley, a native of Henning, Tennessee, spent the last fourteen years of his life in East Tennessee. The square also includes a community-built playground, walking trail, and picnic areas.

**Knoxville's Cradle of Country Music Tour** (ages 6 and up), 600 Market Street, downtown. This downtown walking tour focuses on Knoxville's role in the lives and careers of several country music stars. Brochures are available at the Gateway Regional Visitors Center, and the East Tennessee Historical Society Museum or by calling the Tourism and Sports Corporation at (865) 522–3777.

**Old City Historic District** (all ages), Jackson Avenue and Central Street, at the north end of downtown. Knoxville's renovated downtown district features several restaurants, shops, and boutiques.

## Where to Eat

**Bel Air Grill,** 9117 Executive Park Drive; (865) 694–0606. Family-friendly restaurant with burgers, steaks, and other all-American favorites. $–$$

**Buddy's Bar-b-que,** 5806 Kingston Pike; (865) 584–1924. 8402 Kingston Pike; (865) 691–0088. 121 West End Avenue; (865) 675–4366. $

**Calhoun's Restaurants,** 10020 Kingston Pike; (865) 673–3444. 6515 Kingston Pike; (865) 673–3377. 400 Neyland Drive; (865) 673–3355. Great ribs and barbecue. $–$$$

## Where to Stay

**Days Inn Campus,** 1706 West Cumberland Avenue; (865) 521–5000 or (800) DAYSINN. $$

**Holiday Inn Select, West-Cedar Bluff,** 304 Cedar Bluff Road; (865) 693–1011 or (800) HOLIDAY. On-site restaurant. $$$

**Marriott Knoxville Hotel,** 500 Hill Avenue; (865) 637–1234 or (800) 233–1234. $$$–$$$$

## For More Information

**Knoxville Tourism and Sports Corporation,** 900 East Hill Avenue, Suite 390, Knoxville, TN 37915; (865) 522–3777. www.knoxville.org. Open 8:30 A.M. to 5:00 P.M. Monday through Friday.

# Lenoir City/Loudon

### Fort Loudon Dam (ages 6 and up)
**Highway 321 along the Tennessee River; (865) 986–3737. Free.**

This is the northernmost dam on the Tennessee River built by the Tennessee Valley Authority during World War II. Although for security reasons the dam facilities are no longer open to tourists, you can drive around the dam and walk over it to enjoy some spectacular views. The property adjacent to the dam has family-friendly amenities such as picnic areas, swimming areas, and a boat ramp, which you can enjoy for free. Nearly a dozen marinas dotting the shoreline of the lake offer boat rentals.

### Melton Hill Dam and Lake (all ages)
**Highway 95, 1 mile north of I–40; (865) 988–2440. Free.**

The Melton Hill Dam and Lake, part of the Clinch River, offers a visitor center, a campground, swimming and picnic areas, and boat ramps.

### Carmichael Inn Museum (ages 6 and up) 
**Poplar Street on Courthouse Square, Loudon; (865) 458–1442 or (865) 458–9020. Free.**

This 1810 log cabin served as the local stagecoach inn for years. It is now the county history museum.

# Amazing
# Tennessee Facts

Much of downtown Lenoir City was destroyed in a March 1999 fire. There were no personal injuries, but the fire spread throughout an entire city block, destroying six buildings, including the hundred-year-old former hotel. The only building left standing was the library.

### Historic Downtown Loudon Walking Tour (ages 8 and up)
**501 Poplar Street, Loudon; (865) 458–1442. Free.**

A self-guided walking tour of the downtown area, the county seat of Loudon County, features quite a few pre–Civil War restored homes and buildings. Brochures are available at the Carmichael Inn Museum.

## Other Things to See and Do

**Liberty Park** (all ages), Highway 11, Loudon; (865) 458–2033. Open sunrise to sunset. **Free.** Features swimming pool, jogging and fitness trails, tennis and basketball courts, a baseball and softball field, and a playground.

**Riverside Park** (all ages), Ferry Street, downtown Loudon; (865) 458–2033. Open sunrise to sunset. **Free.** Offers picnic facilities, a boat launch, and fishing piers.

## Where to Eat

**Crosseyed Cricket,** 751 Country Lane, between Lenoir City and Oak Ridge, 2½ miles off I–40 at exit 364; (865) 986–5435. Open March through October. This resort complex has a restaurant, trout lake, catfish lake, campsites, a pool, and more. Catch your own dinner, or order from the menu. One of the dining rooms is in a restored 150-year-old gristmill; another is in a restored 50-year-old cabin. $

**Calhoun's at the Marina,** 100 City Park Drive, (865) 673–3366. This dining establishment has a great view of Fort Loudon Lake and serves a variety of seafood, chicken, and steaks. It has a buffet every Thursday—and it is not to be missed! $

## Where to Stay

**The Captain's Retreat on Fort Loudon Lake,** 3534 Lakeside Drive, Lenoir City; (865) 986–4229 or (877) 541–7421. Four guest rooms with private baths and whirlpools, antique decor, and skylights on winding lake frontage. Overlooks a 75-foot restored antique paddlewheel boat. Children twelve years old and up welcome.

**Crosseyed Cricket (camping),** 751 Country Lane, between Lenoir City and Oak Ridge, 2½ miles off I–40 at exit 364; (865) 986–5435. Open March through October. forty-seven campsites. $

**Ramada Limited,** 400 Interchange Park Drive, off I–75 at exit 81; (865) 986–9000 or (800) 272–6232. $

THE MOUNTAINOUS EAST 55

# For More Information

**Loudon County Chamber of Commerce,** Angel Row, Loudon, TN 37774; (865) 458–0267; www.loudoncounty.net. Open 8:30 A.M. to 4:30 P.M. Monday through Friday.

**Loudon County Visitors Bureau,** 1075 Highway 321 North, Lenoir City, TN 37771; (865) 986–6822. Open 9:00 A.M. to 5:00 P.M. Monday through Saturday. Summer hours are 8:30 A.M. to 5:00 P.M. Monday through Saturday and 1:00 to 5:00 P.M. Sunday.

# Sevierville

### Dolly Parton Statue (all ages)
Sevier County Courthouse lawn. Free.

Dolly Parton grew up outside Sevierville and attended the local high school. It's quite obvious the community is proud to claim her as its own, and it should be. Since making it big, the country star has brought millions of dollars back into the community, both through tourism and through personal contributions to the educational funds in the county. The life-size bronze statue of Dolly is one of the most photographed attractions in town. Dolly herself unveiled the statue on May 2, 1987.

### Sevierville Historic Walking Trail (ages 8 and up)
866 Winfield Dunn Parkway; (865) 453–6411 or (888) SEVIERVILLE. Free.

The downtown section of Sevierville has retained most of its small-town atmosphere. In a walking tour of twenty-six of its historic structures, you can learn about the history of the area.

## Amazing
# Tennessee Facts

Sevierville was named for John Sevier, the first governor of Tennessee. The town was founded in 1795 and incorporated in 1901.

### The Apple Barn and Cider Mill (all ages)
230 Apple Valley Road, just off Route 441; (865) 453–9319. Open daily. Free.

At this working apple orchard, the barn was converted into a mill in 1981, and the owner's farmhouse was converted into a restaurant in 1987. Today, in addition to two restaurants and the cider mill, there's a bakery, an apple butter kitchen, a fudge kitchen, a candy factory, a smokehouse, and a gift shop.

### Smoky Mountain Deer Farm and Exotic Petting Zoo (all ages)
478 Happy Hollow Lane, 5 miles from Sevierville on Highway 411 North; (865) 428–DEER. Open 10:00 A.M. to 5:00 P.M. November through April, 10:00 A.M. to 7:00 P.M. May through October. $–$$.

Buy a cup of feed before walking into the pen with the animals, and you'll be the most popular person there. It's a great opportunity to get close to these tamed critters and quite an experience for the younger ones in your family.

In addition to the deer, you'll get a chance to see and pet zebras, guanaco, llamas, miniature horses, pygmy goats, sheep, miniature Sicilian donkeys, peacocks, and Vietnamese potbellied pigs. Bring your camera because photo opportunities abound.

## Other Things to See and Do

**Forbidden Caverns** (all ages), 455 Blowing Cave Road; (865) 453–5972. Open daily April through November. Call for rates. You can take a guided tour of one of the country's most interesting caves. Special effects make it even more fun.

## Where to Eat

**Applewood Farm House Restaurant,** 250 Apple Valley Road; (865) 429–8644. Applewood Farm House is one of the finest restaurants in this part of the state. There's something tasty here to satisfy the entire family. On the menu are traditional items such as steaks and prime rib, but there are also local favorites such as fried biscuits and fresh Smoky Mountain trout. And you can't go wrong with the fried chicken, turkey and dressing, and country ham.

If it's a nice day during the winter or between Memorial Day and Labor Day, chances are you'll have to wait for dinner. Reservations aren't accepted, so come early, give the hostess your name, and kill the time by browsing through the other parts of the complex. It's worth the wait! Breakfast, lunch, and dinner are served daily year-round. Also on the property is the Applewood Farmhouse Grill, which serves a similar menu. $ (breakfast and lunch), $–$$$ (dinner)

## Where to Stay

**Clarion Inn Willow River,** 1990 Winfield Dunn Parkway; (865) 429–7600 or (800) 610–0565. Balconies overlooking river; some rooms have fireplaces. $$–$$$$

## For More Information

**Sevierville Visitor Center,** 3099 Winfield Dunn Parkway, Sevierville, TN 37876; (865) 453–6411 or (888) SEVIERVILLE; www.visitsevierville.com. Open 8:30 A.M. to 5:30 P.M. Monday through Saturday and 1:00 to 5:00 P.M. Sunday.

# Pigeon Forge

Considering its nickname, Action-Packed Pigeon Forge, one has a tendency to expect a lot when driving into this tourist town, located a few miles from Gatlinburg and the Great Smoky Mountains.

This place brings out the kid in all of us. A drive down Pigeon Forge Parkway is like a drive through the middle of an amusement park. There indeed is an amusement/entertainment park, plus waterparks, go-cart tracks, and carnival rides. If it's fun, it's probably here.

Combine all that with the Elvis Museum, Carbo's Smoky Mountain Police Museum, music theaters, and no less than a dozen miniature golf courses, and you're sure to please everyone in your family.

A word of warning: This place becomes a virtual parking lot during the peak seasons, so it's a smart decision to utilize the Fun Time Trolley, Pigeon Forge's nostalgic answer to mass transit.

Shopping for bargains? Pigeon Forge is a true mecca for outlet aficionados, and if you're lucky enough to have a bunch of shoppers in the family, it's a great addition to a family vacation. It's also great for rainy-days, when you'd rather not be out hiking or riding a horse through the nearby mountains.

The outlet stores are popping up all over, and it's hard to keep track of them all, but a rough count shows there are six outlet malls, with more than 200 stores among them. In addition, there are smaller shops along the parkway selling everything from Christmas items to dolls and toys. There are also several music theaters featuring live family entertainment every night.

### Carbo's Smoky Mountain Police Museum (all ages)

**3311 Parkway; (865) 453–1358. Open 10:00 A.M. to 5:00 P.M. April through October (Friday through Sunday in April, Friday through Wednesday May through October). $–$$.**

Carbo's Smoky Mountain Police Museum houses the Bufford Pusser collection, including the 1974 Corvette in which the Tennessee "Walking Tall" sheriff was killed. Other displays include police badges, uniforms, weapons, and other items from around the world.

### Dollywood (all ages)

**1020 Dollywood Lane, off the parkway at traffic light No. 8; (865) 428–9488 or (800) DOLLY-WOOD; www.dollywood.com. Open early April through December; closed Tuesday and Thursday in April and September, closed Tuesday the month of May, and closed Thursday the month of October. $$$$. Group rates and season passes are available.**

Country music star Dolly Parton came back to the mountains several years ago, purchased part of a local theme park, and renamed it Dollywood. Today, after millions of dollars of ride and entertainment expansions, the park is one of the premier live music show parks in the country. Along with its 1950s-themed area and various rides—including a looping roller coaster, log flume, river rapids ride, and train rides up the mountain—Dollywood offers some of the best in-park musical entertainment and some of the best in-park shopping in the country.

The park offers its own lineup of musical shows, and it brings in some of the biggest names in country music for a series of celebrity concerts during the summer months. It also offers several mountain festivals, including the Harvest Festival and Southern Gospel Jubilee in October. Many regional crafts, including blacksmithing, glassblowing, and wood-working, can be viewed (and items purchased) in the park's Craftsmen Valley.

You will pay a price for all this fun: $39 for each adult, $35 per senior sixty and over, and $29 per child four to eleven.

# Tennessee **Tornado**

If you're a roller coaster fanatic, you'll want to check out Dolly-wood's Tennessee Tornado coaster. The one-of-a-kind coaster takes you on several thrilling twists and turns, upside down loops, and a "double butterfly loop" in honor of Dolly Parton. It even takes you through the side of a mountain. The coaster reaches a maximum speed of 63 miles per hour with 3.7 Gs. Hang on!

### Dixie Stampede Dinner and Show (all ages)
**3849 Parkway; (865) 453–4400 or (800) 356–1676. Open year-round. Admission: $$$$.**

My family especially enjoyed the Dixie Stampede Dinner show, located along the parkway. Here, in an old-looking building, you'll find one of the most original dinner show concepts in the world. You sit at tables facing a large dirt-floor arena and enjoy eating a barbecued chicken dinner with your fingers while watching cowboys, racing pigs, and trick riders per-form. It's a fast-paced, interactive show. The place fills up quickly, so be sure to make a reservation as soon as you know your travel plans.

### Dolly's Splash Country (all ages) 🌊
**2146 Middle Creek Road; (865) 428–9488. Open Memorial Day through Labor Day; hours vary according to weather. $$$.**

Adjacent to Dollywood, this new waterpark sprawls across twenty-five acres, with a 25,000-square-foot wave pool, sixteen water slides, and a winding "Lazy River" tubing ride for those in need of relaxation more than thrills. There are two children's play areas.

### Fun Time Trolley (all ages)
**2910 Middle Creek Road; (865) 453–6444. Open daily 8:30 A.M. to midnight April through Octo-ber, 10:00 A.M. to 10:00 P.M. November and December. Closed January through March. $.**

Pigeon Forge's nostalgic answer to mass transit, the Fun Time Trolley is a great way to get around. For a quarter you can ride the trolley, which makes more than one hundred stops. There is also a handicap van on call; rides are 50 cents.

### The Track (all ages)
**2575 Parkway, at traffic light No. 3; (865) 453–4777 or (865) 428–2675. Open year-round 10:00 A.M. to 11:00 P.M. Monday through Friday, 10:00 A.M. to midnight Saturday and Sunday. Hours sometimes vary. $$–$$$.**

There's all kinds of fun stuff here, including go-cart tracks (even a three-story wooden track), bumper boats and bumper cars, two miniature golf courses, bungee jumping, and an arcade. Part of the complex is called Kid's Country; it features numerous kiddie rides and attractions.

## Mountain **Music**

Driving along the Parkway, it's hard to miss the many music theaters. It seems that one of Pigeon Forge's biggest attractions is music. Here's a rundown of some of the area's live entertainment theaters.

- Black Bear Jamboree Theater, 119 Music Road, (800) 985–5495.
- The Comedy Barn, 2775 Parkway; (865) 428–5222.
- Country Tonite Theatre, 129 Showplace Boulevard; (865) 453–2003 or (800) 792–4308.
- Dixie Stampede, 3849 Parkway; (865) 453–4400 or (800) 356–1676.
- Louise Mandrell Theater, 2046 Parkway; (865) 453–6263 or (800) 768–1170.
- Memories Theater, 2141 Parkway; (865) 428–7852 or (800) 325–3078.
- Ole Smoky Hoedown, 2135 Parkway; (865) 428–5600.
- Smoky Mountain Jubilee, 2115 Parkway; (865) 428–1836.

### Twin Mountain Outdoor Resort (all ages)
**304 Day Springs Road; (865) 453–8181 or (800) 848–9097. Call for rates.**

The resort offers 150 shady campsites on the Little Pigeon River. It features a swimming pool, kiddie pool, tennis and basketball courts, three large bathhouses, a recreation hall, a laundry room, a camp store, cable TV, fishing access, and tubing on the river. The Pigeon Forge Trolley makes a stop here, so you can pull into camp, park your car, and not worry about traffic until you're ready to leave town.

### Dinosaur Walk Museum (all ages)

**106 Showplace Boulevard; (865) 428–4003. Hours vary by season, open every day except December 24 and 25. $–$$.**

This natural science museum contains more than fifty true-to-life dinosaur re-creations. The murals on the walls help create the illusion of a dinosaur world. Most kids' favorites are the *Tyrannosaurus Rex*, near the entry, and the 70-foot-long *Apatosaurus*.

### Professor Hacker's Lost Treasure Golf (ages 5 and up)

**3010 Parkway, (865) 453–0307. Hours and days of operation vary according to season. $–$$.**

Ride a mining train through caverns, past ancient ruins, and beneath waterfalls as you enjoy a round of miniature golf.

### Veterans Memorial Museum (ages 10 and up)

**110 Showplace Boulevard; (865) 908–6003. Hours vary according to season; open daily except December 24 and 25. $-$$.**

This facility is an American military museum, with artifacts dating from the War of 1812 to current conflicts. Among its highlights are some very substantial bronze sculptures, made by the museum owner. The most amazing is a life-size statue of a dozen American World War II soldiers storming a beach.

## Other Things to See and Do

**Belz Factory Outlet World,** 2655 Teaster Lane; (865) 453–3503.

**Christmas Place,** 2470 Parkway; (865) 453–0415 or (800) 445–3396. Huge Christmas village fantasyland, filled with decorated trees, ornaments, lights, clocks, and thousands of other items from around the world.

**Flyaway,** 3106 Parkway; (865) 453–7777. Open daily. If you've ever wondered what it would be like to skydive, this is your chance to find out without having to jump out of a plane. After a short orientation class you can go flying in an indoor skydiving simulator. Flights last three minutes. You must weigh at least forty pounds. The price is $27.57 per person.

**Pigeon Forge Factory Outlet Mall,** 2850 Parkway; (865) 428–2828.

**Tanger Outlet Center,** 161 Wears Valley Road, Sevierville; (865) 408–5775.

## Where to Eat

**The Old Mill & Restaurant,** 160 Old Mill Avenue; (865) 429–3463. Bring a big appetite when you come here. Try the turkey and gravy, pot roast, or fried chicken. All lunches come with corn fritters and corn chowder, and the dinners come with those plus salad and dessert. $$

## Where to Stay

**Holiday Inn Resort,** 3230 Parkway; (865) 428–2700 or (800) 782–3119. Indoor pool with waterfall; also arcade and restaurant. $$–$$$$

**Music Road Hotel,** 303 Henderson Chapel Road; (423) 429–7700 or (800) 429–7700, ext. 888. The mini water park will be a hit with the kids. $$–$$$$

**Willow Brook Lodge,** 3035 Parkway; (865) 453–5334 or (800) 765–1380. This lodge has more than 150 spacious rooms, with an out-door activity center and new indoor pool. $$

## For More Information

**Pigeon Forge Department of Tourism,** 2450 Parkway, P.O. Box 1390, Pigeon Forge, TN 37868; (865) 453–8574 or (800) 251–9100; www.mypigeonforge.com. Open 8:00 A.M. to 5:30 P.M. Monday through Saturday and 1:00 to 5:00 P.M. Sunday. Summer hours are extended Monday through Friday until 6:00 P.M.

# Gatlinburg

You could spend a week here and not see everything that this Gateway to the Smokies has for the tourist. It's a fun family town because its offerings include everything from the totally tacky to the refined, one-of-a-kind piece of mountain folk art.

During peak season traffic jams along the main parkways through town get quite bad. The city has set up a trolley route, complete with old-fashioned trolley cars, to provide transportation throughout the area, so park your car and let someone else fight the traffic as you enjoy the scenery. You'll see the well-marked trolley stops. The cost to ride the trolley is 25 cents per person.

Traffic lights are numbered in Gatlinburg to help you locate attractions.

## Smoky Mountain Winterfest

The fun and excitement in this area of the state don't slow down during the winter months anymore since Gatlinburg, Pigeon Forge, and Sevierville have joined together to present the Smoky Mountain Winterfest from mid-November through February. There are probably a million lights put up for the holidays in these three adjoining communities. It's a beautiful and colorful sight. In addition to all the holiday decorations, numerous events and celebrations take place during this period. For a Winterfest brochure call (800) 255–6411.

## Hillbilly Golf (all ages)

**On the parkway, near traffic light No. 2; (865) 436–7470. Call for schedule and prices.**

Let's start out with some unique fun first. Hillbilly Golf may well be the world's most unusual miniature golf course. In keeping with the theme of the area, the course is built into the side of a hill. To get to the first hole, you have to take an incline railroad up to a point 300 feet above the rest of the city. Two eighteen-hole courses, with "traditional mountaineer hazards," work their way down to the bottom. You even have to putt around a genuine mountain outhouse.

## Guinness World Records Museum (all ages)

**631 Parkway, B-11, Baskins Square Mall; (865) 436–9100. Open 9:00 A.M. to 11:00 P.M. daily April through November, 10:00 A.M. to 8:00 P.M. Monday through Thursday and 9:00 A.M. to 10:00 P.M. Friday through Sunday December through March. Admission: $–$$.**

As you wind your way through downtown Gatlinburg, you might want to stop at the Guinness World Records Museum. You'll see thousands of exhibits on astounding feats, as recorded in the famous *Guinness Book of World Records*, and memorabilia from celebrities including Michael Jackson, Elvis, and the Beatles. The museum is stroller and wheelchair accessible.

## Mysterious Mansion (ages 8 and up)

**424 River Road; (865) 436–7007. Open 10:00 A.M. to 11:00 P.M. May through October, and weekends only during other months. Call for admission prices.**

For some spooky fun visit this attraction, a classic "haunted house."

## Ripley's Believe It or Not! Museum (all ages)

**904 Parkway; (865) 436–5096. Open 9:00 A.M. to 11:00 P.M. Sunday through Thursday, 9:00 A.M. to midnight Friday and Saturday. Hours may change in the winter. Admission: $–$$.**

Always a fun place to stop, Ripley's Believe It or Not! Museum features three floors of exhibits. There are thousands of oddball artifacts and "curiosities" from around the world, plus rare film footage from the collection of Robert Ripley.

## Ripley's Moving Theater

**904 Parkway; (865) 436–9763. Open 9:00 A.M. to 11:00 P.M. Sunday through Thursday and 9:00 A.M. to midnight Friday and Saturday. Winter hours are subject to change. $$$, price covers both films. Children must be at least 43 inches tall.**

This full-size theater has a giant screen featuring Surround Sound and seats that move in sync with the film. There are two films, each about five minutes long.

## Old Gatlinburg Golf and Games (all ages)

**716 Parkway, Reagan Terrace Mall; (865) 430–GOLF. Call for updated schedule and admission prices.**

You can learn about the history of Gatlinburg and the Smokies as you make your way through these two eighteen-hole miniature golf courses.

### Space Needle Family Fun Center (all ages)

**115 Historic Nature Trail; (865) 436–4629. Open 9:00 A.M. to midnight; hours vary in the winter. Admission: $–$$.**

The Space Needle takes you nearly 350 feet above Gatlinburg in a glass elevator. At the street level, there's an arcade with all sorts of games.

### The Ober Gatlinburg Ski Resort and Amusement Park (all ages)

**1001 Parkway; (865) 436–5423; www.obergatlinburg.com. Hours vary depending on season and weather. Admission to the park is free, with each activity on a pay-per-play basis. Tram rides are $–$$.**

This is a fun stop. You'll find a bevy of activities, such as bungee jumping, batting cages, and an alpine slide ride that takes riders down an 1,800-foot track through woods and across ski trails. A scenic chairlift takes you to the top of the alpine slide, so it's really two rides in one. There's also an indoor ice-skating arena, wintertime downhill snow skiing, go-cart racing, a huge indoor arcade with some great games, a gift and crafts shop, live entertainment, and a dinner theater. A new black bear habitat can be seen at the tramway exit.

The unique thing about Ober Gatlinburg is that it's located 2¼ miles up the mountain, but you won't have any problems getting to all the action and attractions. The famous aerial tramway, with a station on the main parkway, takes you up the mountain from downtown Gatlinburg. Trams depart at twenty minutes after and twenty minutes before the hour. The ride is quite a lot of fun. If you want to save that money and spend it on something else at the facility, you can drive your car up Ski Mountain Road to the attractions.

### Christus Gardens (ages 5 and up)

**510 River Road; (865) 436–5155; www.christusgardens.com. Open daily 8:00 A.M. to 9:00 P.M. April to October, 9:00 A.M. to 5:00 P.M. November through March. Admission: $–$$$.**

One of the most visited attractions in the area is Christus Gardens. Calling itself America's number-one religious attraction, it was created in 1960 after founder Ronald Ligon recovered from a life-threatening case of tuberculosis. He vowed if he were to regain his health, he would build "some type of significant memorial as a permanent expression" of his gratitude to "divine providence."

Today the attraction portrays the life of Christ in various scenes and through various stories, including the Nativity and the Sermon on the Mount.

Each scene has custom-crafted, life-size figures dressed in garments faithful to the Bibles descriptions. It's quite a moving collection of scenes.

## Great Smoky Arts and Crafts Community (all ages) 🔒
**Highway 321 North/Glades Road/Buckhorn Road; (865) 671–3600. Free.**

The craftspeople of Gatlinburg have made it easy for you to shop for their authentic crafts. More than eighty artisans, all members of the Great Smoky Arts and Crafts Community, have their studios located along an 8-mile loop outside town, each with plenty of parking directly adjacent to their workshops. To make it even easier to visit and shop, the Arts & Crafts Trolley makes the loop every half hour during the season. It leaves City Hall and the Park & Ride lot on Highway 321 North.

Along the route you'll find just about everything, including quilts, copper fountains, cornhusk flowers, stained glass, pottery, local watercolor scenes, log cabin birdhouses and feeders, and fireplace mantels. The kids will especially enjoy the dollmakers and toymakers located along the trail. Maps listing the various craftspeople can be found throughout the area. The group of artisans brings its wares into town twice each year for crafts shows at the Gatlinburg Convention Center over Easter and Thanksgiving weekends.

# Other Things to See and Do

**Fort Fun** (ages 5 and up), 716 Parkway; (865) 436–BEAM. Call for updated schedule and prices. Laser tag for the whole family.

**Sugarlands Riding Stables** (ages 6 and up), 1½ miles from downtown on Highway 441 South, near the park headquarters; (865) 430–5020.

**Camp Thunder Fun Center** (ages 5 and up), 542 Parkway; (865) 430–8680. Call for schedule and admission prices. Indoor go-carts and indoor miniature golf.

**Smoky Mountain Stables** (ages 6 and up), 2 miles east of Gatlinburg on Highway 321; (865) 436–5634.

# Where to Eat

**Best Italian Restaurant,** 968 Parkway; (865) 430–4090. A favorite with locals and visitors. Two of the specialties are lasagna and fettucine. They have a good children's menu with lots of kids' favorites. $–$$

**The Park Grill,** 1110 Parkway; (865) 436–2300. Delicious moonshine chicken and fried trout. $$

# Where to Stay

Gatlinburg has thousands of hotel and motel rooms, cabins, chalets, bed-and-breakfast rooms, and other accommodations. Here are a few to get you started.

**Clarion Inn and Suites,** 1100 Parkway; (865) 436–5656 or (800) 933–0777. One of Gatlinburg's newest hotels, the Clarion features an indoor pool and penthouse suites. Only a step away from the city's best shopping, dining, main attractions, and the national park. $$–$$$$

**Holiday Inn SunSpree Resort Gatlinburg,** 520 Historic Nature Trail; (865) 436–9201 or (800) 435–9201. Two blocks from downtown Gatlinburg. Swimming pools, store/deli, pizza take-out. Children ages twelve and under eat **free** in the on-site restaurant. Activity staff plans children's activities daily. $$–$$$$

**Mountain Rentals and Realty, LLC,** 1228 Ski Mountain Road; (865) 430–3030 or (800) 430–3030. Offers more than sixty different chalets and cabins, all including kitchens, grills, and cable TV. Most include fireplaces (with firewood included) and hot tubs. $$$–$$$$

**Park Vista Resort Hotel,** 705 Cherokee Orchard Road; (865) 436–9211 or (800) 421–PARK. This fifteen-story hotel offers

great views from every room, swimming and wading pools, indoor and outdoor play areas, basketball and volleyball, and a **free** shuttle to downtown. Children ten and under eat **free** in the on-site restaurant. $–$$$$

## For More Information

**Gatlinburg Chamber of Commerce,** 811 East Parkway, Gatlinburg, TN 37738; (865) 436–4178 or (800) 56–VISIT; www.gatlinburg .com. Open 8:30 A.M. to 5:00 P.M. Monday through Friday.

# Great Smoky Mountains

## Great Smoky Mountains National Park

107 Park Headquarters Road; (865) 436–1200; www.nps.gov/grsm. Open year-round. **Free.**

If there's a heaven on Earth, it must be the Great Smoky Mountains. Located within the Appalachian Mountain range, Great Smoky Mountains National Park is half a million acres of great wilderness.

At an elevation of 6,642 feet, Clingman's Dome is the tallest peak in the park and the second tallest in the eastern United States. In all, there are sixteen peaks towering above 6,000 feet. The park features more species of plants than any other area on the continent and is an official international biosphere reserve—as such, it is one of the largest protected areas in the East.

There are more than 800 miles of hiking trails, ranging in difficulty from a relatively flat walk to the famous Appalachian Trail, which forms the Tennessee–North Carolina state line, at the top of the park. There are also several trails accessible to the disabled. Although the inner secrets and beauty of the park lie off the major byways, you don't have to devote a lot of time or energy to appreciate its magnificent offerings.

## Amazing Tennessee Facts

There are approximately 700 black bears in the Great Smoky Mountains National Park.

There are plenty of designated scenic pull-offs and observation areas along the road system within the park. Those along the Foothills Parkway provide some of the best sightseeing from your car. The best view in the park comes after a short walk through the wilderness to the observation tower at Clingman's Dome.

A listing of the best observation areas and a map of the trail and road system are available at the Sugarlands Visitor Center, located 2 miles inside the park from Gatlinburg. The center also has plenty of other information on the park and an exhibit area with displays of many of the flora and fauna you're apt to see during your visit.

There are entire books written on the Smoky Mountains, and it would be impossible to do the area total justice in just a few paragraphs. Suffice it to say that a family visit to the Great Smoky Mountains National Park should be included in your trip to this part of the state. It will be a highlight in your family's vacation history. There are campgrounds, hundreds of sparkling mountain streams and waterfalls, plenty of planned activities, and many fabulous photo opportunities.

If you're visiting the Smokies, you should definitely plan to see Cades Cove, a thriving mountain community of the 1850s. At that time it had about 685 residents in 137 different households and 15,000 usable acres of farmland under cultivation. Now, the entire area is as it was, with the original buildings still in their original locations, giving visitors a true sense of the spaciousness of early mountain life. An 11-mile, self-guided auto loop tour gives the best idea of the culture of the region. The loop is also open to bicycle traffic. Most of the homes, churches, and stores are open to the public. Today the area is administered by the National Park Service as a pioneer homestead, and the auto loop follows many of the grades and turns of the old wagon roads. You'll even need to forge a stream or two.

The best way to make the most of a visit to the park is to round up information before getting here. Plan your route, your hikes, your meals, and your rest periods. For the benefit of everyone in your family, you might want to break up your visit into several half days, spending the rest of your time at the attractions and other activities in the areas surrounding the park.

# Cades Cove Sights

Cades Cove has been described as an open-air museum. Covering 1,800 acres of open space nestled along the base of the Smoky Mountains, the cove has rolling hills, waterfalls, and abundant plants and wildlife. There are a handful of structures remaining from its first settlers in 1819, including the John Cable Mill, built in 1868; John Oliver Place, built in 1826; and Primitive Baptist Church, the first of three churches built in the area.

# Townsend

Known as the "Peaceful Side of the Smokies," the area around Townsend has plenty of action but is not as commercially built up as Pigeon Forge and Gatlinburg, which are "just over the ridge on the other side."

## Amazing
## Tennessee Facts

Townsend was named for W. B. Townsend from Pennsylvania, who set up the Little River Lumber Company and logged in the area for nearly fifty years. In the early 1900s, Townsend was the capital of the lumber industry in the eastern United States.

The area, situated adjacent to the Great Smoky Mountains National Park, is just 9 miles from Cades Cove and has several different scenic routes out of town, including one to Clingman's Dome, the highest peak in the Smokies. If it can be done outdoors, it can be done in Townsend. There are miles of hiking trails into the Smokies, with trails classified as easy, moderate, or strenuous, and there are eight biking trails running from 3 to 28 miles in length. Brochures list both hiking and biking trails.

Beware: This is the wilderness, and the animals you see are not behind barriers. If you happen to spot bears on any of the paths, never throw anything at them, attempt to feed them, or approach them. All park bears are potentially dangerous and should be viewed only at a distance. If you run into one accidentally, make a lot of noise and wave your arms, and it'll go away. Poison ivy is also quite prevalent, so be careful.

### Wood–N–Strings Dulcimer Shop (all ages)
**77327 East Lamar Alexander Parkway; (865) 448–6647. Open Monday through Saturday 10:00 A.M. to 6:00 P.M. Free.**

Not just a shop, this is a place where you and the kids can actually watch a dulcimer being created from walnut, cherry, or butternut wood— and then hear the owner play some music on it. Other gifts, especially musical ones, are available for sale as well.

### Cades Cove Riding Stables (ages 6 and up)
**4035 East Lamar Alexander Parkway; (865) 448–6286. Open March through October. Call for hours and rates.**

There are several registered riding stables in the area. This one is located in Cades Cove and offers guided horseback and carriage rides through the foothills of the Smokies as well as hayrides around the cove.

### Davy Crockett Riding Stables (ages 6 and up)
**505 Old Cades Cove Road, off Highway 321; (865) 448–6411. Open mid-March through mid-November on a first-come, first-served basis, 9:00 A.M. to 5:00 P.M. Call for rates. Reservations and advance deposit required for overnight, half-day, and all-day rides.**

Guided trail rides through the mountains will take you to areas with spectacular views.

### Tuckaleechee Caverns (all ages)
**825 Caverns Road, off Highway 321; (865) 448–2274. Open mid-March through mid-November. $–$$.**

One of Tennessee's underground treasures is Tuckaleechee Caverns, which bills itself as the "greatest sight under the Smokies." There are plenty of rock formations, river passages, and stalagmites to keep the family oohing and aahing for an hour or so. Pay special attention to what the owners call Flowstone Falls; it's a curtain of beautiful flowing onyx.

## Other Things to See and Do

**Lee Roberson Gallery** (ages 10 and up), 758 Wears Valley Road; (865) 448– 2365 or (800) 423–7341. Gallery of Smoky Mountain artist Lee Roberson.

**Little River Railroad and Lumber Company Museum** (all ages), 7747 East Lamar Alexander Parkway (Highway 321); (865) 448–2211; www.littleriverrailroad.org. This museum displays artifacts and memorabilia of the area's railroad and lumber operations.

## Where to eat

**Carriage House Restaurant,** 8310 Highway 73; (865) 448–2263. Country-style breakfasts, lunches, and dinners. Friday and Sunday buffets. $–$$

**Deadbeat Pete's,** 7613 Old Highway 73; (865) 448–0900. Features Tex-Mex food. Dine inside or on the quaint porch that overlooks the Little River.

**Tuckaleechee Trout Farm,** 142 Tipton Road; (865) 448–2290. Catch trout with your kids at the farm's well-stocked ponds, then the staff will cook 'em up for you. You can also enjoy the "fresh-catch" menu or choose chicken, steak, or hamburgers, all served up with the usual sides. There are some great southern-style home-cooked vegetables, too. $–$$

## Where to Stay

**Bear'ly Rustic Cabin Rentals,** 7807 East Lamar Alexander Parkway; (865) 448–6036 or (888) 448–6036; www.townsendcabin.com. Bear'ly offers fifty furnished cabins, each with a fireplace, hot tub or Jacuzzi, kitchen, cable TV, and phone. $$$

**Best Western Valley View Lodge,** Highway 321; (865) 448–2237 or (800) 292–4844. Free breakfast, outdoor and indoor pools, fifteen acres of gardens. $–$$$$

**Little River Village Campground,** 8533 Highway 73; (865) 448–2241 or (800) 261–6370. Open year round. Call for rates.

Offers 145 campsites, a grocery store, laundry facilities, and a playground.

## For More Information

**Smoky Mountain Convention and Visitors Bureau,** 201 South Washington Street, Maryville, TN 37804; (865) 983–2241 or (800) 525–6834; www.smokymountains.org. Open 9:00 A.M. to 5:00 P.M. Monday and 8:00 A.M. to 5:00 P.M. Tuesday through Friday.

**Townsend Visitors Center,** 7906 East Lamar Alexander Parkway, Townsend, TN 37882; (865) 448–6134. Open daily, but hours vary according to season.

# Vonore

### Sequoyah Birthplace Museum (all ages)
**Citico Road (Highway 360); (423) 884–6246. Open Monday through Saturday 9:00 A.M. to 5:00 P.M., Sunday noon to 5:00 P.M. Admission: $, under 6 admitted free.**

Sequoyah, an uneducated Cherokee Indian, is the only person to single-handedly develop and perfect an alphabet, and by doing so he endowed the entire Cherokee nation with learning. In 1821 he introduced an alphabet that had taken him twelve years to develop. It was simple and took the average person only a few hours to learn. As a result of the alphabet, it wasn't long before the Cherokees were more literate than most of the white settlers living in the area.

Sequoyah's story is told at the Sequoyah Birthplace Museum, and it's an amazing tale. Shunned by his peers when he was younger, he dedicated his life in the Little Tennessee Valley to self-learning. During his life he was a soldier, a statesman, and a silversmith.

The museum, owned and operated by the Cherokee, is located on the shores of the majestic Tellico Lake. It tells the story of the Cherokee Nation and its culture through artifacts, exhibits, and displays. Through interactive displays you'll be able to hear some fascinating Cherokee stories and legends that have been passed down through generations, thanks to Sequoyah's alphabet.

### Fort Loudon State Historic Park (all ages)
**Highway 360, 1 mile off Highway 411; (423) 884–6217. Open daily 8:00 A.M. to sunset. Free.**

Fort Loudon was the first planned British fort on the western frontier and played a significant role in helping Great Britain secure the trans-Appalachian region from France during the French and Indian War. Construction took place between 1756 and 1757. The Fort was located near several Cherokee towns and was built to help protect them from other tribes, as well as from French forces.

Today an authentic reconstruction of the fort as it was between 1756 and 1760 stands on the location, and the archaeological ruins of the circa-1794, military-built Tellico blockhouse are open to the public.

A visitor center houses historic displays, offers audiovisual presentations, and has knowledgeable guides who can tell you all about exciting events that took place through the years. The Independent Company of South Carolina, a group of reenactors, uses the fort on a regular basis for camp-outs and garrison weekends. Each December, a pioneer Christmas celebration is re-created, and the fort is decorated with the items of the day, including live greenery such as holly and ivy.

## Where to Eat

**Countryside Restaurant,** 2021 Highway 411; (423) 884–6673. Casual, home-style dining. $–$$

## Where to Stay

**Notchy Creek Campground,** Corntassel Road; (423) 884–6280. Open April through mid-October. The campground has fifty-two campsites plus a boating, swimming, and fishing area. Call for rates.

**Grand Vista Hotel,** 117 Grand Vista Drive; (423) 884–6200. Amenities include an outdoor pool and free full, hot breakfast. $$–$$$

## For More Information

**Monroe County Tourism Council,** 4765 Highway 68, Madisonville, TN 37354; (423) 442–9147 or (800) 245–5428; www.monroecounty.com. Open 8:00 A.M. to 5:00 P.M. Monday through Friday.

# Sweetwater

## Lost Sea (all ages)
**140 Lost Sea Road, at exit 60 off I–75; (423) 337–6616. Open daily at 9:00 A.M. Closing time varies according to season. $–$$$.**

The *Guinness Book of World Records* says that the Lost Sea is the world's largest underground lake. The four-and-a-half-acre "bottomless" lake is certainly the main attraction here, but the walk down to it is quite beautiful in itself. Almost half the world's known supply of rare anthrodites, or "cave flower" formations, line the walls. For that distinction the cave is a Registered Natural Landmark. Be sure to take your time studying the cave flowers; they are unique and beautiful.

Glass-bottomed boats will take you on a short tour of the lake. Be on the lookout—strange-looking white trout will usually swim up to greet the boat as it approaches their end of the lake. The tour guides are a lot of fun and relate some stories that probably get better with each telling. They'll even try to scare you a couple of times.

On top of all that, this is probably the most accessible underground attraction in the state. The fifty-five-minute tour is an easy walk down to the lake, and there is not a single stair. It's all graded with sloping paths and plenty of handrails. The lake is 300 feet underground, but it is only 1,000 feet by pathway from the front entrance. The cave's temperature is 58 degrees Fahrenheit at all times.

The folks here will be glad to recommend nearby camping and other lodging. There are also a gift shop, restaurant, ice cream parlor, picnic grounds, nature trails, and a play area aboveground.

# Niota

A few miles down Highway 11 from Sweetwater is the little town named Niota, which you may remember from national news reports a few years back. It was put on the map when the town was run by an all-female government. Coincidentally, this was the home of Harry Burn, the Tennessee legislator who cast the deciding vote to ratify the amendment to the U.S. Constitution that gave women the right to vote.

The main attraction in town is the Niota Depot, the oldest standing railroad depot in the state. Built in 1853, the building now houses the town offices. If you'd like a tour, stop by and someone will take you on a guided walk through the historic building.

## Where to Stay

**Best Value Sweetwater Hotel and Conference Center,** 180 Highway 68; (423) 337– 3511 or (800) 523–5727. Room service, outdoor pool, and an on-site restaurant. Pets allowed. $$

## For More Information

**Monroe County Tourism Council,** 4765 Highway 68, Madisonville, TN 37354; (423) 442–9147 or (800) 245–5428; www.monroe county.com. Open 8:00 A.M. to 5:00 P.M. Monday through Friday.

# Coker Creek

**Coker Creek Village Adventure and Retreat Center** (all ages)
**Just outside town on Highway 68; (423) 261–2310 or (800) 448–9580. Hours vary by season; prices vary by activity program. Please call for hours and prices.**

In the late 1820s, more than twenty-five years before the famous California Gold Rush, gold was found here in Coker Creek, and by the time the Civil War began, more than 1,000 men were believed to have been working the creeks and the mines of the area. Due to the difficulty in separating the gold from the ore because of the gold's fineness, the industry didn't establish deep roots in the area.

Today gold can still be found along Coker Creek, or you can stop by Coker Creek Village Adventure and Retreat Center, get a few pointers on how to pan for your own, then try that knowledge out in the sluice. The 300-acre village is in the Smoky Mountains, totally surrounded by the Cherokee National Forest.

Sanford Gray and his wife, Esther, own and operate the retreat. If you're looking for adventure, Sanford can fix you up for local activities including rafting on the mighty Ocoee River, rappelling, mountain biking, horseback riding, or tubing and canoeing on the Ocoee or Hiwassee Rivers. If you don't want too much adventure, he can point out nature's tranquillity, from misty waterfalls to sight-seeing trips.

Weather curtails most of the activity during the winter months, but the well-stocked and countrified general store and bed-and-breakfast are open year-round. There's a USDA Forest Service interpretive center on the grounds, staffed with an expert who can tell you anything you need to know about sights and activities on all the federal lands in the area.

## The Cherohala **Skyway**

One of the most beautiful scenic drives in America is the Cherohala Skyway, which connects eastern Tennessee to western North Carolina. The 40-mile route travels through the Cherokee and Nantahala National Forests and climbs from 800 to 5,300 feet in elevation, meandering across some of the highest mountain peaks in the region. The skyway's name comes from a combination of the names of the two forests.

The skyway took more than thirty years to build and cost $100 million. The route opened in October 1996 and was designated a National Scenic Byway. Tellico Plains, in Monroe County, anchors the route in Tennessee.

As you drive along the skyway, there are numerous opportunities to view the magnificent scenery, stop for a picnic, stroll short trails, and observe nature. Take your time and enjoy the ride. Allowing for a few stops, it takes about two hours to travel the length of the skyway.

For more information on the Cherohala Skyway, contact the Monroe County Tourism Council (423–442–9147 or 800–245–5428).

**Autumn Gold Festival** (all ages)
Coker Creek Village Adventure Center and Mountain Ranch; (423) 261–2310 or (423) 261–2242. Second full weekend in October. Admission: $.

Two types of gold are featured at this festival: the kind you'll find in the creek beds and the golden color of the leaves as they turn for the winter. You can pan for gold, dance and sing to mountain music, or find one-of-a-kind mountain crafts at the large crafts fair. Call the Grays at Coker Creek Village Adventure Center and they can fill you in on the event, which has been held since 1968.

## Other Things to See and Do

**Coker Creek Crafts Gallery** (ages 8 and up), 206 Hot Water Road; (423) 261–2157.

**Ducktown Basin Museum** (ages 8 and up), Burra Burra Hill, Highway 68, Ducktown; (423) 496–5778. Open Monday through Saturday. Winter hours 9:30 A.M. to 4:00 P.M., summer hours 10:00 A.M. to 4:30 P.M. Located at the Burra Burra Mine Site, Ducktown Basin Museum traces the history of copper mining in the basin.

## Where to Eat

**Tellihala Cafe,** 128 Bank Street, at the end of the Cherohala Skyway, Tellico Plains; (423) 253–2880. This popular eatery serves home-cooked lunches and dinners daily. $

## Where to Stay

**Coker Creek Village,** 12528 Highway 68; (423) 261–2310 or (800) 448–9580. A bunkhouse-type, rustic inn. $–$$$

**The Company House,** 125 Main Street, Ducktown; (423) 496–5634 or (800) 343–2909; www.bbonline.com/tn/company house. Mike and Margie Tonkin purchased this historic home in 1994 and turned it into a bed-and-breakfast inn with six rooms, each with a private bath. A full country breakfast is served each morning. It's a popular lodging spot for Ocoee River rafters. $$–$$$

**Mountain Garden Inn,** Highway 68; (423) 261–2689. This three-story log home is located high up in the Cherokee National Forest, where you can look out over the mountains of North Carolina, Georgia, and Tennessee. There are two suites and two cozy bedrooms. Owners Stephen and Pam Wentworth serve a full breakfast each morning. $–$$$

## For More Information

**Monroe County Tourism Council,** 4765 Highway 68, Madisonville, TN 37354; (423) 442–9147 or (800) 245–5428; www.monroe county.com. Open 8:00 A.M. to 4:30 P.M. Monday through Friday.

# Plateaus and Valleys

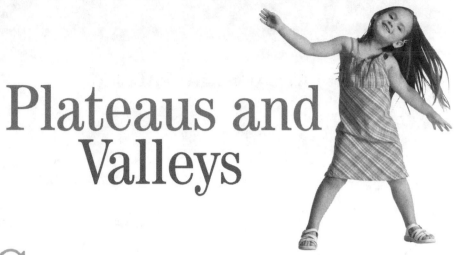

G eographically speaking, this region is the most diverse area of the state. It offers rolling hills, a bevy of spectacularly beautiful commercial caves, including the second largest cavern system in the country, the highest waterfall in the eastern United States, and many breathtaking picture-perfect vistas.

Forested and rugged, the plateau spans the width of the state, forming the western boundary of the Tennessee Valley. The foothills provide majestic backdrops to many of the small historic villages that have been preserved through the years, thanks to grassroots efforts of proud citizens.

The numerous rivers and streams, filled to the brim each spring with crystal clear waters from mountain run-offs, have carved a series of gorges and valleys that today provide magnificent areas for the sports-minded. Several of the rivers are known nationally by white-water enthusiasts and were used for white-water events during the 1996 Summer Olympics in Atlanta.

# Etowah

### L&N Depot/Railroad Museum (all ages)
**Tennessee Avenue, downtown; (423) 263–7840. Open Tuesday through Saturday 10:00 A.M. to 4:00 P.M. Free.**

At the turn of the twentieth century, the site of present-day Etowah on Highway 411 was muddy farmland. Then news came that the Louisville and Nashville Railroad was to build a new line between Cincinnati and Atlanta. The land was purchased to build a rail center. A boomtown soon sprang up, and the L&N Depot, built in 1906, became the community's central point. Social, economic, and cultural life revolved around the depot and railroad activities for many years.

As passenger travel declined, the depot's influence on the community died, and it was eventually abandoned in 1974. In 1978 the town purchased the depot, restored it, and had it added to the National Register of Historic Places. It houses a railroad museum and is open to the public. The elegant Victorian structure looks more like a hotel or an elegant private home than a railroad depot. It is made of yellow pine and has eighteen rooms.

# PLATEAUS AND VALLEYS

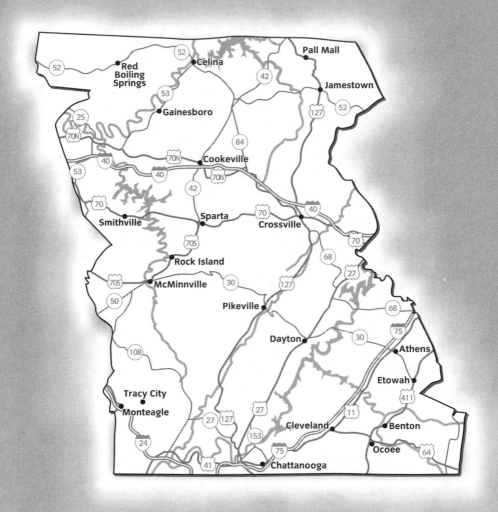

The museum examines what it meant to be a railroad town in the "New South" and focuses on the railroad's impact on ordinary people of the community. In addition to the museum, the depot is home to the Etowah Chamber of Commerce, the Tennessee Overhill Heritage, an office of the USDA Forest Service, and the Depot Gift Shop.

The grounds surrounding the depot are a popular gathering place for the community. Fairs, festivals, weddings, and all sorts of activities, including train watching, take place here. The train yard is still active and can provide rail buffs a fun time watching all the switching and maneuvering. There are picnic tables, public restrooms, a walking track, and lots of parking.

## Gem Theater (all ages)

**Seventh and Tennessee Avenues, downtown; (423) 263–7608. Admission varies depending on the event.**

The city of Etowah purchased the circa-1918 Gem Theater and have beautifully restored it to its cultural splendor. At one time the Gem was considered the largest privately owned theater in eastern Tennessee. Today it has a full schedule of film presentations. The Etowah Arts Commission Art Gallery is next door.

# Birding in Tennessee

Tennessee's a great state for bird-watching. The state is the year-round home of the robin, eastern bluebird, cardinal, meadowlark, Carolina chickadee, and mockingbird, the state bird. Other birds you can see from time to time include the yellow-shafted flicker, whippoorwill, Carolina wren, sparrow hawk, and several species of woodpeckers. The summer bird residents include the brown thrasher, scarlet tanager, indigo bunting, rose-breasted grosbeak, and species of warblers, sparrows, thrushes, flycatchers, hawks, and swallows. Migratory birds include sandhill cranes and Canada Geese.

## Where to Eat

**Castillo's Mexican Restaurant,** Highway 411 North; (423) 263–6562. If you and your kids are in the mood for something south of the border, this is the place the locals recommend, with good reason. Mexican-style home-cooking with kids' specials, too. Olé! $

**Memories,** Highway 411 North; (423) 263–7820. Burgers, steaks, chicken, and a children's menu. $

**Savannah Grille,** Highway 411 South; (423) 263–9153. A full menu includes burgers, steaks, fish, and chicken. Children's menu, too. $

## Where to Stay

**Windswept Farm,** 2889 Highway 163, Delano (about 5 miles south of Etowah on Highway 411, then 1⅒ miles west on Highway 163); (423) 263–0440. Furnished log home and contemporary A-frame. $$$–$$$$

## For More Information

**Etowah Area Chamber of Commerce,** P.O. Box 458, 727 Tennessee Avenue, Etowah, TN 37331; (423) 263–2228; www .etowahcoc.org. Open 8:30 A.M. to 4:30 P.M. Monday through Friday.

# Athens

### McMinn County Living Heritage Museum (ages 8 and up) 🏛

**522 West Madison Avenue; (423) 745–0329. Open Monday through Friday 10:00 A.M. to 5:00 P.M. and Saturday and Sunday 2:00 to 5:00 P.M. $.**

The McMinn County Living Heritage Museum is one of the few museums in the state that provides you with a great in-depth look at the local scene, while making sure you can see the whole picture as well. Here, within the thirty rooms of exhibits, you can experience the growth of the area and at the same time follow the settlers through the various periods of Tennessee history, from the Cherokee and pioneer days to the Civil War to today.

Fom a log cabin to a Victorian parlor, the different rooms reflect the different eras and help set the mood for the exhibits. The museum has an extensive glassware collection, including several rare, one-of-a-kind pieces. Among all of its offerings, the museum is probably best known for its quilt collection. One of the best times to visit is during the spring quilt show. It's one of the South's largest. Another fun time to visit is during the annual doll show in December. More than 5,000 artifacts are on display.

### Mayfield Dairy Farms Visitors Center (all ages)

**4 Mayfield Lane; (423) 745–2151, ext. 2253, or (800) MAYFIELD. Tours available Monday through Saturday 9:00 A.M. to 4:00 P.M. (Saturday tours end at 1:00 P.M. during winter). There is no milk production on Wednesday and no ice cream production on Saturday. Free.**

The Mayfield Dairy has been serving the folks in this part of the state for more than seventy-five years with fresh milk and some of the best ice cream you've ever had. Now **free** tours of the dairy are available, allowing all of us to see how it's done. The tours start in the visitor center. It's best to look around at the historical exhibits and some of the other displays before taking the tour. You and the kids will have a better understanding of what you see inside if you have some background.

On your way to Mayfield, ask the kids how they think the stick is put inside the ice cream bar. Then bet an ice cream sundae on who is right. You'll see it being done during your visit. After the tour, you'll be able to sample the products of the dairy and visit the gift shop.

### Swift Air Museum (all ages)

**McMinn County Airport, off Highway 30 on County Road 552; (423) 745–9547. Open Monday through Friday 9:00 A.M. to 5:00 P.M. Free.**

The Swift Air Museum has several vintage Swift aircraft on exhibit as well as other displays. These classic airplanes are a favorite among airplane aficionados, and there are fewer than 800 still in existence. You'll also get an occasional opportunity to see Swift planes landing and taking off. A full-time shop is attached to the museum, and at any one time there will be two or three planes being reconditioned or renovated.

## Amazing Tennessee Facts

Tennessee's state flower is the purple iris. The state wildflower is the passion flower.

## Other Things to See and Do

**Historic Downtown Athens** (all ages), Courthouse Square. **Free.** Specialty shops, antiques shops, and restaurants.

## Where to Eat

**Gondolier Pizza and Steak,** 2241 Congress Parkway; (423) 745–5303. Excellent pizza, with a buffet at noon on weekdays. Children's menu. $

**Riddle & Wallace Drugstore,** 8 Washington Avenue Northeast, downtown square; (423) 745–3382. Features an old-fashioned soda fountain. $

## Where to Stay

**Homestead Inn East,** 1827 Holiday Drive, just off I-75; (423) 744–9002. $

**Homestead Inn West,** 2808 Decatur Pike; (423) 745–9002 or (800) 673–4481. $

**Majestic Mansion,** 202 East Washington Avenue; (423) 746–9041. This bed-and-breakfast in historic Athens welcomes children of all ages. Roomy accommodations have unusual decor—one room is decorated in authentic Japanese style, and another is "country" style, complete with a barn door. $$$–$$$$

## For More Information

**Athens Area Chamber of Commerce,** 13 North Jackson Street, Athens, TN 37303; (423) 745–0334; www.athenschamber.org. Open 8:30 A.M. to 4:30 P.M. Monday through Friday.

# Benton

The Ocoee River in Polk County, long known by white-water enthusiasts for its exhilarating rapids, was the site of the white-water events during the 1996 Summer Olympics in Atlanta. Each year thousands of people, from first-timers to professional athletes, come here to challenge the river in kayaks, canoes, and rafts.

## The **Ocoee**

The Ocoee River is divided into three areas. The Upper Ocoee was the site of the 1996 Olympic course and is occasionally open for commercial rafting. The Middle Ocoee has been the site of commercial rafting since 1976; both the Middle and Upper offer class III and IV rapids. The Lower Ocoee (below Parksville Lake Dam) is the best spot for tube floating.

Not all the action on the river, however, needs to be a challenge. In certain areas the waters are more docile, and entire families can have a fun time on canoe and rafting trips. Be careful in booking trips for the kids, as most of the specific river runs have minimum age limits. There are several professional outfitters in the Benton area that can set you up for a memorable family adventure. Two are listed here. Costs of trips vary, but most are in the $27 to $40 range per person.

### Ocoee Inn Rafting (ages 12 and up)
**Lake Ocoee Inn and Marina, Highway 64 on Lake Ocoee; (423) 338–2064 or (800) 272–7238. Open late March through early November. Days and hours vary depending on season. Closed Tuesday and Wednesday during the summer. $$$.**

With motel rooms, cabins, a restaurant, and white-water rafting, the Lake Ocoee Inn and Marina can be a one-stop fun spot.

### Sunburst Adventures (ages 12 and up) Ⓐ
**Welcome Valley Road, north of Highway 64; (423) 338–8388 or (800) 247–8388. Open late March through October. Days and hours vary depending on season. Closed Tuesday and Wednesday during the summer. $$$.**

Rafting trips on the Middle Ocoee last about two hours, plus break time. When the Upper Ocoee is available, you can do a full river trip with about four hours on the water.

**Old Fort Marr** (all ages)
**Highway 411 North; (423) 263–0050 or (423) 745–3573. Open daily. Guided tours of the building are available by inquiring at the sheriff's office or at the state parks office. Free.**

Old Fort Marr, the oldest original blockhouse in the United States, still stands along Highway 411 near the Polk County sheriff's office. Built in 1814 to safeguard Andrew Jackson's shipping trains, the structure also was used as protection for the Cherokees who were fighting the Creek Indians at the time. As part of a larger structure, it was used as a stockade to detain the Cherokees prior to their forced removal on what became known as the Trail of Tears.

## One Lake, **Two Names**

Don't be confused by the dual names: Lake Ocoee and Parksville Lake are one and the same.

## Other Things to See and Do

**Benton Antique Mall** (all ages), Highway 411; (423) 338–8318. Open Tuesday through Saturday.

## Where to Eat

**Lake Ocoee Inn Restaurant,** Highway 64; (423) 338–2064 or (800) 272–7238. Open from late March through early November. Sandwiches, barbecue, seafood, and steaks. $

**Wildwater Steak House,** 1620 Highway 64 East; (423) 338–4433 or (800) 372–7031. Steaks, burgers, and dining inside or outside by the shores of the Ocoee River. $–$$

## Where to Stay

**Chilhowee Recreation Area,** 7 miles off Highway 64; (423) 338–5201 or (800) 280–CAMP. Open May through October. Campsites, including RV and tent sites; bathhouse; boating, fishing, and swimming area. $

**Lake Ocoee Inn and Marina,** Highway 64, off I–64; (423) 338–2064 or (800) 272–7238. Motel rooms and cabins. Boat rentals. $–$$ (motel), $$$–$$$$ (cabins)

**Welcome Valley Village,** Welcome Valley Road, between Highway 64 and Highway 411, about 3 miles from Benton and 4 miles from Ocoee; (423) 338–9499. Furnished cabins in the woods along the Ocoee River. $$–$$$$

## For More Information

**Polk County–Copper Basin Chamber of Commerce,** East office: P.O. Box 988, Ducktown, TN 37326; (423) 446–9000 or (877) 790–2157. West office: P.O. Box 560, Town Plaza, Highway 411, Benton, TN 37307; (423) 338–5040 or (800) 633–7655. www.ocoeetn.org. East office is open 9:00 A.M. to 4:00 P.M. Thursday through Saturday; west office is open 8:00 A.M. to 5:00 P.M. Monday, Tuesday, and Thursday and 8:00 to 11:00 A.M. and 2:00 to 4:00 P.M. Wednesday.

# Cleveland/Ocoee

### Cherokee National Forest (all ages) ⬛ ⬛ ⬛

Ranger Station, Highway 64 east of Highway 411, across from Lake Ocoee; (423) 476–9700; www.r8web.com. Open year-round. **Free.**

As one of the gateways to the beautiful Cherokee National Forest, Cleveland is the doorway to some of the best outdoor activities in the state. In Tennessee, when you mention forests, fantastic views, and hundreds of miles of hiking trails, people usually think of the Great Smoky Mountains. That's why this 640,000-acre forest remains virtually untouched by the crowds. It's the state's largest tract of public land.

When you enter the forest, you won't find any gas stations, fast-food restaurants, motels, or organized "touristy" activities, so be prepared to rough it. From tall, virgin stands of forests to campgrounds and ranger stations built by the Civilian Conservation Corps, the natural and cultural heritage of the southern Appalachians is nurtured throughout. This area is home to more than 20,000 species of plants and animals. Water sports include white-water rafting, kayaking, canoeing, and skiing. Commercial outfitters throughout the area are there to rent equipment and to provide guide service on the Ocoee and Hiwassee Rivers.

There are several modern campgrounds, with some requiring fees, but primitive camping throughout the forest is **free.** No off-road vehicles are permitted in the forest.

A good place to start your visit is at the ranger station on Highway 64 east of Highway 411 across from Lake Ocoee. There, the rangers will tell you that the lower forest area is divided into three distinct sections, each having its own series of trails, swimming lakes and beaches, boating areas, scenic views, and fishing opportunities. The upper forest area continues on the eastern side of the Smokies and runs northeast to Bristol.

## Amazing
# Tennessee Facts

Tennessee covers a total geographic area of 42,146 square miles and ranks as the thirty-sixth largest state in the United States. In land area, the state covers 41,219 square miles and ranks thirty-fourth.

There is a tremendous amount of wildlife roaming through the forest, so be on the lookout as you drive down the roads. Among the species living here are the black bear, Russian boar, turkey, grouse, white-tailed deer, and red wolves, which were recently reintroduced to this area by conservation groups. Remember, these animals are wild and should never be approached.

There is so much diversity to this area that entire books have been written about it. It's a gem of which Tennesseans are quite proud.

In all, the Forest Service maintains twenty-nine camping areas, many horse trails, and 105 hiking trails. There are more than 1,100 miles of roads cut through the dense forest. Cleveland is just one of the gateways. Tellico Plains in the Mountainous East is another, as are Erwin and several other cities in the First Frontier.

## Ocoee Scenic Byway (all ages)
**Route 64, between Highway 411 and Ducktown; (423) 338–5201.**

A nice way to see a section of the forest without going in too deep is to take a drive along the Ocoee Scenic Byway. Along the way you'll get some great views of the Ocoee River.

The road is narrow, and being a main route between Chattanooga and the Smokies, there is quite a bit of traffic, so be careful and pull over at the designated observation areas if you want to savor any of the sights. Several other less-traveled roads, including Forest Service Road 77, which you can pick up at the Highway 64 ranger station, take you into total wilderness.

## Historic Downtown Cleveland Walking Tour (all ages)
**Ocoee Street; (423) 472–6587. Walking tour maps are available at tourist locations and at the chamber of commerce office, 225 Keith Street, and at the Main Street Cleveland office, in city hall on Second Street. Free.**

The city of Cleveland has much to offer the wandering family. Beginning in Johnston Park in the heart of downtown, the walking tour includes twenty historic sites, which feature several restored churches and buildings. While in Johnston Park, be sure to stop at the *Cherokee Chieftain*, a sculpture by internationally known Native American artist Peter "Wolf" Toth.

## Cherokee Heritage Wildlife Tour (all ages)
**Maps available at the chamber of commerce office at 225 Keith Street; (423) 472–6587. Free.**

This area was a geographic center for Native American culture in the Southeast, and you'll find much history, especially about the Cherokees, throughout the region. To get a better idea of the role the county played in the everyday life of the Cherokee, two self-guided tours have been developed, with maps and additional information to guide you.

The Cherokee Heritage Wildlife Tour points out the best locations in the area to view wildlife and allows you to get a good feel for the Cherokee heritage. The Cherokee Scenic Loop Tour begins and ends in Cleveland and takes you throughout the county, where you'll visit many of the areas mentioned in this chapter, including Red Clay and the Ocoee River. Both maps offer a well-organized way to see the best the county and region have to offer.

## Red Clay State Historical Area (all ages) 🚻 🏛 🧗

Off Highway 60, about 12 miles south of Cleveland; (423) 478–0339. Open daily year-round. Free.

A little south of Cleveland, off a series of back roads, you'll find the Red Clay State Historical Area. (If you see a sign that reads WELCOME TO GEORGIA, you've gone about ½ mile too far.) This was the site of the last council ground of the Cherokee Indian Nation before its forced removal in 1838 by the U.S. government. That action was a 1,000-mile wintertime journey in which a reported 4,000 of the 18,000 who were forced to leave perished along the way. That was one-fourth of the Cherokee population.

The Trail of Tears, the path that they followed, began here at Red Clay and ended in Oklahoma. The state historical area encompasses 260 acres and includes the great council spring, or blue hole, that the Cherokees used for their water supply during the eleven national councils that were held here.

The James Corn Interpretive Center houses the exhibits, along with a theater and a resource reading room. Outside, a Cherokee farmstead and council house have been replicated to show how the area might have looked more than 150 years ago. There's a picnic shelter with tables, an outdoor picnic area with grills, a 2-mile hiking trail, and a self-guided nature trail.

## Other Things to See and Do

**Cleveland Speedway** (all ages), 2420 South Lee Highway; (423) 479–8574. Open March through August. $–$$

**Museum Center at Five Points** (all ages), Inman Street; (423) 339–5745. Open year-round. Admission charged. A regional history museum and cultural center.

**Primitive Settlement** (all ages), Kinser Road; (423) 476–5096. Open April through October from 9:00 A.M. to 4:00 P.M. Free. Collection of log homes furnished with household and farm items used by early settlers.

## Where to Eat

**Gardner's Market,** 262 Broad Street; (423) 478–3906. Delicious deli sandwiches, forty-five kinds of coffee, 120 kinds of tea, and fantastic muffins. $

**Jenkins' Deli,** 88 Mouse Creek Road; (423) 478–1648. $

**Stadfeld's Family Restaurant,** 1430 Twenty-fifth Street; (423) 479–3123. Daily buffet, good fried chicken. $

## Where to Stay

**Baymont Suites,** 107 Interstate Drive, off I–75 at exit 25; (423) 339–1000 or (800) 428–3438. $$

**Holiday Inn,** 2400 Executive Park Drive, off I–75 at exit 25; (423) 472–1504 or (800) HOLI-DAY. Family-style restaurant. $$

## For More Information

**Cleveland/Bradley County Chamber of Commerce,** P.O. Box 2275, 225 Keith Street, Cleveland, TN 37320; (423) 472–6587 or (800) 472–6588; www.clevelandchamber.com.

**Polk County–Copper Basin Chamber of Commerce,** East office: P.O. Box 988, Ducktown, TN 37326; (423) 446–9000 or (877) 790–2157. West office: P.O. Box 560, Town Plaza, Highway 411, Benton, TN 37307; (423) 338–5040 or (800) 633–7655; www.ocoeetn.org. East office is open 9:00 A.M. to 4:00 P.M. Thursday through Saturday; west office is open 8:00 A.M. to 5:00 P.M. Monday, Tuesday, and Thursday and 8:00 to 11:00 A.M. and 2:00 to 4:00 P.M. Wednesday.

# Chattanooga

There are a lot of fun things for families to do here in the state's fourth-largest city. Located along a 7-mile bend in the Tennessee River, the city was made internationally famous by the song "Chattanooga Choo Choo."

## Chattanooga Visitors Center (all ages)
**2 Broad Street, next to the Tennessee Aquarium; (423) 756–8687. Open daily. Free.**

A nine-minute video is shown continuously at the Chattanooga Visitors Center. This is also a good place to start your visit of the area. You can buy tickets to area attractions, make reservations for accommodations, pick up information, and buy souvenirs in the gift shop.

## Chattanooga Choo Choo (all ages)
**1400 Market Street; (423) 266–5000 or (800) TRACK–29.**

The city's old Terminal Station, now known as the Chattanooga Choo Choo, has been restored and houses unique shops, restaurants, and a Holiday Inn, all playing on the train theme. Among the 360 guest rooms in the hotel are forty-eight Victorian family suites aboard vintage railroad sleeping cars. What a great experience for the entire family!

Elsewhere in the Choo Choo complex is one of the world's largest working model railroads. Covering 3,000 square feet, there are more than 100 miles of HO gauge track in the layout, which was created by the Chattanooga Area Model Railroad Club. The fully automated layout features more than 300 authentically detailed model engines and cars. If there's a train lover in your family, this is a must-stop.

## Amazing Tennessee Facts

The Chattanooga Choo Choo's lobby, built in 1909, is considered an architectural wonder. It features an 85-foot-tall freestanding brick dome, the largest of its type in the world.

### Downtown Arrow (all ages)
**Terminal Station, 1400 Market Street; (423) 894–8028. Runs weekends June 9 through July 29. Catch a ride at the Choo Choo or at the Tennessee Valley Railroad Museum. $–$$.**

The Downtown Arrow passenger train leaves Terminal Station once a day on Saturday and Sunday afternoons during the summer and takes you out of town along an original Civil War train right-of-way. On the way you'll pass the Chattanooga National Cemetery, where you'll see a replica of a Civil War locomotive. The Downtown Arrow ride takes you out to the Tennessee Valley Railroad Museum, where there are exhibits and an audiovisual presentation on the early days of railroading.

### Tennessee Valley Railroad Museum (all ages)
**4119 Cromwell Road; (423) 894–8028 or (800) 397–5544; www.tvrail.com. Schedule varies according to season. Train rides available daily from late March through November. $–$$.**

Since the Downtown Arrow runs only on weekends, you might want to consider the Tennessee Valley Railroad Museum's train rides. The Tennessee Valley Railroad Museum is the South's largest operating historic railroad, and its entire operation has been placed on the National Register of Historic Places. Tickets to the museum include a forty-five-minute round-trip ride, a walking tour, and a video presentation. There are also several daylong excursions and occasional evening trips available for an extra charge. The museum has an impressive collection of classic railroad equipment on display.

During the Christmas holiday season, the Polar Express comes to life. This special train ride includes storytelling, cookies, hot chocolate, and an appearance by jolly old Saint Nicholas himself. This two-hour ride runs from the museum to the Chattanooga Choo Choo and back, from Thursday through Sunday in November and December. All tickets are $20.

## Amazing
# Tennessee Facts

In 2000 Tennessee was the sixteenth largest state in terms of population. The state's estimated population that year was 5,689,283.

### Incline Railway (all ages)
**3917 St. Elmo Avenue (lower station); (423) 821–4224. Open daily. $–$$.**

Let's stay on track now and head up to Lookout Mountain via the Incline Railway, promoted as "America's most amazing mile." What a great view you get of the city below as the train takes you up the mountain. As you near the top, you're at an amazing 72.7 percent grade in the track, which gives it the distinction of being the steepest passenger railway in the world.

At the upper station there's a **free** observation deck, which is the highest overlook on the mountain. On a clear day you can see the Great Smoky Mountains 200 miles away. While you're at the top, be sure to visit the machine room, where you'll be able to see the giant gears and cables, made in 1895, that operate this historic mode of transportation.

The Incline makes three or four trips per hour. There's plenty of **free** parking at the lower station at 3917 St. Elmo Avenue. It's best to take the round-trip on the Incline, enjoy the nice views, then drive to the attractions you want to see at the top of the mountain.

## Point Park (all ages)
**110 East Brow Road, Lookout Mountain, Georgia; (423) 821–7786. Open 9:00 A.M. to sunset. $. Free for children 16 and under.**

While you're up there on the Incline, you can take a 3-block walk to Point Park. This is where the Civil War Battle above the Clouds took place in 1863. It was a decisive Union victory over the Confederates, who had held the mountain during most of the war. A fun thing to do while here is to get a picture of your family standing on the same bluff that Gen. Ulysses S. Grant stood upon while he surveyed the area prior to the battle. Point Park Visitor Center also offers a seven-minute narrative on the battle, played every fifteen minutes, as well as a mural entitled *The Battle of Lookout Mountain*.

# Chattanooga's Claims to Fame

Chattanooga has quite a history beyond its Cherokee heritage and its role in the Civil War. Other claims to fame include the innovation of putting Coca-Cola in a bottle, the blues artistry of Bessie Smith, and the engineering mastery of the Tennessee Valley Authority.

## Rock City (all ages)
**1400 Patten Road, Lookout Mountain, Georgia; (706) 820–2531. Open daily. $$–$$$.**

Here's your chance to do what the directions on barn roofs have been telling you to do for years: "See Rock City." High atop the mountain, this is a one-of-a-kind piece of true Americana. With its delightful blend of nature and fantasy, Rock City has been a traditional vacation destination for families for more than sixty years. This is truly a great family activity.

One of the activities your children may especially like is the Underground Enchantment, where you walk through Fairyland Caverns and Mother Goose Village, both of which have fantasy figures and dramatic underground lighting. Then there's the Fat Man's Squeeze along the walking trail; amazing rock formations, some twenty stories high; and beautiful gardens. You can see seven states from Lover's Leap—Tennessee, Georgia,

Alabama, Kentucky, Virginia, and North and South Carolina. Every year from mid-November to the end of December, from 6:00 to 9:00 P.M., Rock City hosts the Enchanted Garden of Lights, in which Rock City becomes illuminated with more than 500,000 lights to celebrate the holidays.

## Ruby Falls (all ages)

**1720 South Scenic Highway, on Lookout Mountain; (423) 821–2544; www.rubyfalls.com. Open daily except Christmas. $$–$$$.**

Three miles down the road from Rock City on Lookout Mountain Scenic Highway is the beautiful Ruby Falls. Located deep within the heart of the mountain, the falls are in the deepest commercial cavern in the United States. The 145-foot-high falls are illuminated by colorful lights and are quite breathtaking. Along the walkway to the falls, you'll encounter glistening stalagmites made from white onyx.

Outside the cavern, the Fun Forest is a great place to let the kids play for a while as you enjoy a snack or drink from the concession stand. The playground is full of opportunities to jump, crawl, hide, climb, and scream before getting back into the car. From mid-November through the end of December, Ruby Falls hosts its brand-new holiday production, Deck the Falls, which transforms Ruby Falls for the holiday season by an array of enchanting lights and sound effects.

## Tennessee Aquarium (all ages)

**1 Broad Street; (423) 265–0695 or (800) 262–0695. Open daily. Special combination ticket prices are available for those planning to also visit the IMAX 3-D Theater and/or Creative Discovery Museum. $$–$$$.**

The Tennessee Aquarium is located next to the Tennessee River and is dedicated to the life along and within the river. The five galleries showcase more than 9,000 living specimens of fish, mammals, reptiles, and amphibians. Billed as the "world's first major freshwater life center," the facility salutes the 300-plus fish species found in the state. Along your tour of the aquarium, guides will tell you that Tennessee has a greater variety of native fish than any other state in the United States, and the state is one of the most biologically diverse in the country.

Your family will ooh and aah even before you get inside. With pyramid-shaped skylights on top of the twelve-story building, the facility and the well-landscaped park around it create a marvelous sight.

## Tennessee Aquarium IMAX 3-D Theater (all ages)

**201 Chestnut Street, next door to the aquarium; (800) 262–0695. Open daily. Discounts are available to those buying tickets to two or three films, and various combination tickets are available for the theater, Tennessee Aquarium, and Creative Discovery Museum. $–$$.**

Put on your 3-D glasses and get ready—images seem to pop right off the six-story screen. This place is a blast, and most films are educational, too.

### Creative Discovery Museum (all ages)
**321 Chestnut Street, downtown at the corner of Fourth and Chestnut; (423) 756–2738. Open daily. $–$$.**

Your kids will love this 42,000-square-foot fun spot, filled with interactive, hands-on learning activities. They can dig for dinosaur bones, record music, make sculptures, paint, and create their own inventions. When they've done all that, there's plenty more for them to do! A brand-new exhibit called *RiverPlay* is great for kids. They can pilot a kid-size riverboat, scale a crow's nest high atop a two-and-a-half story climbing structure, build sailboats, and make a waterwheel turn.

## Other Things to See and Do

**Bluff View Art District** (all ages), 411 East Second Street; (423) 757–0117. For families who like to see a city on foot, this area offers views of lovely homes, inns, charming cafes and restaurants, and several art galleries, including an outdoor sculpture garden. The stroll is **Free.**

**Chattanooga Regional History Museum** (all ages), 400 Chestnut Street; (423) 265–3247. Open 10:00 A.M. to 4:30 P.M. Monday through Friday, 11:00 A.M. to 4:30 P.M. Saturday and Sunday. Through dramatic, interactive exhibits, the CRHM tells the story of people from all walks of life in the Chattanooga and tri-state region, from 10,000 years ago to the present day. $

**Cherokee Removal Memorial Park** (all ages), near Blythe Ferry Landing off Highway 60 in Meigs County, about 45 miles outside of Chattanooga; (423) 756–8687 or (800) 322–3344. The park has a walking trail and a memorial wall containing the names of the Cherokee who were forced to travel on the Trail of Tears. When completed, the park will have a Cherokee genealogy library and wildlife overlook.

**Coolidge Park** (all ages), 2 Broad Street; (423) 756–8687. Open year-round. This ten-acre park in Chattanooga's Riverpark features the Chattanooga Carousel and an interactive play fountain, plus an overlook area, picnic facilities, and benches along the riverwalk. **Free.**

**International Towing and Recovery Hall of Fame and Museum** (all ages), 3315 Broad Street; (423) 267–3132. Open 10:00 A.M. to 4:30 P.M. Monday through Friday, 11:00 A.M. to 5:00 P.M. Saturday and Sunday. Learn about the history of the towing and recovery industry. Features antique towing and recovery equipment, along with antique vehicles and toys. Gift shop. $

**Southern Belle Riverboat** (all ages), 201 Riverfront Parkway, Pier 2; (423) 266–4488 or (800) 766–2784. Runs February through November; schedule varies according to season. The 500-passenger *Southern Belle* offers a variety of sight-seeing, lunch, and dinner cruises on the Tennessee River, including a family-night dinner cruise that allows one child **free** with each paying adult. Rates range from $5.50 to $16.95 per child three to ten and $11.00 to $33.95 per adult.

**Walnut Street Bridge** (all ages), connects downtown to Coolidge Park, (423) 756–8687. Open year-round, all hours. **Free.** After a dinner downtown or a visit to the city's attractions, there's no better way to cap off the day than a stroll over this bridge that spans the Tennessee River. The kids will be impressed to know that they're walking across the world's longest pedestrian bridge (it's ¾ of a mile across).

**Chattanooga Zoo at Warner Park** (all ages), 1101 McCallie Avenue; (423) 697–1322. Open 9:00 A.M. to 5:00 P.M. seven days a week, April through October, then 10:00 A.M. to 5:00 P.M. November through March. Closed major holidays. Come see why this has been hailed as "the best little zoo in the world." Some of the exhibits include an African aviary, Gombe Forest and reptile house. $

## Surf Tennessee **State Parks**

If you're looking for something fun to do, you can't go wrong with a state park. You can check out Tennessee's state parks online at www.state.tn.us/environment/parks. Pick your park, then hit the road!

## Where to Eat

**Big River Grille and Brewing Works,** 222 Broad Street, near the Tennessee Aquarium; (423) 267–BREW. Chicken, seafood, salads, and sandwiches; cavernous and casual microbrewery/restaurant. $–$$

**Sweeney's Pit Barbecue,** 3147 Broad Street; (423) 267–1390. Award-winning barbecue. $

**The Loft,** 328 Cherokee Boulevard; (423) 266–3061. Voted Chattanooga's number-one fine-dining restaurant for more than twenty years. Seafood, pasta, chicken, steaks, Cajun specialties, soups, and salads. $$$

## Where to Stay

**Chattanooga Choo Choo Holiday Inn,** 1400 Market Street; (423) 266–5000 or (800) TRACK–29. $$$–$$$$

**The Chattanoogan,** 1201 South Broad Street; (877) 756–1684 or (423) 756–3400. $$–$$$

**Stonefort Inn,** 120 East Tenth Street; (423) 267–7866. $$$$

## For More Information

**Chattanooga Area Convention and Visitors Bureau,** 2 Broad Street, Chat-

tanooga, TN 37402; (423) 756–8687 or (800) 322–3344; www.chattanoogafun .com. Open 8:30 A.M. to 5:30 P.M. daily.

# Monteagle/Tracy City

### Best Western Smokehouse Restaurant
**Highway 64-41A, off I–24 at exit 134; (931) 924–2268 or (800) 489–2091.**

Save your appetite for your visit to Monteagle, the well-known mountain along I–24 where the highways close often during winter weather. At the top you'll find the Jim Oliver's Best Western Smokehouse complex, which includes a wonderful family restaurant, a general store with all kinds of fun and funky items, and a motel.

The restaurant is known for several dishes, but you may especially enjoy the catfish dinner, complete with hush puppies and vegetables. Other popular items include the sugar-cured ham dinner and the hot food bar that offers at least two meats, vegetables, breads, and homemade vegetable beef soup. There's a children's menu, but the best deal for the little ones is a trip to the hot bar. That's discounted as well, and the selection is much better. Check out the swimming pool behind the hotel. It's shaped like a country ham!

### Blue Water Lodge (all ages) 
**901 West Main Street; (931) 924–7020. $–$$ for lunch and dinner; no extra cost to watch the show.**

This is a restaurant with a "meat and three" attitude. Every Friday night there's a radio performance, *The Mountain Goat Radio Show*, which airs live from the lodge, and it's quite entertaining to watch.

### South Cumberland State Park and Natural Area (all ages)
**Highway 41, Monteagle (visitor center); (931) 924–2980 (park office), (931) 692–3887 (Stone Door Ranger Station), (931) 779–3532 (Savage Gulf Ranger Station).**

Located atop the southern end of the Cumberland Plateau, this park is made up of a visitor center complex and seven separate areas located in Franklin, Marion, Grundy, and Sequatchie Counties. It covers approximately 16,000 acres throughout a 100-square-mile region and is managed as a single park. The visitor center serves as the headquarters and there's a small museum inside. You can pick up maps, trail information, and directions to park areas any day of the week.

Areas of the park include Savage Gulf, Grundy Lakes, Foster Falls, Sewanee Natural Bridge State Natural Area, Carter State Natural Area, Hawkins Cove Natural Area, and Grundy Forest Natural Area.

### Dutch Maid Bakery (all ages)
**111 Main Street, Tracy City (6 miles from Monteagle); (931) 592–3171. Open daily. Tours are free, but advance notice is requested.**

Ever try an applesauce fruitcake? Here's your chance if you haven't. Take your family to the Dutch Maid Bakery in Tracy City, the state's oldest family-operated bakery, established in 1902 by Swiss immigrant John Baggenstoss. Through the years all of Baggenstoss's six sons have been involved in the business, and now the operation is in the hands of a cousin.

In addition to the famous applesauce fruitcake that they bake year-round, the bakers create salt-rising bread and other regular items. There is also a nice selection of local crafts, a sampling of local honey, and other products made in this part of the state.

## Where to Eat

**Best Western Smokehouse Restaurant,** Highway 64-41A, off I–24 at exit 134; (931) 924–2268 or (800) 489–2091. $

**High Point Restaurant,** 224 West Main; (931) 924–4600. This is said to be the former 1920s-era home of Al Capone's mistress and is on the National Register of Historic Places. Excellent filet mignon, crab legs, trout, chicken, and a children's menu. Reservations are recommended. $$

## Where to Stay

**Best Western Smokehouse Restaurant and Lodge,** Highway 64-41A, off I–24 at exit 134; (931) 924–2268 or (800) 489–2091. Motel rooms and cabins. $–$$$ (motel rooms), $$$$ (cabins)

**Monteagle Inn,** 204 West Main; (931) 924–3869. Just down the street from High Point Restaurant is this lovingly restored 1940s-era home. Twelve guest rooms, with king or queen beds and full private baths. $$–$$$

## For More Information

**Monteagle Mountain Chamber of Commerce,** 19 East College Street, Monteagle, TN 37356; (931) 924–5353; www.monteagle chamber.com. Open 8:00 A.M. to 4:00 P.M. Monday through Friday.

# McMinnville/Rock Island

Warren County, which serves McMinnville as county seat, is known as the Nursery Capital of the World. More than 400 commercial nurseries throughout the county grow trees, shrubs, and plants. Many of the nurseries are located along the major highways and provide miles of flowering beauty for you to see as you drive along. Many of the nurseries are open for tours, and several have small retail outlets. For a listing of those open to the public, call the chamber of commerce at (931) 473–6611.

### Cumberland Caverns (all ages)

**1437 Cumberland Caverns Road, 7 miles southeast of McMinnville off State Highway 8; (931) 668–4396. www.cumberlandcaverns.com. Open daily May through October, 9:00 A.M. to 5:00 P.M. Call for current tour schedule. $–$$.**

Cumberland Caverns is the second-largest cave system in the United States. (The largest is Mammoth Cave, a couple hours' drive north of here in Cave City, Kentucky.) In addition to being a large cavern, Cumberland has some unusual elements , including a 15-foot-high crystal and brass chandelier that measures 8½ feet in diameter. It hangs from the rocky ceiling of a huge dining room 500 feet below ground. During the one-and-a-half-hour tour, the guide will point it out and tell you that it came from the Loews Metropolitan Theater in Brooklyn, New York. Another interesting room is called the Hall of the Mountain King, the largest cavern room in the eastern United States. It's 600 feet long, 150 feet wide, and 140 feet high. While in the hall, you'll be treated to the spectacular light-and-sound show "God of the Mountain."

You'll also get a chance to see a remarkable number of giant stalactites and stalag-mites, towering stone columns, and enormous flowstone deposits, as well as several beautiful pools and waterfalls. Because of the extent of the cave and its variety of forma-tions, the cavern has been designated a National Landmark by the U.S. Department of the Interior. If this great family attraction won't get the kids to take off their Walkmans, noth-ing will.

### Historic Falcon Manor (ages 8 and up)

**2645 Faulkner Springs Road; (931) 668–4444; www.falconmanor.com. Accommodations for children under 12 by prior arrangement only. The owners provide a casual tour of the facil-ity daily at 1:00 P.M. Tour rates: $–$$.**

In 1896 the entrepreneur Clay Faulkner told his wife, Mary, that he would build her the finest house in Warren County if she would move next to their woolen mill 2½ miles out-side McMinnville. She agreed, and less than a year later, the Faulkners and their five chil-dren moved into the 10,000-square-foot Queen Anne–Victorian mansion. In 1946 the house was converted into the Cumberland Valley Sanitarium and Hospital, and in 1989 George and Charlien McGlothin bought the old house at auction and spent four years restoring it to its Victorian grandeur. They have now opened one of the most splendid bed-and-breakfast inns in the state. Historic Falcon Manor is listed on the National Regis-ter of Historic Places and is part of Tennessee's Heritage Trail. PBS (Public Broadcasting Service) has referred to it as "Tennessee's Biltmore."

### Rock Island State Park (all ages)

**82 Beach Road, off Highway 70S, Rock Island, about 13 miles south of Sparta; (931) 686–2471. Open year-round. Free.**

Another magnificent waterfall can be seen at the Rock Island State Park. The Great Falls of the Caney Fork River plunge into an imposing limestone gorge that provides a great place for fishing, rock hopping, and exploration. Located at the upper end of Center Hill Lake, the park also has a white-sand swimming beach and boat launching areas on the lake, as well as cabins, campsites, and picnic pavilions. The annual Sandbar Arts and Crafts Show is held each October.

### Big Bone Cave Natural Area (all ages)
**Bone Cave community, about 7 miles from Rock Island State Park; (931) 686–2471. Open year-round, by appointment. Free tours available from the ranger's office at Rock Island State Park.**

The Big Bone Cave Natural Area is located near Rock Island State Park. This is where Pleistocene mammal fossils, as well as the bones of a jaguar and a giant ground sloth, were discovered. The area is also historical in that it was mined for saltpeter during the War of 1812 and the Civil War.

## Amazing
# Tennessee Facts

Tennessee's state motto is "Agriculture and Commerce."

## Other Things to See and Do

**Black House** (ages 8 and up), Downtown McMinnville, at the corner of West Main and South High Streets; (931) 668–5050. Open during May Day celebration each year, during Christmas, and on other special occasions. Other times, tours are available by appointment. Call for admission prices. Historically significant home built before the Civil War.

## Where to Eat

**The Collection Mall and Cafe,** 216 East Main Street; (931) 473–1666. A collection of antiques and gift shops under one roof, with a cafe nestled in the center providing lunch, weekend breakfasts, and candlelight dinners. $–$$

**The California Doggery,** Corner of Main Street and South Court Square; (931) 473–

6611. A fast, inexpensive hot dog lunch is yours when you see this mobile kiosk that parks here every weekday and on special occasions that bring crowds to downtown. The hot dogs are huge and will satisfy an adult, especially with all the fixin's. $

## Where to Stay

**Historic Falcon Manor,** 2645 Faulkner Springs Road; (931) 668–4444; www.falcon manor.com. Buffet breakfast. $$–$$$$

**The Inn at Harvest Farms Lake,** 825 Tom Grissom Road, Morrison; (931) 668–1099. Located just outside McMinnville proper, this 7,000-square foot Victorian manor has four bedrooms. Grounds are professionally landscaped and delight the eye with a Victorian gazebo, an arched bridge, and a dock on the lake. Prices include evening refreshments with the hosts and full breakfast. $$–$$$

**The Tree City Inn,** 809 Sparta Street; (931) 473–2159. So named because of its location in the Nursery Capital of the World, this inn offers an indoor pool and spa, exercise rooms, and beautifully decorated guest rooms. A great free continental breakfast comes with your stay. $-$$

## For More Information

**McMinnville/Warren County Chamber of Commerce,** 110 South Court Square, P.O. Box 574, McMinnville, TN 37111; (931) 473–6611; www.warrentn.com. Open 8:00 A.M. to 4:30 P.M. Monday through Friday.

# Sparta

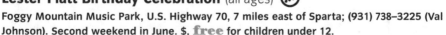

### Rock House Shrine (all ages)
**Highway 70, about 4 miles east of Sparta; (931) 738–9966, (931) 738–5691, or (931) 836–3552. Open Wednesday, Friday, and Saturday 10:00 A.M. to 3:00 P.M., March through November. Free.**

Back when this part of the state was known as the New Frontier, the Wilderness Trail was the main highway through the state, connecting the frontier settlements to the west and the more settled areas to the east. The Rock House stagecoach inn and tollhouse was strategically built at the point where an early railroad connection crossed the Trail. Built between 1835 and 1839 of Tennessee limestone, the inn soon became a gathering place for a "who's who" of the American frontier.

Preserved through the years, this piece of Americana, now known as the Rock House Shrine State Historic Area, is cared for by the Rock House chapter of the Daughters of the American Revolution.

### Lester Flatt Sign (all ages)
**Corner of East Bockman Way and Baker Street, Sparta. Free.**

Sparta is the hometown of legendary bluegrass entertainer Lester Flatt. There's a historical sign honoring him and his contribution to the musical genre at the corner of East Bockman Way and Baker Street.

### Lester Flatt Birthday Celebration (all ages) 🎵
**Foggy Mountain Music Park, U.S. Highway 70, 7 miles east of Sparta; (931) 738–3225 (Val Johnson). Second weekend in June. $, free for children under 12.**

If you're a bluegrass fan, you'll want to visit the two-day Lester Flatt Birthday Celebration in June. There's plenty of music and plenty of room for the kids to run around, as well as crafts, music memorabilia, and bluegrass competition.

### Virgin Falls (all ages) 🚶
**11 miles east of Sparta off U.S. Highway 70; (931) 836–3552 or (931) 336–7424. Open daily. Free.**

The unique Virgin Falls offers a different type of waterfall to enjoy. It comes from nowhere, it falls, and then it disappears! The falls are formed by an underground stream that emerges from a cave, drops over a 110-foot cliff, and then immediately goes back into another cave. Surrounding the falls is the 317-acre State Natural Pocket Wilderness Area, which includes many spectacular overlooks, streams, and caves. If you're up to it, the 8-mile hike, which takes you past many of these natural attractions, is the best way to see the entire area. This trail is designated as both a National Recreation Trail and a State Recreation Trail and is adjacent to the Bridgestone/Firestone Centennial Wilderness Trail System.

### Bridgestone/Firestone Centennial Wilderness (all ages)

**Southeastern White County (follow Highway 70 east through Sparta for 11 miles, turn right at Eastland Road, go 7 miles, then look for the signs); (931) 836–3552.**

This 10,000-acre area was a gift from the Bridgestone/Firestone Tire Company in the fall of 1998. It's in Scott's Gulf, a favorite area for hiking, kayaking, hunting, fishing, and horse-back riding. Scenic bluffs overlook the Caney Fork River Gorge.

## Where to Eat

**The Beechwood,** 673 Charles Golden Road, just off Highway 111; (931) 738–4488. Reasonably priced gourmet food served in an elegant antebellum mansion. Limited children's menu. Sunday brunch. $$

**The Foglight Foodhouse,** 11716 Old McMinnville Highway (State Route 1), about 1½ miles from Rock Island State Park, Walling; (423) 657–2364. Catfish, steaks, Cajun specialties, and coconut shrimp, plus unique specials like alligator tails and ostrich. Children's menu. $$

## Where to Stay

**Royal Inn,** 803 Valley View Road, off Highway 111, Sparta; (931) 738–8585. Kitchens and hot tubs available. $$

## For More Information

**Sparta/White County Chamber of Commerce,** 16 W. Bockman, 38583; (931) 836–3552; www.sparta-chamber.net. Open 9:00 A.M. to 5:00 P.M. Monday through Friday.

# Smithville

### Joe L. Evins Appalachian Center for Crafts (all ages)

**1560 Craft Center Drive (take the Highway 56 exit off I–40 and go south across the Hurricane Bridge of Center Hill Lake, then take the first left after the bridge and go about a mile up the hill); (615) 597–6801. Open 9:00 A.M. to 5:00 P.M. daily year-round, except major holidays and the week between Christmas and New Year's. Free tours available when staff permits, during special events, and on Monday and Tuesday in June and July.**

The Joe L. Evins Appalachian Center for Crafts is an exhibit and sales gallery as well as a teaching institution for Appalachian and contemporary crafts. The center showcases the work of Tennessee craftspeople and artisans from thirteen Appalachian states. You'll find some great one-of-a-kind gift items here, including quilts, baskets, jewelry, clay, and handblown glass. Festivals are held on the Sunday following Thanksgiving Day and on Mother's Day.

## Old-Time Fiddler's Jamboree and Crafts Festival (all ages)

**Smithville town square; (615) 597–4163 or (615) 597–8500. Early July. Free.**

The internationally famous Old-Time Fiddler's Jamboree and Crafts Festival is a country and Appalachian music fan's version of heaven. Patricipants vie for prizes in twenty-eight categories of traditional music and dancing, including old-time bluegrass, clogging, buck dancing, old-time fiddle bands, five-string banjo, dulcimer, dobro, fiddling, and flat-top guitar. The fiddle players have a fiddle-off to determine the grand champion. In addition, there are seven categories for musicians under the age of twelve. There are dozens of traditional craft booths, food stands, and fun things to do. This is a great educational experience as well as a fun event.

## Where to Eat

**Sundance,** 107 East Main Street, just off the town square; (615) 597–1910. Daily lunch specials; homemade pies and cakes. $

## Where to Stay

**East Side Inn,** 598 East Broad Street; (615) 597–4503. $

**Green Brook Inn Bed and Breakfast and Lakehouse,** 810 South College Street; (866) 705–7714 or (615) 597–2998. This bed-and-breakfast is an 1830s-era log home, with a very comfortable feel. The home has three guest rooms with private baths, and the lake house has two bedrooms, and two baths with a fireplace and hot tub overlooking Center Hill Lake. It's a great place to relax after your travels, and the breakfasts are delicious and bountiful. On request, the owner will play the piano while dog Nadine sings along. $$$–$$$$

**Lakeside Resort,** at Center Hill Lake, 7 miles north of Smithville; (615) 597–4298. Twelve furnished cottages and guest houses, plus a group facility. Weekly bookings all year $$$

## For More Information

**Smithville/DeKalb County Chamber of Commerce,** P.O. Box 64, 301 North Public Square, Smithville, TN 37166; (615) 597–4163; www.smithvilletn.com. Open 9:00 A.M. to 4:00 P.M. Monday through Friday.

# Cookeville

### Arda Lee's Hidden Hollow Park (all ages)

1901 Mt. Pleasant Road; (931) 526–4038. Open daily 8:30 A.M. to 10:30 P.M. $.

Looking for some funky, laid-back outdoor fun? Hidden Hollow fills that bill. This place is hard to explain. Back in 1972, Arda Lee retired in order to live out his childhood dream and transformed an old, eighty-six-acre discarded farm into a great place to picnic and have fun. Among its offerings are a small petting zoo with deer, rabbits, and birds; a dandy beach complete with kiddie swimming pool; and a pond perfect for cane-pole fishing.

A gingerbread tree house and a tepee, which adjoin the kiddie pool, offer a fun place for the smaller kids to have a party or a picnic. There's a covered bridge, a waterwheel, a wedding chapel, rock gardens, and fountains. From Thanksgiving through Christmas, the 50-foot-high windmill is lit to resemble a Christmas tree, and the hills are transformed with thousands of lights and figurines. This is a day-use park (no camping), but there is a snack bar.

### City Lake Natural Area (all ages)

Bridgeway Road, off I–40 at exit 290; (931) 526–9591. Open year-round. Free.

This forty-acre natural park features a fishing pier, shaded picnic areas, hiking trails, and a waterfall with an overlook. There are also several preserved water-treatment buildings from the 1920s, when the lake was the city's main water source.

### Cane Creek Park (all ages)

201 C. C. Camp Road, about 3 miles off I–40 at exit 286; (931) 526–9591. Open year-round. Park Admission: free.

Cane Creek Park has a fifty-six-acre lake as the centerpiece of its 260 acres and is the largest municipal park in the upper Cumberland region. Among its offerings are hiking trails; a boat ramp; a paved bike trail; a concession stand; a softball complex; two fishing piers; volleyball, basketball, and horseshoe courts; and a lot of space and playground equipment. Canoe and paddleboat rentals are $2.00 per half hour.

### Burgess Falls State Natural Area (all ages)

State Route 135, 8 miles south of Cookeville; (931) 432–5312. Open daily 8:00 A.M. to sunset. Free.

At the Burgess Falls State Natural Area, the Falling Water River provides several magnificent waterfalls amid acres of old forests. Various mills along the river played important roles in the development of the surrounding region. An early gristmill provided meal and flour to settlers, and later a sawmill was powered by the river and offered precision-cut lumber to homesteaders.

The city of Cookeville purchased the area in the early 1920s and constructed a dam and powerhouse to produce electricity for the city, which it did until 1944. The dam still exists, and remains of the old powerhouse can be seen. To see the natural areas and the falls, take the ¾-mile-long riverside trail. It dead-ends into the 130-foot-tall falls. Along the way you'll see several other cascading talls and interesting rock formations within the river gorge. Other trails lead to areas above the dam, where you get a great view of the entire river and its rapids far below. The river action is awesome here and should be seen, but keep an eye on the kids; there are a lot of unprotected limestone overhangs and cliffs.

Plenty of picnic areas below the dam offer nice scenic views of the river. Rest room facilities and grills are available.

## Muddy Pond Mennonite Community (all ages)
**Between Monterey and Clarkrange on Highway 62; (931) 526–2211. Free.**

The Muddy Pond Mennonite Community provides a glimpse into the fascinating world of the Mennonites. You'll be able to watch true craftsmen create fine horse-drawn buggies and wagons and the harnesses and saddles that go with them. Several homes in the area sell wonderful fresh-baked breads and pies. Fresh eggs are available as well. A major draw each fall is the making of molasses, produced the old-fashioned way with mule power. Look for signs throughout the area for items for sale.

## Cookville History Museum (all ages)
**144 Lowe Avenue; (931) 520–5455. Open 10:00 A.M. to 4:00 P.M. Tuesday through Friday. Free.**

This interesting collection offers historical data. artifacts, old photos, clothing, and other tidbits related to life in Putnam County and the Upper Cumberland region in bygone days.

## Other Things to See and Do

**Circle K Horse Pavilion** (ages 6 and up), 4775 Bohannon Lane; (931) 528–2287. Guided trail rides, riding instructions, and a summer day camp.

**Cookeville Depot Museum** (all ages), corner of Cedar and Broad, off I–40 at exit 286 or 287; (931) 528–8570. Open year-round Tuesday through Saturday. **Free.** This depot was built in 1909 by the Tennessee Central Railroad and is on the National Register of Historic Places. Railway artifacts, old photos, and two of the Tennessee Central's cabooses are on display.

## Where to Eat

**The Diner on First,** 120 West First Street; (931) 520–0173. Features sandwiches, salads, and daily lunch specials like vegetable lasagna and red beans and rice. $

**Mamma Rosa's Pizzeria and Italian Restaurant,** 230 South Lowe Avenue; (931) 372–8694. $

## Where to Stay

**Hampton Inn,** 1025 Interstate Drive; (931) 520–1117. $$

**Holiday Inn,** 970 South Jefferson; (931) 526–7125. Family-style restaurant. $$$

## For More Information

**Cookeville/Putnam County Chamber of Commerce,** 1 West First Street, Cookeville,

TN 38501; (931) 526–2211; www.cookeville chamber.com. Open 8:00 A.M. to 4:30 P.M. Monday through Friday.

# Celina/Gainesboro

Gainesboro was once called the Switzerland of the Upper Cumberland, and there is still a kind of Old World charm to this town. There are lots of celebrations, but one of the best is the Poke Sallet Festival, which honors the tasty weed with a three-day event the second weekend in May. You'll see outhouse races, get to ride in horse-drawn carriages, listen to music, and play games from the nineteenth century. Contact the chambers of commerce listed at the end of this section for more information.

### Dale Hollow Lake and Dam (all ages)

**5050 Dale Hollow Dam Road, Celina; access to the lake is on secondary roads off Highways 42, 52, and 53; (931) 243–3136.**

Often referred to as the cleanest, most pristine, most beautiful lake in the Southeast, Dale Hollow Lake spreads across four counties adjacent to the Kentucky border. With more than 600 miles of unspoiled shoreline, the lake is an all-season favorite for those who prefer fresh air and natural winds to air-conditioning and forced-air heating.

With small coves and inlets galore, fishing here is magnificent. In fact, the world-record smallmouth bass (eleven pounds, fifteen ounces) was taken from the lake. Each year the Dale Hollow Bass Classic is held, and anglers from all over come for a shot at that record.

In the wintertime the American bald eagle is a regular visitor to the lake. The U.S. Army Corps of Engineers conducts an annual eagle watch and invites visitors to come along. Reservations are needed.

The corps also maintains seven different recreation areas along the lake, where you'll find picnic areas, hiking, campgrounds, lake access, and boat ramps. There are several commercial marinas on the Tennessee side of the lake offering fishing and pleasure-boat rentals, houseboat rentals, Jet Ski rentals, and just about anything else you need to enjoy a day on the lake—or under it, for that matter. Because of its clean water, the lake is popular with scuba divers.

The lake was created in 1943 when the U.S. Army Corps of Engineers built the Dale Hollow

Dam just east of Celina along Highway 53. The dam is an imposing sight, at 200 feet high and 1,717 feet wide. A panoramic view of the lake and its environs can be had from the top of the dam.

### Historic Gainesboro (ages 8 and up)
**100 Hull Avenue, Gainesboro; (931) 268–0971 (Gainesboro/Jackson County Chamber of Commerce).**

Tourism has saved the little town of Gainesboro, located on the Cumberland River about 25 miles south of Celina on Highway 56. Just a few years ago, the town was faced with hard times and financial difficulties. Creative thinking by local officials and several business leaders shook off the death throes of the sluggish agrarian economy. Today the downtown antiques district has brought new life and a lot of visitors to the town.

In addition to the many antiques shops and antiques malls, there are two drugstores—both of which still have old-fashioned soda fountains—a hardware store, and several arts and crafts shops. A special Cumberland Heritage Christmas celebration takes place each December.

## Carthage's **Claim to Fame**

The town of Carthage, seat of Smith County, is the hometown of former vice president Al Gore.

## Other Things to See and Do

**Clay County Courthouse** (all ages), 100 Courthouse Square, Celina; (931) 243–2161. **Free.**

**Clay County Museum,** 805 Brown Street, Celina; (931) 243–4220. **Free.**

**Dale Hollow National Fish Hatchery** (all ages), 50 Fish Hatchery Road, north of Celina on Highway 53; (931) 243–2443. Open year-round. **Free.** This hatchery produces rainbow, brown, and lake trout for stocking federal waters.

**Fort Blount/Williamsburg** (all ages), Smith Bend Road, on State Highway 262, 10 miles outside Gainesboro; (931) 268–0971. **Free.** Located on the banks of the Cumberland

River, this site was originally known as the Crossing of the Cumberland. In 1791 it was an important link between eastern Tennessee and the Cumberland settlements.

## Where to Eat

**City Cafe,** 112 Main Street, Gainesboro; (931) 268–2777. A favorite since the 1970s, known for its affordable lunches. $

**Crow's Nest,** 820 East Lake Avenue, Celina; (931) 243–3333. Family-style restaurant. Friday and Saturday night seafood buffet. $

**Sherry's Restaurant,** 911 East Lake Avenue, Celina; (931) 243–6565. This eatery serves down-home country cooking at its best. The locals' favorite is the catfish with mashed potatoes and slaw. $

## Where to Stay

**Horse Creek Resort,** 1150 Horse Creek Road, about 4 miles from Celina, off Highway 52; (931) 243–2125 or (800) 545– 2595. One of several resorts on Dale Hollow Lake. Furnished cabins and eight motel rooms. Houseboats and fishing boats. $$–$$$$ (cabins), $ (motel). Houseboats accommodate ten to twelve people and range from basic to luxurious. All have central heat and air-conditioning, and all have water slides. $$$$

## For More Information

**Clay County Partnership Chamber of Commerce,** 476 Brown Street, Celina, TN 38551; (931) 243–3338; www.claycountytn .com. Open 8:00 A.M. to 4:00 P.M. Monday through Friday.

**Gainesboro/Jackson County Chamber of Commerce,** 402 East Hull Avenue, Gainesboro, TN 38562; (931) 268–0971. Open 8:00 A.M. to 4:00 P.M. Monday through Friday.

# Red Boiling Springs

During the early 1900s, Red Boiling Springs was a bustling health and vacation resort made famous by its medicinal waters. Today the quiet little village is known for its tranquillity, its two covered bridges, and the great southern hospitality and tasty food at its three restored hotels (Armour's, the Donoho, and the Thomas House), which are now bed-and-breakfast inns and listed on the National Register of Historic Places.

The town was famous for its four types of water: black, red, double and twist, and free stone. Each is different in its mineral analysis, and each was considered a "cure" for different ailments.

## Log Cabin Visitors Center (all ages)
**East Main Street; (615) 666–5885. Free.**

The Log Cabin Visitors Center houses exhibits on the area's history. You can pick up a driving-tour map of the area.

## Historic Red Boiling Springs (all ages)
**Highway 52; (615) 699–2011. Free.**

Take a walking and driving tour to learn all about this area's heritage. You can sample the famous "healing waters" at several pumps around town.

## Armour's Red Boiling Springs Hotel
**321 East Main Street; (615) 699–2180.**

Armour's Red Boiling Springs Hotel is one of the three surviving original hotels from the days when the town had six hotels and no fewer than ten boardinghouses. It has twenty modern guest rooms, each with air-conditioning and private bath, with rates starting at $40 per person per night, including dinner and breakfast. Laban and Reba Hilton own the hotel and still operate the only bathhouse in town where you can "take the cure." A one-hour treatment in the water, including a massage, is $40.

The kids can play in a creek across from the hotel, and a small park nearby has playground equipment.

### Donoho Hotel (all ages)

**500 East Main Street, (615) 699-3141; www.donohohotel.com. Lodging $$–$$$; dining $$–$$$.**

This circa-1914 hotel was closed for many years and has undergone extensive renovations. Now restored to its original elegance, the hotel offers a 200-foot long old-southern-style veranda, home cooking, and a beautiful, old-fashioned family-style dining room. Many people come in just to tour the hotel, and even if you're not a guest, you can eat here if you make a reservation. Live entertainment every Friday and Saturday night.

## Other Things to See and Do

**City Park** (all ages), 190 Dale Street; (615) 699–2011. **Free.** Scenic park with playgrounds, covered bridges, and a public community center.

## Where to Eat

**The Dinner Bell,** 213 Market Street, downtown; (615) 699–3299. Good daily lunch specials and Friday and Saturday night catfish dinners. $

**RBS Bar-B-Q,** 111 Whitley Hollow Road; (615) 699–3633. Open Friday, Saturday, and Sunday for breakfast, lunch, and dinner. $

## For More Information

**City of Red Boiling Springs,** 166 Dale Street, Red Boiling Springs, TN 37150; (615) 699–2011; www.redboilingsprings.com. Open 8:00 A.M. to 4:30 P.M. Monday through Friday.

# Pall Mall/Jamestown

Tucked away in the Cumberland Mountains, Pall Mall is a small community that gave birth to a legend. Sgt. Alvin York gained international fame for his exploits during World War I when he led a small patrol in the Argonne Forest, killed 25 German soldiers, and helped in the capture of 132 more. The Congressional Medal of Honor was among the forty Allied decorations he received.

Soon the humble mountain boy became an international hero. But upon his return, he shunned the publicity and returned to his mountain homestead. He did, however, give consent to a movie based on his life, Sergeant York, which starred Gary Cooper.

York spent most of his life in public service, working to better the lives of the mountain folk in the Pall Mall and Jamestown areas. In 1929 he established the Alvin York Institute in Jamestown, which is still thriving. Through the years the school has provided local children with educational and vocational opportunities that would have otherwise been unavailable to them.

### Sergeant Alvin C. York Mill and Burial Place (all ages)
**Highway 127, Pall Mall, about 7 miles north of Jamestown; (931) 879–6456 or (931) 879–5366 (ranger office). Open daily. Free.**

Located along the banks of the Wolf River, the Sergeant Alvin C. York Mill and Burial Place is a state historic site. The area consists of the family farm and the gristmill that York operated for years. Today the site is run by York's son, Andy, who loves to show guests around and talk about his father. Talking with Andy is really the highlight of the visit. It's an interesting experience and one that your family shouldn't miss.

# Big South Fork National River
# and Recreation Area

Big South Fork National River and Recreation Area brings many rugged, outdoorsy types to Pall Mall and Jamestown. Big South Fork sprawls over 125,000 acres from East Tennessee to the Jamestown area, north into Kentucky. Visitors are attracted to the beauty of the Cumberland Plateau and for the opportunities for bird-watching, camping, white-water rafting, biking, hunting, and fishing. On the Tennessee side, Bandy Creek Visitor Area, located 2 miles off Tennessee Highway 297 between Oneida and Jamestown, is a good place to find out more about the area. Its number is (423) 286-7275.

### Highland Manor (ages 8 and up)
**Highway 127, just south of Jamestown; (931) 879–9519. Open 10:00 A.M. to 5:00 P.M. Monday through Saturday year-round; also open 1:00 to 5:00 P.M. Sunday in the summer. Free.**

This is the state's oldest winery. The best time to see the entire wine-making process is in the fall, shortly after the harvest. You can watch the wine making, tour the wine cellar, and picnic and play on the grounds for free. A wine and gift shop is located in the authentic Tudor manor house.

## Where to Eat

**Ruth's Family Restaurant,** 331 North Main Street; (931) 879–8182. This wonderful restaurant close to town, has a varied menu with a great buffet. If you go once, that won't be your last time! $

## Where to Stay

**Wildwood Lodge Bed and Breakfast,** 3636 Pickett Park;(931) 879–9454. You can even bring your horses to board in the stables here while you enjoy the more civilized

amenities, including a library with fireplace, three decks from which to enjoy the view, and twenty-seven acres of woodland. The breakfasts are sumptuous and satisfying. $$–$$$

## For More Information

**Jamestown/Fentress County Chamber of Commerce,** P.O. Box 1294, 114 Central Avenue West, Jamestown, TN 38556, (800) 327–3945; www.jamestowntn.org. Open 8:00 A.M. to 4:30 P.M. Monday through Friday.

# Crossville

The Highway 127 corridor through Crossville is part of the world-famous 450-mile-long "yard sale" held the third weekend in August each year. The sale starts in Covington, Kentucky, and runs through Tennessee on Highway 127 to Gadsden, Alabama. People who live along the highway fill their yards with merchandise. Nonresidents sell out of portable stands and from the back of pickup trucks. It's quite a sight and a great place to find a lot of bargains.

## Cumberland County Playhouse (all ages)

**221 Tennessee Avenue, 3 miles west of Crossville on Highway 70; (931) 484–5000. Call for a schedule and ticket prices.**

Founded in 1965, the Cumberland County Playhouse is one of the state's cultural treasures and one of the largest rural professional theaters in the country. There's a professional, family show being performed on one of the facility's two stages just about any time you come through the area. From *Phantom of the Opera* to *The Mikado* to *Amadeus* to *Brigadoon,* a wide variety of shows are available for your family's enjoyment.

## Cumberland General Store (all ages)

**1 Highway 68, at the junction of Highways 127S and 68, 4 miles south of Crossville; (931) 484–8481. Open Monday through Saturday year-round and Sunday afternoons from mid-March through December.**

This is a fun store where you can pick up some unique items. Its slogan is "Complete Outfitters with Goods in Endless Variety for Man and Beast."

Everything in the store is an exact, new reproduction. You'll find apple peelers, cuspidors, spinning wheels, carbide lamps, jelly strainers, livestock brushes, country hams, woodstoves, Victorian and colonial hardware, and thousands of other items. You'll also be able to pick up a set of *McGuffey's Readers*. If you're not interested in shopping or browsing, you can buy an ice-cold root beer and sit out on the porch in a rocking chair to watch the world go by as you wait.

## Cumberland Homesteads Tower Museum (ages 6 and up)

**96 Highway 68; (931) 456–9663. Open March through December, 10:00 A.M. to 5:00 P.M. Monday through Saturday and 1:00 to 5:00 P.M. Sunday. $.**

Across the street from the Cumberland General Store is the Homesteads Tower Museum. It's located in the building that served as the administrative office of President Franklin D. Roosevelt's Cumberland Homesteads Project, widely referred to as the "showplace of the New Deal." Of the 102 New Deal projects, the Cumberland Homesteads was considered one of the most successful.

The museum tells the story of the Homesteads community through photos, memorabilia, newspaper clippings, and rare documents. The plan to construct Homesteads was formulated during the 1930s, to furnish the people of Cumberland County with employment and to provide a total of 256 families a low-cost means of purchasing a home. The 29,000 acres were divided into small farms, from five to fifty acres each. Soon picturesque stone cottages were being built, many of which still stand.

The tower and the building in which the offices were located have been restored and are open to the public. A beautiful panoramic view of the area can be seen from the top of the 80-foot-tall octagonal tower.

## Cumberland Mountain State Park (all ages) 

**Highway 127, south of Crossville and I–40; (931) 484–6138 or (800) 250–8618. Open year-round. Free.**

Part of the Homesteads plan was the creation of recreational facilities. One of those areas is the 1,562-acre Cumberland Mountain State Park. Created by the Civilian Conservation Corps (CCC) and the Works Progress Administration (WPA), many of the buildings still standing were made of Crab Orchard stone, an indigenous sandstone that is still used in construction throughout the area. The state's grandest CCC project is a seven-arch Crab Orchard sandstone bridge in the park that spans the fifty-acre Byrd Lake, created by a Crab Orchard sandstone dam. It is spectacular and provides a nice photo opportunity.

In addition to its dense forests, the park offers nearly 15 miles of walking trails, one of which winds between tall pines and hemlocks and circles the lake. A state-operated restaurant overlooks the lake and is open year-round; for my money, it's one of the best places in this part of the state to enjoy a nice, relaxing, tasty meal with your family.

There are a lot of picnic tables located throughout the park, an Olympic-size swimming pool, numerous play areas, canoe and paddleboat rentals, and plenty of fishing opportunities.

## Ozone Falls State Natural Area (all ages)

**Highway 70 East; (931) 484–6138. Open year-round. Free.**

Old-growth forests dominate the Ozone Falls State Natural Area, managed by the Cumberland Mountain State Park. The highlight here is the magnificent waterfall where Fall Creek cascades into the deep gorges below. From the trail at the top of the falls, take a look west. It's one of the most beautiful vistas you'll find anywhere. Be very careful as you walk along, and keep an eye on the little ones here. There are quite a few unprotected drop-offs in the area. The falls and natural area are named after the small community of Ozone, in which they are located. You'll find the pull-off for the area along U.S. Highway 70 between Rockwood and Crab Orchard. The best time to see the falls and creek in full glory is during late winter and spring.

## Crabtree House (all ages)

**Pigeon Ridge Road; (931) 484–8529. Open Monday through Saturday from 10:00 A.M. to 5:00 P.M., Sunday noon to 5:00 P.M. $, under age 6 free.**

Crabtree House's Homestead Tower and Museum tells about the Homestead Project of the 1930s. There is a renovated and period-furnished homestead house on the property.

## Wilson's Wildlife Adventures (all ages)

**2262 North Main Street; (931) 707–WILD; www.wilsonwildlifemuseum.com. Open Monday through Thursday 9:00 A.M. to 6:00 P.M., Friday and Saturday 9:00 A.M. to 7:00 P.M. $–$$.**

Stroll around the largest wildlife museum in the Southeast, and take an up-close-and-personal look at animals from around the world in spectacular natural habitats. .

## Palace Theatre (all ages)

**72 South Main Street; (931) 484–6113. Call for ticket prices and show information.**

Local theater hosts concerts, events, and various entertainment.

# Other Things to See and Do

**Crab Orchard Stone Quarries** (all ages), Highway 70; (931) 484–6222. Call in advance for a tour. **Free.**

**The Crossville Depot** (all ages), North and Main Streets; (931) 456–2586. Open 9:00 A.M. to 5:00 P.M. Monday through Saturday. **Free.** Site of Sgt. Alvin C. York's celebrated return from World War I in 1921.

**Pirates Plateau** (all ages), 3818 Peavine Road; (931) 456–1544. Open daily mid-May through Labor Day; weekends only late March through mid-May and after Labor Day through Thanksgiving. Closed other months. **Free** admission, pay per attraction. Miniature golf, go-carts, bumper boats, and a game room.

**Simonton's Cheese House** (all ages), Highway 127 South (in the South Main Mini-Mall); (931) 484–5193. Open 8:00 A.M. to 5:00 P.M. Monday through Saturday. More than 500 gourmet food items and cheeses.

## Where to Eat

**Cumberland Mountain State Park Restaurant,** in the park, overlooking the stone bridge; (931) 484–7186. Open mid-January through early December. Buffet-style lunch and dinner. Nightly specials. Discounts for children and seniors. $–$$

**Halcyon Days Restaurant,** 2444 Genesis Road; (931) 456–3663. The signature dish for this restaurant is —all of them. This place specializes in freshness—whether it's steak, seafood, or pasta. Although they don't have a children's menu, they offer smaller versions of grown-up meals for the small fry in your bunch. This is a nice break from the fast-food chains. $$–$$

## Where to Stay

**Fairfield Glade Resort,** Peavine Road (Highway 101), off I–40 at exit 322; (931) 484–7521. This resort spans 12,251 acres and offers golf, swimming, tennis, and other activities. Accommodations include a lodge, condos, villas, and time-share units. $$$–$$$$

**La Quinta Inn Crossville,** 4038 Highway 127 North; (931) 456–9338. $$

**Ramada Inn,** Highway 127 North, off I–40 at exit 317; (931) 484–7581 or (800) 228–2828. On-site restaurant. $$

## For More Information

**Crossville–Cumberland County Chamber of Commerce,** P.O. Box 453, 34 South Main Street, Crossville, TN 38555; (931) 484–8444 or (877) 465–3861; www.crossville .com/thechamber. Open 8:00 A.M. to 4:30 P.M. Monday through Friday.

# Pikeville

### Fall Creek Falls State Park (all ages)
**Highways 111 and 30, east of Pikeville; (423) 881–3297, (800) 250–8610 (inns and cabins), or (800) 250–8611 (campground). Open year-round. Free.**

With more than 16,000 acres, Fall Creek Falls State Park is the largest and probably the most beautiful park within the state system. Throughout you'll find majestic cascades, deep gorges, acres of virgin timber, and the fabulous Fall Creek Falls. With a drop of 256 feet, it's the highest waterfall east of the Rocky Mountains. The park's four other falls, although not as high, are just as impressive.

Just about anything you'd want to do in the outdoors you can do here. The nature center is a great place to start your visit. You'll find exhibits that depict the natural and cultural history of the park. In addition, there are miles of hiking, biking, and horseback riding trails. Bikes and horses, as well as paddleboats, canoes, and fishing boats, can be rented for use on the 345-acre Fall Creek Lake. The state record channel catfish (fifty-two pounds) and bluegill (two pounds, twelve ounces) were both caught here.

The 4-mile-long Woodlands Trail is an easy family walking path that takes you along the top of the Fall Creek Falls and down to the large pool below. You are permitted to swim there, at your own risk. The rangers say the water is so cold that few stay in for long.

Better swimming conditions exist in the village green area, where there's an Olympic-size pool, as well as a wading pool for the young ones.

There's a 144-room inn, a full-service restaurant, thirty rental cabins, and 227 campsites in the park. Its eighteen-hole golf course was named one of the top twenty-five public golf courses in the United States by *Golf Digest* magazine. The park is open year-round and is **free.**

## For More Information

**Pikeville–Bledsoe County Chamber of Commerce,** 125 Spring Street, Pikeville, TN 37367; (423) 447–2791; www.pikeville bledsoe.com. Open 9:00 A.M. to 4:00 P.M. Monday through Friday.

# Dayton

### The Scopes Trial Museum and Rhea County Courthouse
(ages 8 and up) 🏛

1475 Market Street; (423) 775–7801. Open Monday through Friday during courthouse hours. **Free.**

The eyes of the world focused on Dayton in 1925 when William Jennings Bryan and Clarence Darrow took part in the famous Scopes evolution trial. The Rhea County Courthouse, where the "Scopes monkey trial" took place, has been restored and is now a National Historic Landmark. The second-floor courtroom, the actual venue for the trial, is still in use today and can be visited.

The Rhea County Museum is located in the courthouse and contains exhibits, news clippings, and photos of the famous trial. Scopes was accused of teaching the Darwinian theory of evolution to a high school biology class in violation of a state statute that made it unlawful "to teach any theory that denies the story of the divine creation of man as taught in the Bible." Scopes was found guilty and fined $100, a fee he never paid.

### Scopes Trial Play and Festival (all ages) 🎵

(423) 775–0361 (Dayton Chamber of Commerce). Held in mid-July. Reserved seats. $–$$.

While serious debates were going on inside the courthouse, locals were having a good time outside. That's why the Scopes Trial Play and Festival, held each July, is such good fun. It gives the whole picture of what really took place in this little Tennessee town, not just what the newspapers reported. The play, *The Scopes Trial: Destiny in Dayton*, is a dramatization that takes place in the same courtroom where the actual trial took place, using court transcripts as the scripts for the actors.

## Annual Tennessee Strawberry Festival (all ages)

**Downtown Dayton; (423) 775–0361 (Dayton Chamber of Commerce). Second and third weeks in May. Free.**

The ten-day Annual Tennessee Strawberry Festival features a children's fair, beauty contest, sporting events, a quilt show, a carnival with a full array of children's and adult amusement rides, and the "World's Longest Strawberry Shortcake," among other attractions and activities.

## Where to Eat

**Watts Bar Resort,** 5757 Watts Bar Highway, about 15 miles from Dayton; (423) 365–9595. Casual, family-style restaurant. Open April through October. $

## Where to Stay

**Watts Bar Resort,** 5757 Watts Bar Highway, about 15 miles from Dayton; (423) 365–9595. Located at 38,000-acre Watts Bar Lake; the resort offers thirty-eight furnished cottages, hiking trails, tennis courts, a swimming pool, and boat rentals. $–$$$

## For More Information

**Dayton Chamber of Commerce,** P.O. Box 634, 107 Main Street, Dayton, TN 37321; (423) 775–0361. Open 8:30 A.M. to 5:00 P.M. Monday through Friday.

**Rhea Economic and Tourism Council,** P.O. Box 634, 107 Main Street, Dayton TN 37321; (423) 775–6171. Open 8:30 A.M. to 5:00 P.M. Monday through Friday.

# the
# Heartland

**M**usic and musicians are everywhere in Tennessee's Heartland, and nowhere are they more plentiful than in the Nashville area. When you have a bevy of banjo pluckers and guitar pickers, you're bound to attract the most important element of country music, the adoring, music-buying fan. Put the star and the fan together and you have an example of the excitement of the region. Music clubs, concert series, and museums and attractions devoted to country music icons are located everywhere.

Although the music industry is important, middle Tennessee doesn't totally revolve around country tunes. The Civil War battlefield sites in Dover, Franklin, and Murfreesboro provide historic, albeit painful, memories of the war in which so many Tennesseans were killed.

History with fonder memories also abounds in the area. A trip to Hermitage, the home of President Andrew Jackson, is a magnificent lesson, as is a visit to the home of another Tennessean who became president, James K. Polk. The historic Natchez Trace Parkway, a 444-mile scenic highway connecting Nashville to Natchez, Mississippi, is a fascinating historic corridor, and the 170,000-acre Land Between the Lakes natural area has much to offer, from buffalo to bald eagles.

The region is dominated by gently rolling hills, sloping green meadows, and miles of river and lake frontage.

## Tennessee **Tunes**

Tennessee has several state songs: "My Homeland Tennessee," "When It's Iris Time in Tennessee," "My Tennessee," "The Tennessee Waltz," "Tennessee," "The Pride of Tennessee," and "Rocky Top."

## Nashville

Some call it Twangtown, a less formal version of its proper nickname, Music City, and most of the top country musicians call it home. Nashville is the state's second most populated city and as its capital serves as the heart of Tennessee.

# THE HEARTLAND

There's a plethora of activities and attractions to choose from around here, with something for everyone, day or night.

Contrary to popular belief, having fun in Nashville goes beyond country music. You don't need to have a love for this musical genre to enjoy visiting or living in the city. But, of course, the city's relationship to country music has created quite a few unique and funky attractions.

Let's start our Music City tour in the northeastern quadrant, 9 miles from downtown off Briley Parkway. That's where you'll find the Opryland area, which includes, among other things, the Opryland Hotel, the Grand Ole Opry, the *General Jackson* showboat, and television studios for TNN (The Nashville Network) and CMT (Country Music Television). Opry Mills, a huge shopping and entertainment destination, is now located on the site of the former Opryland theme park (which closed in 1997).

## Amazing Tennessee Facts

The Grand Ole Opry is the world's longest continuously running live radio program. It was first broadcast in 1925, over station WSM.

### Frist Center for the Visual Arts (all ages)

**901 Broadway; (615) 244–3340. Open daily except Thanksgiving Day, Christmas Day, and New Year's Day. Open Monday through Saturday 10:00 A.M. to 5:30 P.M., Thursday 10:00 A.M. to 8:00 P.M., and Sunday 1:00 to 5:00 P.M. $–$$, free for children 18 and under.**

In April 2001 Nashville saw the opening of this fabulous new arts center. The Frist Center for the Visual Arts, located in the historic downtown post office, offers more than 24,000 square feet of exhibition space for a variety of visual-arts presentations. It features the work of local and regional artists as well as major national and international exhibitions. Special educational programs involve children and families in the visual-arts experience. The center has three different galleries, an auditorium, gift shop, cafe, and resource center for the arts.

### *General Jackson* Showboat (all ages)

**2812 Opryland Drive; (615) 871–6100 or (615) 871–7817. Open year-round.**

The *General Jackson* showboat, considered to be the world's largest, makes regular runs on the Cumberland River. Among its offerings, the nicest trip is the luncheon cruise, which lasts from two to two-and-a-half hours and takes you into downtown Nashville, where you can get a different perspective of the skyline from the river. Prices range from $35 to $50 for adults and from $25 to $45 for children four to eleven, depending on the cruise.

## Opryland Hotel (all ages)

2800 Opryland Drive; (615) 889–1000. Open year-round. **Free.** Parking fee charged.

The 2,883-room Opryland Hotel is an attraction in itself. It's divided into three areas: the Cascades, the Conservatory, and the Delta. Each of the sections has a large atrium. The Cascades covers two acres and includes a waterfall, a stream, and a regularly scheduled dancing water show. The two-acre Conservatory has a two-level walkway through a lush botanical garden. The four-and-a-half-acre Delta is dominated by a lake and river system, complete with flatboats that you can ride.

All three areas are open to nonguests and have restaurants ranging from fine dining to a walk-up food court. On a hot day these air-conditioned areas are wonderful places to take a walk, and there's enough going on to keep the kids amused. If you get the chance, visit during the winter when the hotel is decorated for Christmas, both inside and out. You've never seen anything like it!

## Willie Nelson and Friends Museum (all ages)

2613A McGavock Pike; (615) 885–1515. Open 8:00 A.M. to 10:00 P.M. Memorial Day through Labor Day, 9:00 A.M. to 5:00 P.M. the rest of the year. $.

Along with Willie Nelson's gold and platinum albums, guitars, and personal items, you'll find tributes to Patsy Cline, Audie Murphy, and Elvis Presley in this museum.

## Amazing
# Tennessee Facts

Tennessee's state insects are the firefly and the ladybug.

## Music Valley Wax Museum of the Stars (all ages)

2515 McGavock Pike; (615) 883–3612. Open 8:00 A.M. to 10:00 P.M. Memorial Day through Labor Day, 9:00 A.M. to 5:00 P.M. the rest of the year. $.

The action at Music Valley Wax Museum of the Stars starts outside with the footprints and handprints of nearly 200 stars. Your children might spend as much time out here comparing their feet with the stars' impressions as they might looking at the exhibits inside. It's fun, and I bet you'll end up doing the same. Inside, country music legends are presented in wax.

## Music Valley Amusement Park (ages 3 and up)

2440 Music Valley Drive; (615) 885–2330. Hours vary by season. $–$$$.

While you're in the vicinity of Music Valley Wax Museum of the Stars, check out this new amusement park. This offers old-fashioned fun, with rides you might find in a fair-type of attraction, such as a carousel, bumper cars, and a roller coaster suitable for the kids.

## Grand Ole Golf and Games (all ages)

**2444 Music Valley Drive; (615) 885–8126. Open year-round. Pay per attraction, $–$$$.**

A few blocks from the Music Valley Drive area, Grand Ole Golf and Games has three minia-ture golf courses, plus bumper boats and a fun arcade. The courses range from easy to challenging.

## Nashville Shores (all ages)

**4001 Bell Road, Hermitage, off I–40 at exit 221-B; (615) 889–7050. Open daily from late May through late August (weekends only from May 1 through late May and from late August through late September). $$$–$$$$.**

This water park, located next to Percy Priest Lake, is bound to be a summertime favorite with your kids. Water slides, a pond and activity area for the little ones, a pool area with a waterfall, and a sandy beach with volleyball courts offer plenty of opportunities for water-soaked fun. There's also miniature golf. Pack a picnic lunch and enjoy the day. If you want to spend the day on the lake, you can rent sailboats, pontoon boats, Jet Skis, and paddle-boats at the marina.

## Nashville Zoo at Grassmere (all ages)

**3777 Nolensville Road; (615) 833–1534. Open 9:00 A.M. to 6:00 P.M. daily April through Octo-ber, 9:00 A.M. to 4:00 P.M. daily November through March. $, $2.00-per-car parking fee.**

The Nashville Zoo is located on the grounds of the former Grassmere Wildlife Park. This is a lovely, walk-through park that features animals in natural settings. You can see all sorts of creatures here, including black bears, lions, reptiles, and zebras. There are two new exhibits—exotic hyacinth macaws and gibbons. The kids will enjoy working off some energy at the Jungle Gym, the nation's largest community-built playground park. You can also take a guided tour of an 1810 working farm and renovated historic house.

## The Parthenon (ages 6 and up)

**Centennial Park, West End and Twenty-fifth Avenues; (615) 862–8431. Open 9:00 A.M. to 4:30 P.M. Tuesday through Saturday year-round and Sunday afternoon April through Sep-tember. $, free for children under 4.**

Several decades before Nashville became known for its country music industry, it had a reputation as a regional center of culture and education. The area had many colleges and institutions of higher learning, and it wasn't long before the city was being called the Athens of the South. Therefore, build-ing a replica of the Greek Parthenon for the state's centen-nial celebration in 1896 was a natural thing to do. The exact replica, with a tolerance of less than 1/16 inch, is now open to the public in Centennial Park, just west of downtown on West End Avenue. A 42-foot replica of Athena

Parthenos has been sculpted and is on display inside, as are various art exhibits during the year.

### Tennessee Crafts Fair (all ages)
**Centennial Park, West End and Twenty-fifth Avenues; (615) 665–0502. First weekend in May. Free.**

Centennial Park plays host to several quality events during the year, including the Tennessee Crafts Fair, sponsored by the Tennessee Association of Craft Artists. Nearly 200 Tennessee artists are chosen to display and sell their creations. As part of the celebration, there are craft demonstrations, children's craft activities, a puppet theater, and much more. The same organization sponsors a national, juried crafts show the last weekend of September at the same location.

## Traveling the **Natchez Trace Parkway**

Natchez Trace Parkway is a 444-mile scenic route that commemorates the historic Natchez Trace of the early 1800s. It links Nashville to Natchez, Mississippi.

This is one of the oldest trails in the Western Hemisphere. It began as an Indian trail and was later used by early pioneers who took flatboats loaded with goods down the Mississippi River, then traveled back home on the trace by foot. It was a rough and rugged route. Andrew Jackson and Meriwether Lewis were among those who traveled the trace (and Lewis is buried by the trace as well).

This is a great road to travel on a lazy Sunday afternoon, by car or by bicycle. (Be sure to observe the speed limit.) Start at the northern terminus, at Highway 100 across from the famous Loveless Cafe. Five miles south of the northern terminus, where the trace crosses Highway 96, is the 1,648-foot-long bridge, one of only two post-tensioned, segmented concrete bridges in the world.

For more information contact the Natchez Trace Parkway Heritage Tourism Area in Tupelo, Mississippi, at (800) 305–7417 or (601) 680–4027.

### Tennessee State Capitol (ages 8 and up)
**Charlotte Avenue, downtown Nashville; (615) 741–2692. Open 9:00 A.M. to 4:00 P.M. Monday through Friday. Free.**

Architect William Strickland considered his work on the Tennessee State Capitol building to be his crowning achievement. In fact, he liked it so much that he wanted to be buried there, which he was in 1854, a year before the final stone of the building was laid. He's in the northeast corner above the cornerstone, in a tomb of his own design. President James K. Polk is also buried on the grounds.

The limestone structure has a marble interior and has been restored to its original beauty. A **free** self-guided walking tour is available. Start your visit at the information desk, where you can pick up a brochure explaining the points of interest.

### Ellington Agricultural Center (ages 5 and up)

**E440 Hogan Road; (615) 837–5197. Open 9:00 A.M. to 4:00 P.M. Monday through Friday. Free.**

The history of the state's rich agricultural heritage has been preserved at the Ellington Agricultural Center. Maintained by the Tennessee Department of Agriculture, the museum features more than 2,600 farm implements and rural household items from the time of the first pioneers to the time when electrical power was first introduced to rural communities of the state. There's a special emphasis on the hands-on teaching approach for children, and as a result most of the area's schoolchildren end up here on field trips. It's also an enjoyable place to go as a family. You'll find horse-drawn equipment on display and the large, handmade loom that belonged to Nancy Hanks, the mother of Abraham Lincoln.

The Annual Historic Rural Life Festival is held each May and provides further perspective into the rural life of the state. Activities range from sheepshearing to butter churning to crafts demonstrations.

### Adventure Science Center (all ages)

**800 Fort Negley Boulevard; (615) 862–5160. Open 10:00 A.M. to 5:00 P.M. Monday through Saturday, 12:30 to 5:30 P.M. Sunday. Admission: $–$$. Planetarium show extra.**

Adventure Science Center provides a look at more contemporary life on our planet. Most exhibits are of the hands-on variety and range from environmental technology to health. Kids can walk away from here with some great ideas, such as the environmental message they'll learn at the recycling exhibit.

There's also a planetarium, and there are usually live animal demonstrations in the auditorium. The science museum is just south of downtown.

### Fisk University (ages 8 and up)

**Corner of Jefferson Street and D. B. Todd Boulevard; (615) 329–8720. Free.**

Nashville's Fisk University is one of the nation's oldest African American schools. It was established 1865, when Governor Clinton Fisk met with various representatives to plan a school for the education of the children of former slaves. Today it's a private, coeducational, liberal arts college.

Fisk was created in the changing social order of the Reconstruction, and the campus buildings reflect this in their variety and scale. Jubilee Hall, the first permanent structure on the campus and today a National Historic Landmark, sits prominently on a hill overlooking one of the original, clapboard Civil War–era buildings that was used as a hospital. Restored, it now serves as the Little Theater. The extant building that is most impressive is the Fisk Memorial Chapel. With Romanesque arches and a gigantic Gothic bell tower, it stands out from the rest of the structures on campus.

The university owns and displays one of the largest art collections in the Southeast, as well as one of the most outstanding collections of African American art in the nation. The Carl Van Vechten Art Gallery houses the world-famous Stieglitz Collection of Modern Art. The university has other significant collections on campus. The Fisk Library houses three floors of artwork, special printed collections, and a gallery with objects collected from Africa and the South Pacific. The administration building contains murals by Aaron Douglas, one of the most celebrated artists of the Harlem Renaissance.

Most of the artwork can be seen during the hours school is in session and on most weekends. The brochure, *African-American Historical Sites,* lists more details on Fisk as well on Nashville's other African American sites. Call the Metro Historical Commission (615–862–7970) for a copy.

## Amazing Tennessee Facts

The nation's oldest African American architectural firm, McKissack and McKissack, and the nation's oldest African American financial institution, Citizens Savings Bank and Trust, are located in Nashville.

## Music Row (all ages)

**Sixteenth Avenue South and Seventeenth Avenue South and immediate areas. Free.**

The famous Music Row area is a must-stop while you're in town. This is the heart of Nashville's music industry. Music-related businesses and studios are located along a series of streets with such names as Music Circle, Music Square, and Roy Acuff Place.

Just below Music Row is the touristy strip along Demonbreun Street, where a few stars have had their own museums and gift shops. There aren't as many attractions along the commercial strip as there were a few years ago, but you'll still find the George Jones Gift Shop (615–256– 8299) and one of Nashville's three Ernest Tubb Record Shops (615–244–2845).

## Country Music Hall of Fame and Museum (all ages)

**222 Fifth Avenue South; (615) 416–2001 or (800) 852–6437; www.countrymusichalloffame.org. Open 10:00 A.M. to 6:00 P.M. daily; until 10:00 P.M. on Thursday. Admission: $$–$$$. Free for children under 6.**

If you're a true blue country fan, an interesting stop is the Country Music Hall of Fame and Museum, which moved from its old location on Music Square East to new digs on Fifth Avenue. The building soars high into Nashville's skyline and is huge: The 130,000-plus-square-foot building took two years to complete at a cost of $37 million.

After visitors enter the entryway of the sunny conservatory, they will view an introductory film about the international popularity of country music in the intimate Ford Theater. Then on to the exhibits, which include music and video clips, photographs, artifacts, and personal mementoes from such country music greats as Patsy Cline, Kitty Wells, Reba McEntire, Marty Stewart, and Garth Brooks. (One excellent exhibit is the famous suit embellished with musical notes that was worn by Hank Williams.) Elvis Presley's famous gold Cadillac and Webb Pierce's silver-dollar-studded Pontiac convertible flank the exhibit entrance. A gift shop and restaurant, neither of which require museum admission for entry, are delightful places to shop and relax.

### Second Avenue Historic District (all ages)
**Downtown. Free.**

The Second Avenue Historic District in downtown Nashville features unique shops, restaurants, music clubs, and antiques shops in renovated turn-of-the-twentieth-century warehouses and office buildings.

### Laser Quest (ages 6 and up)
**166 Second Avenue North; (615) 256–2560. Open year-round; hours vary. $$.**

The most advanced version of laser tag can be found at Laser Quest, next to the Spaghetti Factory. Players put on electronic vests with blinking targets, carry a laser gun that shoots an unlimited supply of light beams, and meander through a black-lit, foggy, 8,000-square-foot multilevel maze. Your kids won't want to leave—and neither will you!

## Amazing
# Tennessee Facts

Tennessee's state tree is the tulip poplar.

### Belle Meade Plantation (ages 8 and up)
**5025 Harding Road; (615) 356–0501 or (800) 270–3991. Open 9:00 A.M. to 5:00 P.M. Monday through Saturday and 11:00 A.M. to 5:00 P.M. Sunday. $$–$$$, free for children under 6.**

This 1853 Greek Revival mansion is known as the Queen of the Tennessee Plantations. In the nineteenth century, it was part of a 5,400-acre plantation and world-renowned thoroughbred horse farm. Today, the plantation covers thirty acres and includes the mansion and numerous outbuildings. Antiques, books, toys, and other gifts and souvenirs are available at the visitor center. The Cafe Belle Meade offers a menu prepared by Nashville's famous Loveless Cafe.

## Cheekwood—Nashville's Home of Art and Gardens (ages 8 and up)

1200 Forrest Park Drive; (615) 356–8000. Open 9:30 A.M. to 4:30 P.M. Tuesday through Saturday and 11:00 A.M. to 4:30 P.M. Sunday. Closed Thanksgiving, Christmas, and New Year's Days and the second Saturday in June. $–$$, and free for children under 6. Half-price admission after 3:00 P.M.; $25.00 family price cap.

Beautiful gardens, a historic mansion, and art galleries are the attractions at Cheekwood, a fifty-five-acre estate in West Nashville. The Museum of Art features Cheekwood's own collection plus temporary exhibits of local and regional artists' works. The gardens are beautiful in the spring, but you'll want to return again during the Christmas season, when Cheekwood presents its annual Trees of Christmas event featuring a dozen decorated trees, each with a different theme.

## Belmont Mansion (ages 8 and up)

Belmont University Campus, 1900 Belmont Boulevard; (615) 460–5459; www.belmont mansion.com. Open June, July, and August, Monday through Saturday, 10:00 A.M. to 4:00 P.M.; September through May, closed Monday. $–$$. Offers group rates.

Just before the Civil War, a young, beautiful woman named Adelicia married a much older gentleman by the name of Acklen. Together they built Belle Monte (today it's Belmont), an Italianate-style villa. Belmont became one of the most elaborate antebellum homes in the entire South, with thirty-six rooms and 19,000 square feet. The estate contained an art gallery, conservatories, an aviary, a lake, and lavish gardens. During the war, the newly widowed Adelicia became a pawn between the Union and Confederate Armies, both of which wanted her nearly 3,000 bales of cotton. Young Adelicia shrewdly outwitted both sides, selling her cotton to British concerns and saving her fortune.

Now you can tour the mansion and beautifully landscaped grounds, which include Acklen's huge European art collection, sculptures, and gazebos. It's all here, part of the Belmont University campus, thanks to a very crafty Southern belle who saved it from the ravages of the war.

## Warner Parks (all ages)

7311 Highway 100 West (Nature Center); (615) 352–6299 or (615) 370–8051; www.nashville .gov/parks/warner.htm. Open year-round. Free.

The city has a wonderful lineup of parks featuring the great outdoors. The Percy and Edwin Warner Parks, adjacent facilities named after leading conservationists of the area, were developed under the Works Progress Administration (WPA) program of the 1930s. Today the urban parks still show signs of the original WPA work, including the steeplechase, where the celebrated Iroquois Steeplechase race has been run yearly in May since 1946.

There are numerous scenic drives through the combined 2,500-plus acres, all offering shaded and often panoramic views. There are a number of hiking trails as well, varying in length and difficulty. The nature center is a good place to start your visit to the parks. There you'll find maps, guidebooks, and other information that will help you get the most out of your visit. The nature center contains an interpretive center and a research library. The staff conducts a series of educational programs that are **free** to the public, and visitors can often help out the staff on research programs, such as bird tagging.

Walking along wooded trails is sometimes difficult if you have young children. The Acorn Trail, which starts at the nature center, is a ³⁄₁₀-mile easy walk created for the smaller kids in the family. There's a self-guided trail map.

Other amenities of the park system are a polo field, fishing pond, model airplane field, numerous picnic shelters, two golf courses, stables, and 12 miles of equestrian trails.

### Radnor Lake State Natural Area (all ages)

**Otter Creek Road, off Franklin Road, about 2 miles south of Harding Road; (615) 373–3467; www.radnorlake.org. Open year-round. Free.**

Another natural jewel in the city's park offerings is Radnor Lake State Natural Area. The centerpiece of the 1,000-plus acres is the man-made lake. It was developed in 1914 when the Louisville and Nashville Railroad Company purchased the land, creating a lake that could provide water to its steam locomotives.

There are few signs of the early industrial uses of the area today, and many of the locals consider the lake to be their own private Walden Pond. During spring and fall migrations, the area provides a tremendous opportunity to view several species of songbirds and waterfowl. During the rest of the year, several hundred Canada geese call Radnor home. The wildflowers add a colorful touch to the hillside and trail areas during the spring.

The visitor center houses exhibits and hosts various educational programs, and nearly 6 miles of trails wind around the lake and wooded areas.

### The Hermitage (ages 8 and up)

**4580 Rachel's Lane, Hermitage; (615) 889–2941. Open 9:00 A.M. to 5:00 P.M. daily. Closed Thanksgiving, Christmas, and New Year's Days and the third week of January. $–$$. Free for children under 6. Free admission January 8. Call for group rates and youth education classes.**

A favorite historical home to visit in the Nashville area is The Hermitage, the home of Andrew Jackson, the seventh president of the United States. The national landmark has been beautifully restored, and the grounds offer a wonderful oasis from the hustle and bustle of the area now surrounding the property. The tour includes the mansion, formal

garden, Jackson's tomb, original log cabins, smokehouse, springhouse, Old Hermitage Church, and Tulip Grove Mansion. The visitor center has a restaurant, gift shop, museum, and orientation film.

## Other Things to See and Do

**Alegria,** 307 North Sixteenth Street; (615) 227–8566. Even the little ones will enjoy this colorful and eclectic shop, with a combination of imports and local arts, crafts, and handmade leather goods.

**Bellevue Center** (all ages), Highway 70, off I–40 at exit 196, west of Nashville; (615) 646–8690. Open year-round. **Free.** This large shopping mall has a permanent indoor soft-play playground for kids less than 48 inches tall.

**Davis-Kidd Booksellers** (all ages), 4007 Hillsboro Road; (615) 385–2645; www.davis kidd.com. Open daily. **Free.** Saturday at 11:00 A.M., this Green Hills bookstore sponsors the Kidd's Corner story time.

**Fort Nashboro** (all ages), 170 First Avenue North; (615) 862–8400 (Metro Parks). Open 9:00 A.M. to 5:00 P.M. Tuesday through Sunday. **Free.** A reconstruction of the original log fort Nashville's first settlers built.

**The Mall at Green Hills** (all ages), Hillsboro Road, south of the I–440 outerbelt; (615) 298–5478. Open year-round. **Free.** This mall has a kid's club activity each Saturday at 11:00 A.M.

**Opry Mills** (all ages), off I–24 at exit 43, Opry Mills Drive; (615) 514–1100. This shopping mecca is located right next door to Opryland Hotel. The mall is incredibly huge, with fantastic shops such as Bass Pro Shops, Gibson Bluegrass Showcase (where you can see the company's musical instruments being created), and exotic restaurants such as the Rainforest Cafe.

**RiverSkate** (all ages), Riverfront Park, downtown; (615) 259–4700. Fee charged. From the day after Thanksgiving through early January, you can ice-skate at this rink.

**Wave Country** (all ages), 2320 Two Rivers Parkway, off Briley Parkway; (615) 885–1052. This water park is a great place to cool off on a hot summer day. Admission: $–$$; half price after 4:00 P.M.

## Where to Eat

**Elliston Place Soda Shop,** 2111 Elliston Place; (615) 327–1090. Fun 1950s diner offering great shakes and plate lunches. $

**Hard Rock Cafe,** Broadway and Second Avenue; (615) 742–9900. Lots of rock 'n' roll memorabilia and loud music. $–$$

**Pancake Pantry,** 1796 Twenty-first Avenue; (615) 383–9333. Locals don't mind standing in line. The food is worth the wait. $

**Red Wagon,** 1112 Woodland Street; (615) 226–2527. All kinds of pancakes, omelettes, sandwiches, salads, gourmet coffees, and other goodies await you in this renovated old house.  Casual atmosphere and good service. Open for lunch and dinner. $–$$

**The Spaghetti Factory,** 160 Second Avenue; (615) 254–9010. $

**Wildhorse Saloon,** 120 Second Avenue; (615) 251–1000. Barbecue, salads, sandwiches, and steaks. You can also learn how to line dance for **free.** Lessons are given on the hour from 4:00 to 9:00 P.M. weekdays and from 1:00 to 9:00 P.M. Saturday and Sunday. $–$$

## Where to Stay

**Embassy Suites Nashville,** 10 Century Boulevard; (615) 871–0033 or (800) EMBASSY. $$$$

**Hampton Inn–Vanderbilt,** 1919 West End Avenue; (615) 329–1144. $$$

**The Hermitage Hotel,** 231 Sixth Avenue; (615) 244–3121. Historic hotel. $$$$

**Holiday Inn Express–Opryland Area,** 2516 Music Valley Drive; (615) 889–0086 or (800) HOLIDAY. $$

**Opryland Hotel,** 2800 Opryland Drive; (615) 883–2211 or (615) 889–1000. If you want to splurge on family accommodations, this is the place to do it. There are numerous restaurants, lounges, and shops at the hotel, as well as beautiful gardens. The regular rooms range from about $205 to $255 per night, but occasionally a discounted family rate is available that puts the price range at about $165 to $215. $$$$

**Opryland KOA,** 2626 Music Valley Drive; (615) 889–0282. There are 460 sites and twenty-five cabins. Live country music shows nightly. $

**Sheraton Nashville Downtown,** 623 Union Avenue; (615) 259–2000 or (800) 227–6963. Large rooms on a key-access-only floor; suites available. $$$$

**Shoney's Inn Music Row,** 1521 Demonbreun Street, just off I–40; (615) 255–9977. $$

**Top O' Woodland Bed and Breakfast,** 1603 Woodland Street; (615) 228–3868. This charming and totally renovated Victorian home will take you and the kids back to the grandeur of the early 1900s. Very accommodating to kids, every Saturday they show a silent movie in the parlor and have a piano player for your entertainment. $$$$

**Union Station Hotel,** 1001 Broadway; (615) 726–1001. Historic 1900 train station, beautifully restored. $$$$

## For More Information

**Nashville Convention and Visitors Bureau,** 211 Commerce Street, Nashville, TN 37201, (615) 259–4700, www.musiccityusa .com. Visitor Information Center is located at 501 Broadway, at the Nashville Arena. Open 8:30 A.M. to 5:30 P.M. daily.

# Kingston Springs

Just outside Nashville is Kingston Springs, where you can see a bit of history and "prehistory" in a natural setting.

### Harpeth State Scenic River (ages 6 and up)
**Near Highway 70.**

Harpeth is one of the most historical and scenic rivers of middle Tennessee. The river's name dates back to the end of the eighteenth century, when two bandit brothers, "Big"

Harp and "Little" Harp, terrorized the area. Some of the locals can tell you stories that have been handed down.

This river is significant as a historical site for two reasons: One is that in 1820, a man named Montgomery Bell had his workers tunnel through cliffs where the river doubles back nearly upon itself (this is called the Narrows of the Harpeth). Part of the Harpeth runs through this tunnel and out the other side and results in a 16-foot waterfall, which in the olden days turned the waterwheel used by Bell to create malleable iron bars from pig iron. The other is that prehistoric native peoples drew petroglyphs high up in the limestone cliff faces named, appropriately enough, Paint Rock Bluffs. You can see both of these sights by canoe, and there are several canoe rental places on the river.

# Goodlettsville

### Historic Manskers Station Frontier Life Center (all ages)
**705 Caldwell Road at Moss-Wright Park, off Long Hollow Pike; (615) 859–FORT. Daily tours (except for certain holidays) Monday through Saturday 9:00 A.M. to 4:00 P.M., Sunday 1:00 to 4:00 P.M. $.**

Through interesting living-history demonstrations, visitors are taught history by reliving it at the historic Manskers Station. Costumed docents get visitors involved in the everyday life that would have taken place in a 1779 frontier station, of which this is an authentic reproduction. To help understand the transition that settlers made from fort life to estate living, the Bowen House, located near the fort, is part of the experience and is included in the tours. The oldest standing brick structure in middle Tennessee, the mansion was completed in 1787. The video and tour of the fort and house take about an hour. There is also a visitor center that includes a gift shop.

### Trinity Broadcast Network (all ages)
**1 Music Village Boulevard, Hendersonville; (615) 826–9191. Open Monday through Saturday 10:00 A.M. to 6:00 P.M., Sunday 1:00 to 6:00 P.M. Admission: Free.**

The former home of singing legend Conway Twitty now houses the offices and studio for this Christian television network. The tour includes Church Auditorium, the Twitty Mansion, and the WPGD studio. There is also a Virtual Reality Theater showing original motion pictures filmed on location in Israel. There are TV tapings and concerts throughout the year; call for details.

### Music City Raceway (ages 10 and up)
**3302 Ivy Point Road; (615) 264–0375. Races begin Tuesday through Friday at 6:00 P.M., Saturday at 7:00 P.M., February through October. $–$$, children 12 and under admitted free.**

NHRA drag racing with seven classes, ranging from beginners to semi-pro racers.

### Long Hollow Winery (ages 5 and up)

**665 Long Hollow Pike; (615) 859–5559. Open Monday through Saturday, 9:00 A.M. to 6:00 P.M. Free.**

Long Hollow Winery was established in 2000 by Grand Ole Opry star Stu Phillips and his wife, Aldona. They offer regular tours daily, make gift baskets to order, and have a gift shop on the premises. Even the youngest children love to run among the vineyards and roll in the grass.

### Wanderin' Star Yacht Charters (all ages)

**824 Dry Creek Road; (615) 851–4274. Available by reservation year-round; rates differ by type of charter, so call ahead.**

This unique boating experience will delight everyone from the youngest landlubber to the oldest salt. The company offers three-hour cruises on Old Hickory Lake aboard a 25-foot Catalina sailboat, crewed by a husband-and-wife team who are as full of character as they are experienced sailors. You can try your hand at sailing or just sit back and enjoy a range of food options from simple snacks to a gourmet meal. If weather permits, a stop for swimming at a quiet anchorage is part of the experience.

## Other Things to See and Do

**Antiques malls** (ages 8 and up), along Main Street (Highway 41) in downtown Goodlettsville.

**Museum of Beverage Containers and Advertising** (all ages), 1055 Ridgecrest Drive, Millersville; (615) 859–5236. Open 9:00 A.M. to 5:00 P.M. Monday through Saturday, 1:00 to 5:00 P.M. Sunday. More than 36,000 soda and beer cans, bottles, and advertising items on display. $, under 12 admitted free.

## Where to Eat

**Chef's Market,** 900 Conference Drive; (615) 851–2433. $

**Deedagunks Bellybones,** 919 Conference Drive, Suite 4; (615) 851–5484. Ribs, burgers, award-winning barbecue, and more. $

**Pizza Pro,** 124 Luyben Road; (615) 952 5199. Pizza, hot wings, and homemade bread, kid-friendly atmosphere. $

## Where to Stay

**Comfort Suites,** 621 Rivergate Parkway; (615) 448–2100 or (800) 517–4000. Large indoor pool and spa, continental breakfast. $$

**Econo Lodge,** 123 Luyben Road; (615) 952–2900. Indoor pool; continental breakfast included. $

**Shoney's Inn,** 100 Northcreek Boulevard; (615) 851–1067. $

## For More Information

**Cheatham County Chamber of Commerce,** P.O. Box 354, 101 Court Street, Ashland City, TN 37015; (615) 792–6722; www.cheatham.org. Open 8:30 A.M. to 4:30 P.M. Monday through Friday.

**Goodlettsville Chamber of Commerce,** 100 South Main Street, Goodlettsville, TN 37072; (615) 859–7979; www.goodlettsville chamber.com. Open 8:30 A.M. to 4:30 P.M. Monday through Friday.

# Gallatin/Castalian Springs

### Sumner County Museum (ages 8 and up)
183 West Main Street, Gallatin; (615) 451–3738. Open April through October, 9:00 A.M. to 4:30 P.M. Wednesday through Saturday and 1:00 to 4:30 P.M. Sunday. Group tours by appointment. $, children under 6 free.

As a historical interpretive center, the Sumner County Museum defines the county's place in history. Exhibits in this restored, three-story brick building include 475-million-year-old fossils, military memorabilia, historic clothing, and photography. The exhibits provide a fascinating chronology of the area's growth and evolution.

In all, there are more than 250,000 artifacts from throughout the county. Don't miss the antique toys; be sure the kids get a chance to climb on the fire engine and ring the bell. The city's first traffic light didn't have a yellow light, only red and green. A bell in it would ring just before turning colors. That light is on display, and the bell still rings.

### Wynnewood (ages 8 and up)
210 Old Highway 25, Castalian Springs; (615) 452–5463. Open daily; hours vary by season. Closed January through March. $.

The state's largest remaining log structure, Wynnewood is impressive. Measuring 142 feet long and standing two stories tall, it is believed by many historians to be the largest log cabin ever constructed in the state. It was originally built in 1828 as a stagecoach inn and mineral spring resort. Some of the logs are 32 feet long. All the rooms have outside doors and are entered from a gallery that extends 110 feet across the back of the building.

About 100 yards east of the entrance to Wynnewood is a stone monument marking the location of the giant, 9-foot-diameter sycamore tree in which Thomas Sharp Spencer lived during the winter of 1778–1779. Spencer, the first white settler in the Heartland of Tennessee, called the tree home while he was building a cabin nearby.

### Bledsoe Fort Historical Site (ages 6 and up)
Across Highway 25 from Wynnewood at Rock Springs Road, Castalian Springs; (615) 452–5463. Open for self-guided tours on a limited basis. Gates open from dawn to dusk. Advance notice required to tour the historic cottages. Free.

The Bledsoe Fort Historical Site was developed as Sumner County's 1996 Tennessee State Centennial project, and development is ongoing. During recent archaeological digs, various artifacts have been unearthed and are in the Sumner County Museum in Gallatin.

Remnants of the springhouse have been found, stone steps leading up to the fort have been uncovered, and the Cavern of Skulls, a cave where ancient tribes threw intruders after decapitating them, has been discovered. All the skulls were stolen by trespassers before archaeologists were called in. A couple of 1790s cottages have been relocated here from nearby areas. You can tour these structures, but you must make a reservation first. While your here, stroll the adjacent Bledsoe Cemetery, dating back to the early 1800s.

### The Palace Theater (all ages) ♫
**112 Public Square, Gallatin; (615) 230–0884.**

The Palace Theater is the oldest silent-movie theater in Tennessee still standing in its original location. It operated until 1977 and reopened in 2001. Renovations took nearly eight years, and movies (modern ones) are once again shown. The Palace Theater is also used for live theatrical performances by local and visiting thespian troupes. Although the movies have regular admission prices attached to them and admission for live performances varies, tours of the Palace are available for **free** by calling ahead.

## Other Things to See and Do

**Cragfont** (ages 8 and up), 200 Cragfont Road, Castalian Springs; (615) 452–7070. Open April 15 to November 1, 10:00 A.M. to 5:00 P.M. Tuesday through Saturday and 1:00 to 5:00 P.M. Sunday. Built in 1802, this home was once considered the finest mansion house on the Tennessee frontier. It was built by Gen. James Winchester, a frontiersman, soldier, politician, and one of the founders of Memphis. $

**Trousdale Place** (ages 8 and up), 183 West Main Street, Gallatin; (615) 452–5648. Tours available by appointment. This is the historic home of William Trousdale, Tennessee governor from 1849 to 1851. $

## Where to Eat

**Cherokee Steak House,** 450 Cherokee Dock Road, Gallatin; (615) 452–1515. Locals say this place cooks up the best steaks to be had on the shores of Old Hickory Lake, and after you have tried the fare, you're sure to agree. $–$$

**Jack and Billy's Barbecue Junction,** 1470 Sweetwater Street, Gallatin; (615) 452-9316. Barbecue and fried farm-raised catfish are the house specialties. $–$$

**Three Sisters,** 207 South Water, Gallatin; (615) 452–0902. Pork chops and fried chicken are favorites at this "meat-and-three." $

## Where to Stay

**Comfort Inn,** 354 Sumner Hall Drive; Gallatin; (615) 230–8300 or (800) 228–5150. $$

**The Hancock House Bed and Breakfast,** 2144 Nashville Pike, Gallatin; (615) 452–8431.This is the only colonial Revival log house in the state of Tennessee, and it is on the National Register of Historic Places. All sixteen rooms have fireplaces and private baths and are furnished in period antiques. Enjoy the two courtyards done in traditional

Charleston style. Breakfasts are phenomenal and are served right to your room if you like, at no extra charge. $$$$

**Shoney's Inn,** 221 West Main Street; Gallatin; (615) 452–5433. $$

## For More Information

**Gallatin Chamber of Commerce,** 118 West Main Street, P.O. Box 26, Gallatin, TN 37066; (615) 452–4000; www.gallatintn.org. Open 8:30 A.M. to 4:30 P.M. Monday through Friday.

**Sumner County Tourism,** 118 West Main Street, Gallatin, TN 37066; (615) 230–8474 or (888) 301–7866; www.sumnercounty tourism.com. Open 8:30 A.M. to 4:30 P.M. Monday through Friday.

# Adams

### Bell Witch Cave (ages 8 and up)
**Keysburg Road, off Highway 41; (615) 696–3055. Open 10:00 A.M. to 6:00 P.M. daily May through October and until midnight the last two weeks of October; closed during rainy periods. $$, free for children under 5.**

The most celebrated and most documented ghost in the history of the state calls Adams her home. Now known as the Bell Witch, she taunted John Bell and his family for years by throwing furniture around the house and tearing covers off the beds. Tales of the strange occurrences spread, and Gen. Andrew Jackson traveled from Nashville to Adams to investigate the situation firsthand.

As Jackson approached the farm, all the wheels on his wagon locked, and no amount of effort by his horses and men could move the vehicle, despite the fact that the ground was dry and level. A sharp, mocking voice was heard coming out of nowhere: "All right, General, let the wagon move on. I will see you again tonight."

True to her promise, the ghost was in rare form that night. Jackson returned home and wrote in his journal, "By the Eternal, I saw nothing, but I heard enough to convince me that I would rather fight the British than to deal with this torment they call the Bell Witch!"

Now her presence is more likely to appear in a cave that was part of the Bell property. Known as Bell Witch Cave, it's open for tours, and who knows what will take place? Through the years cave visitors have reported seeing a beautiful young woman with long black hair, and others have been touched, pinched, slapped, and hugged by something unseen. The guide will tell you of these and other colorful tales.

### Tennessee–Kentucky Threshermen's Association Show (all ages)
Old Bell School, Highway 41; (615) 696–8179. Third weekend in July. $, under 12 admitted free.

The Tennessee-Kentucky Threshermen's Association Show is truly a festival honoring Americana. The fields are full of antique tractors and steam engines, crafts booths, live music, square dancing, tractor and mule pulls, magic shows, and, of course, storytelling about the Bell Witch.

### Bell Witch Bluegrass Festival and Arts and Crafts Show (all ages)
Old Bell School, Highway 41; (615) 696–2589. First Friday and Saturday in August. $, under 12 admitted free.

In August the grounds of Old Bell School are alive with the sounds and activities of the Bell Witch Bluegrass Festival and Arts and Crafts Show.

### Bell Witch Opry (all ages)
7617 Highway 41 North, Adams; (615) 696–1222. $.

This has got to be Adams's version of the Nashville Opry. The Bell Witch Opry is held every Saturday night, year-round, in the auditorium of the old Bell schoolhouse. This is an open-forum kind of musical night; you might hear any kind of live entertainment, mostly bluegrass and country, and because some of the performers come from Nashville, who knows who you'll see? It's good old-fashioned, family fun.

### Port Royal State Historical Area (all ages)
Six miles west of Adams on Highway 76 in Montgomery County; (931) 358–9696. Open daily. Free.

The Port Royal State Historical Area provides a glimpse of a once-thriving river town. At the turn of the twentieth century, this area was a stopping point for steamboats, and many businesses lined the waterfront, including a gristmill, cannery, and logging operation. There are plenty of picnic spots and nature trails along the river to keep a family busy for hours. This is a nice, calm, free-flowing area of the river, and if you've ever thought a family canoe trip would be fun, this is the place to do it. Several local businesses rent canoes, and there are several accesses to the river in the park.

# Springfield

### Robertson County Historical Society and Museum (ages 5 and up)
124 Sixth Avenue West, Springfield; (615) 382–7173. Open Wednesday through Friday 10:00 A.M. to 4:00 P.M., and Saturday 1:00 to 4:00 P.M.

Exhibits at this museum pertain to life from the early settlement days to present. New exhibits are presented on occasion.

**Downtown Springfield Walking Tour** (all ages)
**Obtain information at 100 Fifth Avenue West; (615) 384-3800. Free.**

Get the babies in strollers and the older kids ready to stretch their legs as they walk around this beautiful historical downtown, featuring a nice main street, and public square, a 125-year-old courthouse, the museum (above), and shops and cafes.

## Where to Eat

**Burdett's Tea Shop,** 618 South Main Street; (615) 384–2320. Soups, sandwiches, salads, and of course tea are served only during lunch and early afternoon in this quaint tearoom. $

**The Depot,** 1007 South Main Street; (615) 382–8584. This eatery next to the railroad tracks offers everything from finger foods to steaks. $

## Where to Stay

**Springfield Inn,** 2001 Memorial Blvd; (615) 384–1234. $–$$

**Hampton Inn,** 620 Twenty-second Avenue East; (615) 384–1166. $–$$

## For More Information

**Springfield Chamber of Commerce,** 100 Fifth Avenue West, Springfield, TN 37172; (615) 384–3800. Open 8:00 A.M. to 4:30 P.M. Monday through Friday.

# Clarksville/Dover

**Dunbar Cave State Natural Area** (all ages)
**South of Highway 79; (931) 648–5526. Open daily. Free. Guided cave tours $.**

One of the most utilitarian of all caves in Tennessee history is Dunbar Cave, now the centerpiece of the 110-acre Dunbar Cave State Natural Area outside Clarksville off Highway 79. Today it provides the community a link with nature by offering nature programs and guided cave hikes. But the cave itself probably has a more diverse history than just about any cave in the state. Prehistoric Native Americans inhabited the cave entrance 10,000 years ago, and it was being used as part of a mineral springs resort a century ago.

During the 1930s country-music legend Roy Acuff held concerts at the mouth of the cave, and through the years top-name big bands, including Woody Herman and Count Basie, have played here. The singing team of Ozzie and Harriet Nelson once performed on the big wooden stage.

The stately old bathhouse from which nature walks and cave tours depart now serves as a visitor center and museum. There are 4 miles of well-maintained hiking trails, plenty of picnic areas, and fishing in Swan Lake. Each July Children's Mornings are held, with special programs for the younger ones.

Tours are scheduled at different times throughout the year, so it's wise to call ahead to see when they are planned.

### Customs House Museum and Cultural Center (all ages)

**200 South Second Street at the corner of Commerce and South Second, Clarksville; (931) 648–5780. Open 10:00 A.M. to 5:00 P.M. Tuesday through Saturday, 1:00 to 5:00 P.M. Sunday. $, free on Sunday.**

A good place to begin your trek through this part of the state is at the Customs House Museum and Cultural Center. The building that houses the museum was a U.S. post office and customs house erected in 1898 and is one of the state's unique structures. Its eclectic architecture consists of Italianate ornamentation, a Far East–influenced slate roof, Romanesque arches, and Gothic copper eagles perched at each of the four corners.

The exhibits inside are about as eclectic as the building itself. The two model train exhibits are especially popular.

### Walk Clarksville (all ages)

**Brochures available through Clarksville Department of Tourism, off I–24 exit 4, Visitor Center; (931) 647–2331. Free.**

See the best of historic Clarksville in this 2.2-mile self-guided walking tour.

### Drive Clarksville (all ages)

**Brochures available through Clarksville Department of Tourism, off I–24 exit 4, Visitor Center, (931) 647–2331. Free.**

The 17-mile driving tour showcases fifty-two historically significant sites, including the Montgomery County Courthouse, built in 1879, Trinity Episcopal Church, built in 1881, and Madison Street United Methodist Church, built in 1882. All were significantly damaged by a tornado in 1999, and all have been completely restored to their original grandeur.

### Beachaven Winery (ages 5 and up)

**1100 Dunlop Lane; (931) 645–8867. Hours for tours and operation vary by season; call ahead.**

Enjoy free tours and tastings at one of Tennessee's foremost commercial wineries. During summer months every other Saturday night, there is a free live concert called Jazz on the Lawn. Picnic tables under the trees entice visitors to sit and enjoy the shade beside the vineyard. Gift shop on the premises.

### Montgomery County Courts Complex (ages 5 and up)

**1 Millennium Plaza; (931) 648–5787. Open Monday through Friday 8:30 A.M. to 4:30 P.M. Free.**

A combination of new construction and redevelopment following a devastating 1999 tornado, the courthouse, Court Center, and Millennium Plaza serve as a community centerpiece. The corridors adjoining the buildings are lined with 150 photographs illustrating the history and heritage of Montgomery County.

## Fort Campbell Military Reservation/
## Don F. Pratt Memorial Museum (all ages)

**5702 Tennessee Avenue, Fort Campbell, Kentucky; (512) 798–3215. Open 9:30 A.M. to 4:30 P.M. daily. Free.**

The famed 101st Air Assault Division of the U. S. Army calls the Fort Campbell Military Reservation home. The base is open, which means visitors are welcome as long as they pick up a pass at Gate 4 on Highway 41 near the Tennessee/Kentucky border north of Clarksville. Located near Gate 4 is the visitor center, where base tours can be arranged, and the Donald Pratt Museum, which traces the history of the division from World War I to the present. Exhibits also depict the history of Fort Campbell and the surrounding areas.

Guided tours of the base are offered **free** of charge and take approximately two to two-and-a-half hours. There are also four well-marked, well-maintained nature trails designed for light walking. Trailheads are near the post's riding stables.

## Land Between the Lakes National Recreation Area (all ages)

**On the Trace, off Highway 79, 3 miles west of Dover; (270) 924–2000 or (800) LBL–7077; www.lbl.org. Open daily. Free. Fees charged for some attractions and activities.**

Fishing is the top activity for those visiting the huge and beautiful Land Between the Lakes National Recreation Area (LBL), located on a peninsula between Kentucky and Barkley Lakes, two of the most popular fishing lakes in the country. Fishing is also good in the twenty ponds and four lakes on the 270-square-mile peninsula. The burning question of most anglers—"Are they biting?"—can be answered by calling (270) 924–1340. You'll hear a two-minute recording that gives fishing conditions, water levels and temperatures, and other pertinent angler-oriented information.

But the LBL is much more than fishing heaven. Hunting is allowed for fourteen game species, but you must have an LBL permit in addition to a valid hunting license. There are many boat-launch ramps along the 300 miles of undeveloped shoreline, and there are virtually thousands of improved as well as primitive campsites scattered throughout. Nearly all campsites are on a first-come, first-served basis.

There are more than 200 miles of marked hiking trails, ranging from small loop walks to a 65-mile north-south trek. There are also marked equestrian trails, biking trails, and off-road vehicle trails. Special bald eagle–viewing weekends are scheduled during the winter.

The trace is the main north-south byway through LBL and leads to all attractions, including Homeplace 1850, located just south of the Kentucky border. It's a living-history farm where you can get a glimpse of farm life in the mid-1800s. Costumed docents carry out daily routines as homesteaders would have during that period.

There are sixteen log cabins and cultivated fields planted with a variety of crops. An orientation film at the interpretive center gives you an overview of life then and what you are about to see in the village. Special activities include a two-day Folk Festival in June, which offers music, storytelling, and crafts, and an apple festival in October, with cider making, baking contests, and crafts.

Across the trace from the Homeplace is the largest federally owned herd of buffalo east of the Mississippi. If you get there in the morning when it's cool, you'll probably get a good view of them, but once it gets hot, the buffalo have a tendency to disappear back into the deep woods and are hard to find.

About one-third of LBL is located within Tennessee; the rest is in Kentucky. Eleven miles north of the state line, in Kentucky, the Golden Pond Visitor Center acts as the information center for the entire LBL complex. There you'll also find a planetarium with special astronomy programs offered Wednesday through Saturday.

## Fort Donelson National Battlefield (all ages)

**Highway 79, on the west side of Dover, 26 miles west of Clarksville on Highway 79; (931) 232–5706. Open daily. Free.**

The site where the Union forces won their first major victory of the Civil War is now known as the Fort Donelson National Battlefield. The visitor center is where the 6-mile, self-guided auto tour begins. Before leaving, be sure to watch the ten-minute slide presentation that describes the battle and the environs. The earthen fort, river batteries, outer earthworks, historic Dover Hotel where General Buckner surrendered (hence its nickname, Surrender House), and national cemetery have all been preserved and are accessible.

# Other Things to See and Do

**Cross Creeks National Wildlife Refuge,** 643 Wildlife Road; (931) 232–7477 or (931) 232–7495. Open year-round. **Free.** This 9,000-acre refuge, located along the Cumberland River, is a great spot for bird-watching.

**Cumberland RiverWalk,** McGregor Park, Riverside Drive; (931) 645–7476. A nice spot to have a picnic lunch or take a stroll along the river. The newly built Cumberland River-Center, in the heart of the RiverWalk, features a **free** permanent exhibit of the chronology of the Cumberland River and the waterway's significance to the area.

**Historic Collinsville,** 4711 Weakley Road, Southside (about 10 miles south of Clarksville); (931) 648–9141. Open May 15 to October 15, 1:00 to 5:00 P.M. Thursday through Sunday. This restored, nineteenth-century, log settlement offers a look back at the lifestyle of the area's early pioneers. Admission: $, **free** for children under 5.

**L&N Train Station,** Commerce and Tenth Streets; (931) 553–2486. Open Tuesday, Thursday, and Saturday 9:00 A.M. to 1:00 P.M. **Free.** Originally built in 1890, this is now the home of the Montgomery County Historical Society.

## Where to Eat

**Blackhorse Pub and Brewery,** 132 Franklin Street; (931) 552–3726. This charming eatery (and Clarksville's only brewery) in the heart of the old downtown has a home-like atmosphere and makes great pizzas to order. You can "build" your own, choosing from a huge variety of ingredients on the menu. Besides soups, salads, pastas, and a variety of sandwiches, there's also an extensive children's menu. $

**Cafe 541,** 541 Franklin Street; (931) 551–9955. Located along the historic walking tour, this upscale-yet-casual restaurant has a great children's menu and a wide range of appetizers and entrees to please everyone. $

**Cindy's Catfish Kitchen,** 2148 Donelson Parkway, Dover; (931) 232–4817. Children under 3 eat **free**; ages 3 to 8 eat for half-price. $

**Front Page Deli News,** 105 Franklin Street; (931) 503–0325. So called because of its proximity to the oldest daily newspaper in Tennessee, this eatery serves great deli-style sandwiches, salads, and daily specials. $

**The Thai House,** 211 North Riverside Drive; (931) 552–7888. This is real Thai cuisine, cooked by Bangkok-born-and-raised chefs. Most kids' favorite is a dish called pad thai. $

## Where to Stay

**Hachland Hill Inn,** 1601 Madison Street; (931) 647–4084; www.eventsandmeetings .com. This charming inn features three 200-year-old guest cottages that have been moved on-site and renovated. Cottages will accommodate up to twelve people; the main guest house has seven bedrooms with private baths. Children and dogs are welcome. $$

**Holiday Inn,** 3095 Wilma Rudolph Boulevard, off I–24 at exit 4; (931) 648–4848 or (800) HOLIDAY. $$

**Riverview Inn,** 50 College Street, Clarksville; (931) 552–3331. **Free** full American breakfast in the on-site restaurant. $$

**Country Inns and Suites,** 3075 Wilma Rudolph Boulevard, off I–24 at exit 4; (931) 645–1400 or (800) 531–1900. $–$$

## For More Information

**Clarksville/Montgomery County Economic Development Council,** 180 Holiday Road, Clarksville, TN 37040; (931) 648–0001 or (800) 530–2487; www.clarksville.tn.us. Open daily, 8:00 A.M. to 5:00 P.M.

**Stewart County Chamber of Commerce,** P.O. Box 147, Spring Street, Dover, TN 37058; (931) 232–8290. Open 8:00 A.M. to 11:00 A.M. and 1:00 to 4:00 P.M. Monday through Friday.

# Hurricane Mills/New Johnsonville

**Loretta Lynn's Ranch** (all ages)
Highway 13, off I–40 at exit 143; (931) 296–7700. Open daily April through October. Campground is open year-round. Most activities are open Memorial Day through Labor Day. The grounds and shops are **free,** activities are on a pay-as-you-go basis.

When country-music legend Loretta Lynn and her husband, Mooney, decided to go house shopping in 1967, they ended up buying not only a house and farm but also an old mill and the small town of Hurricane Mills. The 3,500-acre Loretta Lynn's Ranch complex is open to the public and includes a campground; Lynn's personal museum, a new 18,000-square-foot building that is open year-round; and a replica of the coal mine her father once worked in, thus earning her the nickname "coal miner's daughter."

A highlight for most visitors is the star's house, a big, two-story antebellum plantation mansion. The kitchen, living room, family room, and original master bedroom are open to the public. A reproduction of her Butcher Holler House has been created, and there's a western store and a gift shop. Other attractions and activities include Saturday night dances, a swimming pool, hiking trails, fishing, horseback riding, miniature golf, and canoeing. Concerts are held on a regular basis throughout the summer, with Lynn usually headlining at least two of them. When she's home, she loves to walk among her fans, talk with them, and sign autographs.

### Johnsonville State Historic Area (all ages)

**Highway 70, New Johnsonville, 9 miles west of Waverly; (931) 535–2789. Open year-round. Visitor center open April through October. Free.**

The spot where the Battle of Johnsonville was fought in 1864 is now known as the Johnsonville State Historic Area. Union redoubts, fortifications, and rifle pits are still discernible on the site. The Confederate victory here is believed to be the only time a naval force was defeated by a cavalry force. Exhibits in the visitor center tell the story of the battle. Outside, the facilities include hiking trails, picnicking areas, and a primitive camping area.

## Amazing
# Tennessee Facts

Tennessee's state rocks are limestone and Tennessee marble.

## Other Things to See and Do

**Humphreys County Museum and Civil War Fort,** 201 Fort Hill Drive, Waverly; (931) 296–1099. Open Thursday through Sunday year-round. Free. A restored 1920s mansion is located on the property of this Civil War fort.

## Where to Eat

**Loretta Lynn's Kitchen and Gift Shop,** 15366 Highway 13 South, Hurricane Mills, off I–40 at exit 143; (931) 296–7589. Breakfast, lunch, and dinner buffets, plus catfish, country ham, steaks, sandwiches, and salads. Children's menu. $

**Marble Oaks Restaurant,** 117 North Court Square, Waverly; (931) 296–8082. Restaurant in a one-hundred-year-old building has an old-fashioned, homelike atmosphere and offers a full menu with Tennessee River catfish, hamburgers, and daily specials. Excellent homemade desserts and a children's menu. $

## Where to Stay

**Deerfield Inn,** 1331 Broadway Avenue, New Johnsonville; (931) 535–3889. $

**Holiday Inn Express,** 15368 Highway 13 South, Hurricane Mills, off I–40 at exit 143; (931) 296–2999 or (800) HOLIDAY. $$

**Loretta Lynn Family Campground,** 44 Hurricane Mills Road; (931) 296–7700. $

## For More Information

**Humphreys County Area Chamber of Commerce,** 124 East Main Street, Waverly, TN 37185; (931) 296–4865; www.waverly.net /hcchamber. Open 8:30 A.M. to 4:30 P.M. Monday, Tuesday, Thursday, and Friday and 8:30 A.M. to 3:30 P.M. Wednesday (closed noon to 1:00 P.M. daily).

# Franklin

### Historic Downtown Franklin (all ages)
**Main Street; (615) 790–7094. Free.**

The folks of Franklin take their history seriously; as a result, the area is one of the nicest restored historic communities in the state. Franklin's entire 15-block original downtown area, including the Main Street shopping district and Town Square, is listed on the National Register of Historic Places. The downtown Main Street area, featuring all original nineteenth-century buildings, is a quaint, bustling shopping district with specialty shops, restaurants, antiques shops, and a lot of Southern hospitality. The Downtown Franklin Association sponsors three wildly popular and **free** community festivals on the streets of downtown each year: the Main Street Arts, Crafts, and Music Festival in late April; a Jazz Festival Labor Day weekend; and the wonderfully Victorian Dickens of a Christmas in early December. Surrounding the shopping district are many beautifully preserved Victorian and antebellum homes, boasting some of the loveliest architecture anywhere. Franklin is the county seat of Williamson County and as locals are fond of saying, "is located 18 miles and one hundred years south of Nashville."

### Carter House (ages 6 and up)
**1140 Columbia Avenue, south of downtown Franklin; (615) 791–1861. Open 9:00 A.M. to 5:00 P.M. Monday through Saturday and 1:00 to 5:00 P.M. Sunday. Admission: $–$$.**

The Carter House was caught in the middle of a Civil War fight, aptly known as the Battle of Franklin, in late 1864. Bullet holes are still evident in the main structure and in the various outbuildings. One of the structures has 203 bullet holes, making it the most battle-damaged building from the war still standing anywhere. The tour includes the museum, a video presentation, and a guided tour of the house and grounds.

### Historic Carnton Plantation (ages 6 and up)
**1345 Carnton Lane, 1 mile south of Franklin off Lewisburg Pike; (615) 794–0903. From April through October, open 9:00 A.M. to 5:00 P.M. Monday through Saturday and  1:00 to 5:00 P.M. Sunday; closes at 4:00 P.M. from November through March. Free admission to the grounds. Guided tours, $–$$.**

Another restored structure from the Battle of Franklin is the Historic Carnton Plantation. Located on the rear lines of the Confederate forces, the estate served as a field hospital during the battle, and at one time the bodies of five slain Confederate generals were laid out on the back porch. The only privately owned Confederate cemetery in the United States is located at the entrance to the mansion's grounds. In addition to the three-story house completed in 1826, there are several fully restored and some reconstructed out-buildings on the grounds. Ask about the ghosts who now roam here. They've been identi-fied and make for a fascinating story.

A great way to show the kids what the holidays were like in the old days is to visit the mansion during the annual Christmas at Carnton Plantation holiday festival, which focuses on nineteenth-century traditions. The house is decorated, the gift shop is stocked, and free hot cider and cookies are served.

### Third Coast Clay (in the Factory) (ages 6 and up)
**230 Franklin Road; (615) 791–1777.**

You can learn how ceramics are made and create your own ceramic masterpiece to take home in this artisan shop, which is on the National Register of Historic Places. No appoint-ment is needed, and groups are welcome.

## Other Things to See and Do

**CoolSprings Galleria** (all ages), 1800 Galle-ria Boulevard, south of downtown, off I–65 at Moores Lane; (615) 771–2128. Open daily. Free. In addition to its 150-plus stores, the CoolSprings Galleria offers "Juniper Junction," a free kid's club event—usually storytelling—each Saturday at 11:00 A.M.

**Recreation World Family Fun Center** (all ages), South of CoolSprings Galleria, exit 68-B off I–65, off Mallory Lane; (615) 771–7780. Open year-round. Prices are pay as you play. Miniature golf, go-carts, batting cages, arcade, food court, and playground.

## Where to Eat

**Dotson's Restaurant,** 99 East Main Street; (615) 794–2805. Great home-cooked breakfasts and plate lunches. $

**Franklin Chop House,** 1101 Murfreesboro Road; (615) 591–7666. American menu, lunch and dinner. $–$$

**Stoveworks, the Factory at Franklin,** 230 Franklin Road; (615) 791–6065. The factory itself once housed a stove manufacturing facility, but now it houses this eatery specializing in southern-style fare. $–$$

## Where to Stay

**Franklin Marriott Cool Springs,** 700 Cool Springs Boulevard, off I–65 at exit 68-A; (615) 771–0889 or (800) 228–9290. $$$–$$$$

**Magnolia House,** 1317 Columbia Avenue; (615) 794–8187. This bed-and-breakfast near downtown Franklin was built in 1905 and welcomes families with older children. Amenities include four bedrooms with queen-size beds and one bedroom with twin beds for the kids. Full southern-style breakfast. $$$–$$$$

**Namaste Acres Barn Bed & Breakfast,** 5436 Leipers Creek Road, just off the Natchez Trace Parkway; (615) 791–0333. This bed-and-breakfast inn offers guided horseback trail rides, a quiet valley setting, in-room coffeemaker, phone, refrigerator, TV, and VCR. Four themed guest rooms, private baths, full breakfast. $$$

## For More Information

**Williamson County–Franklin Chamber of Commerce,** P.O. Box 156, 109 Second Avenue South, Suite 137, Franklin, TN 37064; (615) 794–1225 or (800) 356–3445; www.williamsoncvb.org. Open 8:00 A.M. to 4:30 P.M. Monday through Friday.

# Columbia/Spring Hill

**Polk Ancestral Home** (ages 6 and up) (m)
301 West Seventh Street, Columbia; (931) 388–2354; www.jameskpolk.com. Open 9:00 A.M. to 5:00 P.M. Monday through Saturday and 1:00 to 5:00 P.M. Sunday. Admission: $.

James K. Polk, the eleventh president of the United States, began his legal and political career from his parents' home in Columbia. Today the Polk Ancestral Home, built in 1816, is a Registered National Historic Landmark and is the only existing house, other than the White House, in which Polk lived. The president's sister lived next door, and that house is also open to the public and is part of the tour.

**Mule Day** (all ages)
Maury County Park, 1018 Maury County Park Drive, Columbia; (931) 381–9557; www.muleday.com. Early April. $.

The mule is the king in Columbia the first or second weekend of April each year. That's when the annual Mule Day Festival is held. The celebration, first held in 1934, honors the city's proud heritage as the mule-raising capital of the state. There's a parade like you've never seen before, with mules pulling all sorts of wagons and farm machinery, along with mule shows, a mule sale, and a lot of food and arts-and-crafts booths throughout town.

## Amazing Tennessee Facts

Tennessee's state animal is the raccoon.

### The Athenaeum Rectory (ages 8 and up)
**808 Athenaeum Street; (931) 381–4822. Open 10:00 A.M. to 4:00 P.M. Tuesday through Saturday and 1:00 to 4:00 P.M. Sunday. Admission includes guided tours, $.**

Headquarters for the Association for the Preservation of Tennessee Antiquities, the Athenaeum Rectory is all that remains of an extraordinary school for girls that flourished from 1852 to 1904. Named after the Greek goddess of wisdom (Athena), this school taught girls everything a well-educated young man would have learned at that time, including physics, Latin, and calculus, as well as the more traditional feminine skills of needlework and music. The Moorish-Gothic architecture of the rectory sets it apart from all other buildings in the area; rooms are furnished in period pieces.

### Tennessee Antebellum Trail (all ages)
**Brochure maps available at area attractions or by calling (800) 381–1865.**

Within a 30-mile radius of Nashville lies the highest concentration of antebellum homes in the South today. The driving tour starts and ends in Nashville, and along the way eight of the houses are open to the public. A splendid tour map, which lists and describes each house, is available **free** of charge. Also on the map are lists of bed-and-breakfasts, restaurants, and antiques shops you'll pass along the way, as well as an annual calendar of events.

### Rippavilla Plantation (ages 8 and up)
**5700 Main Street, Spring Hill; (931) 486–9037; www.rippavilla.com. Open 9:00 A.M. to 5:00 P.M. Tuesday through Saturday and 1:00 to 5:00 P.M. Sunday. $–$$.**

Rippavilla, built in 1852, is one of the antebellum houses highlighted on the Tennessee Antebellum Trail. Located north of Columbia in the small community of Spring Hill, the home has been restored and is the headquarters for the Tennessee Antebellum Trails organization. Visitors are welcome to stop by, walk the grounds, and pick up additional information on the area.

The house is located across Highway 31 from the Saturn Corporation, the automobile manufacturer owned by General Motors. The Confederate army was encamped on the property the night before the troops moved north to engage in the Battle of Franklin, one of the last major battles of the Civil War. Legend has it that all five of the Confederate generals killed in the Battle of Franklin had slept at Rippavilla and had breakfast together before heading off to battle.

### Saturn Welcome Center (ages 6 and up)

**Highway 31 South off I–65 between Spring Hill and Columbia; (931) 486-5775 or (800) 326–3321. Open for free tours 8:30 A.M. to 2:00 P.M. Monday, Tuesday, Thursday, and Friday and 10:00 A.M. to 2:30 P.M. Wednesday. Reservations are recommended.**

The Saturn Welcome Center is in a renovated old horse barn, which has items such as t-shirts, key chains, and souvenirs for sale. If you've ever wanted to see how automobiles are manufactured and assembled, now is your chance. During the hour-long tour, visitors ride a tram through the various buildings of the car manufacturing complex. Tour guides will describe the process of building a car. Kids seem to get a kick out of seeing how cars are put together.

## Other Things to See and Do

**Williamsport Lakes Wildlife Management Area** (all ages), Highway 50, about fifteen minutes from Columbia; (931) 626–0336 or (800) 648–8798. Fee charged to fish. Five public fishing lakes, campsites, and more.

## Where to Eat

**Backporch Barbecue,** 900 Hatcher Lane, (931) 381–3463; 200 West Third Street, (931) 381–2225. $

**JJ's Barbecue,** 1122 Hampshire Road; (931) 380–1756. $

**Nolens Barbecue,** 115 East James Campbell Boulevard, (931) 381–4322; 100 West Fifth Street, (931) 490–0007. $

**The Ole Lamplighter Restaurant,** 1000 Riverside Drive; (931) 381–3837. The restaurant is housed in an old log cabin overlooking the Duck River. $–$$

## Where to Stay

**Days Inn,** 1504 Nashville Highway, Columbia; (931) 381–3297. $

**Richland Inn,** 2405 Highway 31 South; (931) 381–4500. More than one hundred suites with Jacuzzis available. Microwaves and refrigerators in most rooms, pet rooms available. Free continental breakfast every morning. $–$$$

**Steeplechase Inn and Suites,** 104 Kedron Road, Spring Hill; (931) 486–1234. $$

## For More Information

**Maury Alliance,** 106 West Sixth Street, Columbia, TN 38401; (931) 388–2155; www.mauryalliance.com. Open 8:00 A.M. to 5:00 P.M. Monday through Thursday and 8:00 A.M. to 4:30 P.M. Friday.

# Murfreesboro

### Cannonsburgh Village (all ages)

312 South Front Street; (615) 890–0355. Grounds open year-round; buildings open May through January, 10:00 A.M. to 5:00 P.M. Tuesday through Saturday and 1:00 to 5:00 P.M. Sunday. Guided tours $, **free** for children under 7.

Directly adjacent to the hustle and bustle of Murfreesboro is the village of Cannonsburgh. When you pass through the gates here, you enter a time when life was lived in a log cabin and electrical power and modern conveniences were nonexistent.

Cannonsburgh, the original name of Murfreesboro, is now a living museum of southern life, complete with log structures, a cotton gin, a chapel, and a blacksmith shop. The village was built in 1976 and was named one of the top sixteen bicentennial projects in the United States that year.

## Stand **in the Center**

It has been determined that the exact center of Tennessee is located on Old Lascassas Pike, 1 mile from downtown Murfreesboro. There's an obelisk marking the spot. For the family with kids who like to be in the middle of everything, here's a unique experience.

The buildings have been collected from throughout the mid-South. With exhibits ranging from a circa-1800 cabin to a century-old telephone office to a 1920s automobile garage, a walk through the village provides a fascinating chronology of growth and evolution.

Throughout the year the village hosts many community and special events and festivals, including Uncle Dave Macon Days the second weekend in July. There's plenty of old-time music and dancing in the village during this weekend. Competition in several areas, including buck dancing, banjo playing, and fiddling, almost guarantees that you'll see some top-notch entertainment. There's a gospel music celebration on Sunday morning and a motorless parade on Saturday, plus a lot of food, crafts, and games.

### Discovery Center at Murfree Spring (all ages)

502 Southeast Broad Street; (615) 890–2300; www.discoverycenteronline.org. Open 10:00 A.M. to 5:00 P.M. Monday through Saturday and 1:00 P.M. to 5:00 P.M. Sunday. $.

A great way to get your younger kids interested in the sciences is to visit the Discovery Center at Murfree spring. It's full of fun, hands-on activities in arts and sciences for children two to twelve, but you'll want to play and learn as well. Who can resist? Among the activities are a water table, where the little ones can climb up and splash around while playing with various toys, and a similar sand table. Be sure to use the available smocks during these two activities, or it may be a cold, wet ride home.

There is also an ample supply of Lego blocks to build with, an animal room with live creatures for the kids to play with, and Nanny's Attic, where they can try on different clothes and primp in front of a mirror. A recently added attraction is the wetlands area.

## Stones River National Battlefield (ages 6 and up)

**3501 Highway 41, 2 miles northwest of downtown Murfreesboro; (615) 893–9501; www.nps.gov/stri. Open daily. Free.**

A Civil War encampment is held each July at the 600-acre Stones River National Battlefield, the site of the Civil War battle where more than 80,000 men fought for three days. Nearly 23,000 casualties make this one of the bloodiest battles fought west of the Appalachian Mountains. An eighteen-minute slide presentation in the visitor center explains that battle and other areas of interest in the park, and you can check out an audiocassette for a two-hour self-guided tour of the battlefield. There are several living-history demonstrations held during the year, mostly during the warmer months.

## Oaklands Historic House Museum (all ages)

**900 North Maney Avenue; (615) 893–0022. Open year-round except for Thanksgiving, Christmas, and New Year's Days. Open Tuesday through Saturday 10:00 A.M. to 4:00 P.M. and Sunday 1:00 to 4:00 P.M. Admission: $.**

This lovely antebellum home served as a base camp for both sides during the Civil War and was headquarters for Confederate president Jefferson Davis while he was in Murfreesboro. Admission includes a guided tour of the home.

## Other Things to See and Do

**Fortress Rosecrans** (ages 6 and up), Old Fort Park at Golf Lane, (615) 893–9501. Open daily. Free. The largest earthen fort of its kind built during the Civil War. Union forces constructed the fort to serve as their supply depot following their victory at nearby Stones River.

**Rutherford County Courthouse and Main Street** (ages 6 and up), Main Street; (615) 895–1887. Free.

## Where to Eat

**Demos' Steak & Spaghetti House,** 1115 Northwest Broad Street; (615) 895–3701. $–$$

**Kleer-vu Lunchroom,** 226 South Highland Street; (615) 896–0520. Soul food. $

**Marina's on the Square,** 125 North Maple Street; (615) 849–8881. Italian. $

**Milano's Ristorante Italiano,** 179 Mall Circle Drive; (615) 849–7999. $$

**Toot's,** 816 Northwest Broad Street; (615) 898–1301. $

## Where to Stay

**Best Western Chaffin Inn,** 168 Chaffin Place; (615) 895–3818. $$

**Doubletree,** 1850 Old Fort Parkway; (615) 895–5555. Indoor pool, hot tub, restaurant. $$$

**Hampton Inn,** 2230 Old Fort Parkway; (615) 896–1172 or (800) 426–7866. $$

**Wingate Inn,** 165 Chaffin Place; (615) 849–9000 or (800) 228–1000. Large rooms and free deluxe continental breakfast. Outdoor pool, whirlpool, exercise room. $$

**Sleep Inn,** 193 Chaffin Place; (615) 396–3000 or (800) SLEEP–INN. Exercise room, outdoor pool, free continental breakfast, in-room coffeemakers. $$

## For More Information

**Rutherford County Chamber of Commerce,** P.O. Box 864, Murfreesboro, TN 37133, 501 Memorial Boulevard, Murfreesboro, TN 37129; (615) 893–6565 or (800) 716–7560; www.rutherfordchamber.org. Open 8:00 A.M. to 4:30 P.M. Monday through Friday. Brochures available outside the front door twenty-four hours a day.

# Bell Buckle

Picture this: a nineteenth-century village with restored homes, tree-lined streets, and a shopping area full of unique shops jammed with quilts, collectibles, fine antiques, and a large selection of local crafts items. Sounds like fun, doesn't it? Well, you've found Bell Buckle, nestled along Route 269, 7 miles off I–24.

Bell Buckle has several fun festivals, including Daffodil Days on the third Saturday of March, the RC and Moon Pie Festival in June, the Quilt Walk and tour of homes on the third Saturday of September, the Webb School Arts and Crafts Festival the third weekend in October, and the Bell Buckle Christmas on the first three Saturdays in December.

### Webb School's Junior Room (all ages)
**Webb Road; (931) 389–9322. Open daily. Free.**

Bell Buckle is home to the Webb School, a preparatory school that has produced ten Rhodes scholars and the governors of three states. The Junior Room, the original wood-shingled, one-room schoolhouse built in 1870, has been preserved as it was then, complete with a potbellied stove and teaching paraphernalia. The widely known and respected Webb School Arts and Craft Festival takes place the third weekend in October each fall and features 150 juried craftspeople, demonstrations, cider making, and beautiful fall weather.

### Bridlewood Farm (ages 8 and up)
**140 Highway 82 East; (931) 389–9388. Open Monday through Saturday 8:00 A.M. to noon. Free.**

A private equestrian community and horse farm specializing in Tennessee walking horses. Tours include a walk through the horse stables, a brief video on this special breed of horses, and horse petting—something the kids especially enjoy.

## Other Things to See and Do

**Louvin Brothers Museum** (ages 6 and up), Railroad Square; (931) 389–9655. Open weekends only. Fifty-seven years of memorabilia from country music's Louvin Brothers. **Free.**

## Where to Eat

**Bell Buckle Cafe,** 16 Railroad Square; (931) 389–9693. Live music Thursday through Sunday nights. $

## Where to Stay

**Bell Buckle Bed & Breakfast,** 17 Webb Road; (931) 389–9371 or (931) 389–9372. Potter Anne White-Scruggs operates this Victorian bed-and-breakfast, decorated in art and antiques. Three guest rooms. Continental breakfast. $$

**Candleshoe Bed and Breakfast,** Webb Road; (931) 389–0646; www.bbonline.com/tn/candleshoe. Built in the late 1800s, this is a six-bedroom Victorian inn within walking distance of historic downtown Bell Buckle. All rooms have private baths and fireplaces. They offer a wonderful multicourse breakfast, ranging from traditional southern fare to a gourmet breakfast. Enjoy the veranda after you've eaten your fill. $$–$$$

## For More Information

**Shelbyville/Bedford County Chamber of Commerce,** 100 North Cannon Boulevard, Shelbyville, TN 37160; (931) 684–3482 or (888) 662–2525; www.shelbyvilletn.com. Open 8:00 A.M. to 4:00 P.M. Monday through Friday.

# Wartrace

Just down a piece from Bell Buckle on Route 269, you'll find Wartrace, which offers a few quaint shops of its own along its century-old Main Street.

### Walking Horse Hotel (all ages)
**101 Spring Street; (931) 389–7050 or (800) 513–8876.**

The Walking Horse Hotel, built in 1917, has seven nice hotel rooms. Out back, the first world-champion Tennessee walking horse, Strolling Jim, is buried under an oak tree. You can walk out and look at the well-marked gravesite.

## Where to Stay

**Historic Main Street Inn,** 207 Main Street; (931) 389–0389. Located in the heart of Tennessee walking horse country, this inn is a beautifully restored Victorian-era home, located within walking distance of gift and antiques stores in downtown Wartrace. $$$–$$$$

**Iris Fields,** 171 Loop Road; (931) 389–9776. Two-story log house; three guest rooms with private baths. Owner Lynn Wilson serves a full breakfast each morning. $$

## For More Information

**Shelbyville/Bedford County Chamber of Commerce,** 100 North Cannon Boulevard, Shelbyville, TN 37160; (931) 684–3482 or (888) 662–2525; www.shelbyvilletn.com. Open 8:00 A.M. to 4:00 P.M. Monday through Friday.

# Manchester

### Foothill Crafts (all ages)
418 Woodbury Highway, just south of exit 110 off I–24; (931) 728–9236. Open daily. **Free.**

Foothill Crafts may be the ultimate quality crafts store. Run by volunteer members of the Coffee County Crafts Association, the shop has an amazing array of handcrafted items for sale. To become a member, each craftsperson must have three items approved by the board. Only approved crafts can be put up for sale. It's a tight procedure, but that juried approach has given the store a reputation for high quality. It now showcases the works of more than 125 local artisans.

### Old Stone Fort State Archaeological Park (all ages)
Highway 41, just north of Manchester; (931) 723–5073. Open daily. **Free.**

The Old Stone Fort, now a state park, was a mystery and a source of intrigue for many generations who saw it on the bluffs high above Duck River. For centuries no one could figure out how the ancient walled enclosure, nearly 1 mile around, came to be. Archaeological research has determined that it was built as a sacred site by prehistoric Woodland Indians about 2,000 years ago.

The old dirt-and-stone fort is now the centerpiece of a 760-acre park that has a museum located in the visitor center. This museum interprets the archaeological and historical features found in the park. A 1¼-mile walk, with interpretive booklet, follows the wall and the cliff perimeter. Facilities include a picnic area, a campground, and an

adjacent golf course. The Coffee County Crafts Association sponsors an annual crafts festival here the last weekend in September.

## Other Things to See and Do

**Arrowheads/Aerospace Museum** (all ages), 24 Campground Road, exit 114 off I–24; (931) 723–1323 or (931) 723–1324. Open daily. Admission is **free.** Lionel trains, toys, Native American artifacts, and Civil War and World War II exhibits.

**Coffee County Courthouse** (all ages), Courthouse Square; (931) 723–5102. Open during courthouse hours. **Free.** On the National Register of Historic Places.

## Where to Eat

**Crockett's Roadhouse,** 1165 Woodbury Highway; (931) 728–2845. $

**Floyd's Family Restaurant,** 82 Paradise Street; (931) 723–4701. $

## Where to Stay

**Hampton Inn,** 33 Paradise Street; (931) 728–3300 or (800) 426–7866. $$

**Ramada Inn,** 2314 Hillsboro Boulevard; (931) 728–0800 or (800) 874–0092. $

## For More Information

**Manchester Chamber of Commerce,** 10 East Main Street, Manchester, TN 37355; (931) 728–7635; www.manchestertn.com. Open 8:00 A.M. to 4:30 P.M. Monday through Friday.

# Shelbyville

**Tennessee Walking Horse National Celebration** (all ages)
**Celebration Grounds, off Madison Street; (931) 684–5915. Begins eleven days before Labor Day. Prices vary per event. $–$$$.**

The Tennessee walking horse emerged from the area's plantations in the late nineteenth century, and today the breed is synonymous with Shelbyville. The town takes that responsibility seriously. Each August more than 120,000 spectators and 3,700 entries gallop here for the ten-day Tennessee Walking Horse National Celebration, which selects the national grand champion of the breed. There's an annual trade fair in which visitors are allowed to browse, a petting zoo for the kids, a special dog show, and plenty of good, southern-style cooking, especially prepared for the guests who come from forty states and foreign countries.

## Amazing Tennessee Facts

The Tennessee Walking Horse Celebration was first held in 1939.

## Other Things to See and Do

**Shelbyville Town Square** (all ages), off Highway 231; (931) 684–3482 (chamber of commerce office). **Free.** This town square was laid out in 1810 as the model for town squares throughout the South and Midwest. It's on the National Register of Historic Places and has restaurants and several shops, including antiques stores.

## Where to Eat

**Legends,** 1609 North Main Street; (931) 680–7473. Children's menu available. $$

**Pope's Cafe,** 120 East Side Square; (931) 684–9901 or (931) 684–7933. Shelbyville's oldest dining establishment. $

## Where to Stay

**Best Western Celebration Inn and Suites,** 724 Madison Street; (931) 684–2378 or (800) 528–1234. $$

**Country Hearth Inn,** 71607 North Main Street; (931) 680–1030 or (888) 693–1030. $

**Super 8 Motel,** 317 North Cannon Boulevard; (931) 684–6060 or (800) 800–8000. $

## For More Information

**Shelbyville/Bedford County Chamber of Commerce,** 100 North Cannon Boulevard, Shelbyville, TN 37160; (931) 684–3482 or (888) 662–2525; www.shelbyvilletn.com. Open 8:00 A.M. to 4:00 P.M. Monday through Friday.

# Lynchburg

### Tennessee Walking Horse Museum (all ages)
Public Square; (931) 759-5747. Open 10:00 A.M. to 4:00 P.M. Tuesday through Saturday. $.

Just recently moved from Shelbyville, this museum showcases the history of the Tennessee walking horse. The Walking Horse has an unusual rhythmic gliding motion in which each hoof strikes the ground separately in an odd one-two-three-four beat. The breed is promoted today as the "world's greatest show and pleasure horse." The Tennessee Walking Horse Museum has been developed to showcase this special breed. Exhibits, interactive videos, artifacts, and photographs tell the interesting story of the only horse breed named for its state. A theater devoted to the ten-day Tennessee Walking Horse Celebration provides a video presentation that gives visitors an overview of what it calls the "world's largest horse show."

### Jack Daniel Distillery (ages 10 and up)
Highway 55; (931) 759–6180. Tours 9:00 A.M. to 4:30 P.M., seven days a week. Closed major holidays. **Free.**

This is the oldest registered distillery in the United States. Guided tours, which welcome children and families, last about seventy minutes.  A statue of Jack Daniel is near the spring he used in the distillery's early days.  The guides say that kids with an interest in science seem to especially enjoy the tour.

The third weekend in October, the distillery hosts its annual World Championship Invitational Barbecue, named one of the top twenty events in the Southeast by the Southeast Tourism Society.

### Lynchburg Old Jail Museum (ages 8 and up)

Public Square; (931) 759–4111. Hours vary by season. Free, but donations are accepted.

Completed in 1893, the jail is preserved as it would have looked back then. Here you can see artifacts pertaining to Lynchburg and Moore County's history and even get an up-close look at a 200-year-old hand loom.

## Where to Eat

**Miss Mary Bobo's Boarding House,** 295 Main Street; (931) 759–7394. Dining by reservation only; call well ahead. Be prepared to enjoy southern cooking as they might have done it in the heyday of boardinghouses. Miss Mary Bobo's is a "must-do" when you're in this part of Tennessee—if you haven't eaten there, then you haven't truly experienced Lynchburg. $

**The Bar-B-Que Caboose,** Public Square; (931) 759–5180. Pulled pork barbeque is the house specialty, along with red beans and rice, Cajun-style, and jambalaya. $

## Where to Stay

**Lynchburg Bed and Breakfast,** 107 Mechanic Street; (931) 759-7158. Located within walking distance of Jack Daniel Distillery and shopping, this rambling two-story home, circa 1877, offers the restful atmosphere of traditional southern hospitality in a small town. Enjoy rocking on the big porch in the early mornings or peaceful afternoons. $$

## For More Information

**Lynchburg-Moore County Convention and Visitors Bureau,** Public Square; (931) 759–4111. Hours 9:00 A.M. to 4:00 P.M. Monday through Friday.

# Tullahoma

Just down the road from Lynchburg is the town of Tullahoma. Don't let its small size or outwardly quiet atmosphere fool you—this is one of the most interesting spots in this part of the state.

### Staggerwing Air Museum (ages 5 and up)

570 Old Shelbyville Highway; (931) 455–1974. Open for tours 10:00 A.M. to 2:00 P.M. Monday through Friday, Saturday and Sunday 1:00 to 4:00 P.M. $, children under 12 admitted free.

The Staggerwing was the first airplane built by aviation pioneer Walter Beech. This biplane's wings are not in total alignment, so the pilot could see better, and it was the Lear Jet of the 1930s and 1940s. A total of eight Staggerwing biplanes and several other vintage planes are on display.

### Arnold Engineering Development Center (ages 10 and up)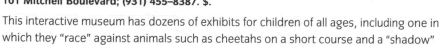
**100 Kindel Drive, on Arnold Air Force Base; (931) 454–7723. Tours are free but are only scheduled Monday through Friday; you must call ahead to schedule.**

The AEDC has dozens of wind tunnels for testing rocket and jet engines. Every spaceship engine in the United States was first tested here. The hour-long tour involves a brief film and a walk through some of the wind tunnels.

### Hands-on Science Center (ages 6 and up)
**101 Mitchell Boulevard; (931) 455–8387. $.**

This interactive museum has dozens of exhibits for children of all ages, including one in which they "race" against animals such as cheetahs on a short course and a "shadow" room, where kids leave their shadows on the walls.

## Where to Eat

**The Stuffed Goose,** 115 North Collins Street; (931) 455–6673. Dine in casual elegance in this two-story house reflecting the warmth of a bygone era. Daily specials, but go early—they're open for lunch only. $$

**Crockett's,** 413 Wilson Avenue; (931) 461–5526. Steaks, hamburgers, and a children's menu. $–$$

## Where to Stay

**Executive Inn,** 1410 North Jackson Street; (931) 455–4501. Jacuzzis in some rooms, pets accepted, outdoor pool, free continental breakfast. $$

**Jameson Inn,** 2113 North Jackson Street; (931) 455–7891. In-room microwaves, coffeemakers, and refrigerators. Free continental breakfast. $$

## For More Information

**Tullahoma Chamber of Commerce,** 135 West Lincoln Street; (931) 455–5497; www.tullahoma.org. Open 8:30 A.M. to 4:30 P.M.

# Lawrenceburg

**David Crockett State Park** (all ages)
Highway 64, ½ mile west of Lawrenceburg; (931) 762–9408. Open year-round. **Free.**

Davy Crockett was truly a Tennessean. He was born in the east, ran a gristmill here in Lawrenceburg, and was elected to Congress from the western part of the state. Over his lifetime, Crockett was a pioneer, soldier, politician, and industrialist. He came here in 1817 and served as a justice of the peace and established a diversified water-powered industry consisting of a powder mill, a gristmill, and a distillery. His entire complex and his financial security were washed away in a flood in 1821, causing him to move farther west.

Today, on the site along the river where Crockett lived and worked, Tennessee has created the David Crockett State Park. The 1,100-acre park has an interpretive center, which is staffed during the summer months and has exhibits depicting Crockett's life here and a replica of the water-powered gristmill he once owned. Facilities include 107 campsites, a restaurant, tennis courts, and an Olympic-size swimming pool.

If you can, plan your visit during the second weekend of August. That's when David Crockett Days take place with a slew of frontier-type activities. Among them are tomahawk throwing, flintlock shooting, blacksmithing, an antique weapons display, fire starting, a gun-making competition, cannon salutes, hide tanning, a Crockett film festival, snake shows, country and bluegrass music shows, and hayrides.

## Amazing
## Tennessee Facts

Lawrenceburg, the county seat of Lawrence County, was named in honor of Capt. James Lawrence, the famous naval hero of the War of 1812, who immortalized the words "Don't give up the ship."

## Other Things to See and Do

**Amish Community** (all ages), off Highway 43 in Ethridge, about 5 miles north of Lawrenceburg. Visitors are welcome, but leave your camera in the car.

**James D. Vaughan Museum** (all ages), Public Square; (931) 762–2484. Open Monday through Friday 10:00 A.M. to 4:00 P.M. Admission is **free,** but donations are accepted.

The U.S. Congress has recognized Lawrenceburg as the Birthplace of Southern Gospel Music. This museum honors the Father of Southern Gospel Music, James Vaughan, and other artists of the genre, with photos, music, and other mementoes.

**Lawrenceburg Public Square** (all ages), (931) 762–4911 (Chamber of Commerce office). **Free.** There's a bronze life-size statue of David Crockett here. You'll also find the Mexican War Monument, several shops, and a gazebo area where festivals are held.

## Where to Eat

**David Crockett Restaurant,** at David Crockett State Park, Highway 64; (931) 762–9408. Open late February through December 20. $

## Where to Stay

**David Crockett State Park,** Highway 64, ½ mile west of Lawrenceburg; (931) 762–9408. 107 campsites. $

**Richland Inn–Lawrenceburg,** 2125 North Locust Avenue; (931) 762–0061 or (800) 742–4526. $$

## For More Information

**Lawrence County Chamber of Commerce,** P.O. Box 86, 1609 North Locust, Lawrenceburg, TN 38464; (931) 762–4911; www.lawrenceburg.com. Open 8:00 A.M. to 9:30 P.M. Monday through Friday.

# Winchester/Cowan/Belvidere/Sewanee

This charming area of the state should be included in your family's list of places to go if you like stepping back in time. Winchester is the Franklin County seat and has a quaint, old-fashioned town square resembling the setting of *The Andy Griffith Show's* Mayberry. You could spend an entire summer in this area and not see everything, but here's a sampling.

### Downtown Winchester (all ages)
**(931) 967–6788 (Chamber of Commerce).**

A stroll around this downtown is worth the trip by itself. One place not to miss is the local combination hardware and five-and-dime, Hammer's. Some of us remember shopping at places like this, where the motto is, "If we don't have it, then you don't really need it." Downtown also offers many colorful antiques and gift shops in the area referred to as Rainbow Row.

### Old Jail Museum (all ages)
**400 Dinah Shore Boulevard, Winchester; (931) 967–6788. Open Tuesday through Saturday from April through October. Hours vary. $.**

This jail was built in 1898 to hold local criminals. You can tour original cells, view collectibles from the history of the area, and see memorabilia belonging to the late Dinah Shore, a former Winchester resident.

### Tims Ford State Park (all ages)
**570 Tims Ford Drive, Winchester; (931) 962–1184 or (888) TN–PARKS. Open year-round. Free.**

Located on the Tims Ford Reservoir surrounded by scenic, rolling hills, this park offers camping, lodging in the cabins (open March 1 through December 1), boating, picnicking, fishing, hiking, and many other kinds of recreation. You can also bring your bike and cruise the paved biking trails.

### The University of the South (ages 6 and up)

**735 University Avenue, Sewanee; (931) 598–1286. Open year-round. Call for special-events schedules and admission prices.**

More commonly known as Sewanee, this campus makes for a breathtaking tour. Most of the buildings are nearly 150 years old, and their Gothic style makes this campus look as if it belongs in England. The university sponsors concerts on occasion.

### Belvidere Market (all ages)

**6334 Davy Crockett Highway, Belvidere; (931) 967–3872. Open Tuesday through Saturday 9:00 A.M. to 5:00 P.M. Sometimes open on Monday.**

Originally established as a farm-equipment supply in 1910, this market, just 6 miles west of Winchester, remains a focal point of the area. Today it offers many locally made crafts, such as carved or painted items, needlework, antiques, glassware, and other collectibles. There are also great sandwiches.

### Falls Mill Museum and Country Store (all ages)

**134 Falls Mill Road, Belvidere; (931) 469–7161. Open year-round Monday through Saturday 9:00 A.M. to 4:00 P.M. and Sunday 12:30 to 4:00 P.M. Closed Wednesday and major holidays. Free.**

This antique mill was built as a cotton and woolen factory and is now used as a gristmill. Your kids will love the cascading falls created by the 32-foot waterwheel, and you can buy stone-ground cornmeal, grits, and flour in the shop on the premises. You can take a self-guided tour that gives the history of the mill, and if you bring a lunch, your family can picnic beside the scenic waterfall.

### Cowan Railroad Museum (all ages)

**On the square, downtown Cowan; (931) 967–7318. Open May through October, Thursday, Friday, and Saturday 10:00 A.M. to 4:00 P.M. and Sunday 1:00 to 4:00 P.M. Admission is free, but donations are accepted.**

This museum is staffed by one of the last true railroad engineers, who will show you a collection of railroad artifacts including an early 1900s-era locomotive, caboose, and model steam locomotive.

# Where to Eat

**Second Avenue Cafe,** 103 Second Avenue Northwest; (931) 962–8599. Serves casual fare of sandwiches and salads. $

**The Corner House,** 401 East Cumberland, Cowan; (931) 967–3910. The specialty of the house is Chicken Divan. They also make a great lasagna and have a variety of fruited teas. $

## Where to Stay

**Best Western Inn,** 1602 Dinah Shore Boulevard, Winchester; (931) 967–9444 or (800) 528–1234. Hot tub and outdoor pool. Continental breakfast included. $–$$

**Falls Mill Bed & Breakfast,** 134 Falls Mill Road, Belvidere; (931) 469–7161. Located at Falls Mill Museum and Country Store, this large log cabin, built in 1895, accommodates six people and has a kitchen and fireplace. Overlooks the mill and waterfall. $$–$$$

## For More Information

**Franklin County Chamber of Commerce,** 44 Chamber Way, Winchester, TN 37398; www.franklincountychamber.com; (931) 967–6788. Open 8:00 A.M. to 4:30 P.M. Monday through Friday.

# Pulaski

### Pulaski Historic Square (all ages)
**100 South Second Street; (931) 363–3789 (Chamber of Commerce office).**

The entire public square area is listed on the National Register of Historic Places and is abundant with preserved and restored eighteenth and nineteenth century architecture.

### Giles County Courthouse (all ages)
**Public square; (931) 363–5300. Open Monday through Friday during business hours. Free.**

The bell that was cast in 1858 and today hangs in the Giles County Courthouse on the public square in Pulaski still strikes the hour, each hour, every day. The sound coming from the cupola is just one of the beautiful elements of this neoclassical building built in 1909. Outside, tall Corinthian columns mark the architecture. Inside, a balcony encircles the third floor, and sixteen caryatids (female faces) hold up the arched vault of the rotunda with its stained-glass skylights.

In front of the courthouse, on the south side of the public square, is a statue of Sam Davis, a young Confederate scout who was captured and executed in Pulaski. Davis was captured behind enemy lines with damaging information in his possession. Instead of betraying the source of that information, he chose to be hanged.

### Sam Davis Museum (ages 8 and up)

Sam Davis Avenue; (931) 363–3789. Hours are sporadic, so it's best to check with the Chamber of Commerce office before visiting. Free.

The Sam Davis Museum now stands on the spot where the "Boy Hero of the Confederacy" was executed on November 27, 1863. The museum contains Civil War memorabilia as well as the leg irons worn by Davis.

### Giles County Historical Museum (ages 8 and up) 

122 South Second Street; (931) 363–2720. Open daily year-round. Free.

This museum houses exhibits, artifacts, and genealogical records of the county.

### American Home Entertainment Museum (ages 5 and up) 

152 Case Road, Prospect (just outside of Pulaski); (931) 424—1212 or (931) 424–0603. Free tours by appointment only; call ahead.

This museum has a great variety of home entertainment dating from the 1800s to today, including a working player piano, pump organ, Edison phonograph, and more. They'll show old movies if your group is large enough. For some parents, this will be a stroll down memory lane!

## Other Things to See and Do

**Brown-Daly Horne House (Colonial Bank of Tennessee)** (ages 8 and up), 307 West Madison; (931) 363–1582. Free. Built in 1855, this is one of the state's best examples of Queen Anne–style architecture.

**Giles County Collectible and Antique Tour** (all ages), 100 South Second Street; (931) 363–3789 (Chamber of Commerce office). Free. Driving tour of area shops. Stop by the Chamber office for a brochure.

**Mama J's Cabin** (all ages), Highway 64, between Lawrenceburg and Pulaski; (931) 762–0678. Free. Three-room log cabin built in the mid-1800s filled with Amish crafts and gifts.

## Where to Eat

**Sarge's Shack,** Highway 64, Frankewing, about 14½ miles from Pulaski; (931) 363–1310. Great steaks and catfish. $

## Where to Stay

**Comfort Inn–Pulaski,** 1140 West College Street at Highway 4; (931) 424–1600 or (931) 428–0192. $$

**Hollow Pond Farm Bed, Barn & Breakfast,** 800 Tight Bark Hollow Road, Frankewing, 2 miles off I–65, (931) 424–8535 or (800) 463–0154. Three rooms, private baths. Overnight stabling for guests with horses.

Full breakfast each morning. Riding trails for guests, plus hiking trails and a swimming pool. $$

**Richland Inn–Pulaski,** 1020 West College Street; (931) 363–0006 or (800) 833–9472. $$

## For More Information

**Giles County Chamber of Commerce,** 110 North Second Street, Pulaski, TN 38478; (931) 363–3789; www.gilescountychamber.com; www.tennesseetourist.com/pulaski.htm. Open 8:00 A.M. to 5:00 P.M. Monday through Friday and 9:00 A.M. to 2:00 P.M. Saturday.

# the
# Western
# Plains

I f it's a taste of the Deep South you're looking for, this region, more than any other in the state, can offer it to you. Separated from the rest of the state by the Tennessee River, the Western Plains has its own distinctive flavor, culture, and folklore.

Through the years many of the state's best-known characters have called this area home. Their roots and their homesteads still dot the landscape. From Elvis Presley, the King of Rock and Roll in Memphis, to Tina Turner, the Queen of Rock and Roll in Nutbush, to the birth of the blues on Beale Street by W. C. Handy, this region has had a significant influence on the musical styles we enjoy.

Add the names of Alex Haley, Casey Jones, Buford Pusser, and Davy Crockett to the list of famous folks, and you get an idea of the diverse heritage of the region. But wait— there's much more than the image of famous people to keep you entertained as you drive through the area.

You'll get an opportunity to visit the National Civil Rights Museum in Memphis, built on the site of Martin Luther King Jr.'s assassination; the National Bird Dog Museum in LaGrange; the Peabody Hotel in Memphis, where famous ducks march twice daily; the Eiffel Tower in Paris, home of the world's largest fish fry; and the world's largest teapot collection in Trenton. Among the hundreds of annual celebrations, you'll be able to enjoy a strawberry festival, a waterfowl festival, and an archaeological festival.

Many say the earthquake in northwestern Tennessee that created Reelfoot Lake is the most severe quake ever recorded. Today the shallow lake is a sporting paradise and the winter home to more than one hundred American bald eagles. Helping to create the eastern border of the area, Kentucky Lake, with more than 2,300 miles of shoreline, is the world's second-largest man-made lake.

# Tiptonville

**Reelfoot Lake** (all ages)
**State Highways 21/22 and 78; (731) 253–2007 or (888) 313–8366 (Reelfoot Lake Tourism Council). Open year-round. Free.**

During the winter of 1811–1812, a series of earthquakes—one the most violent on record in the United States—struck this area. The lands of northwestern Tennessee near the Mississippi

# THE WESTERN PLAINS

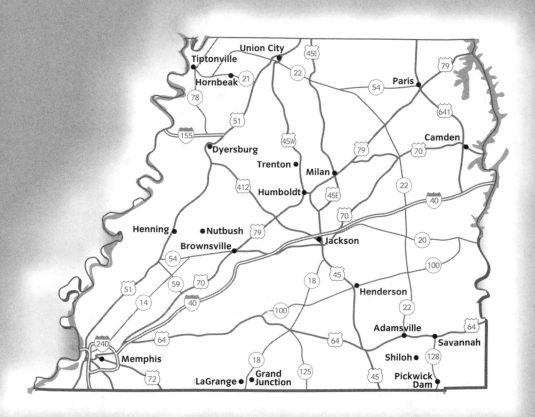

THE WESTERN PLAINS 159

River dropped by as much as 20 feet, and for fifteen minutes the river's water flowed backward to fill this major void that had been a swampy forestland. Known affectionately as Earthquake Lake, this 13,000-acre sportsman's paradise is officially known as Reelfoot Lake.

When the new lake was formed, the forestland was flooded, and the remains of many of the trees can still be found under the waters today, making boating a tricky business. The average depth of the lake is 5.2 feet, and the deepest area is only 18 feet. Because of the shallow water and the abundance of natural cover, the lake is a natural fish hatchery, with fifty-four different species calling it home.

The lake is also the winter home of more than one hundred American bald eagles. The birds, with wingspans of 6 to 8 feet, come from their northern summer homes to spend the winter in a warmer, ice-free environment. There are numerous organized "eagle tours" during the winter months that allow people to get within 50 feet of the nesting birds. Along with the eagles, a wide variety of fowl can be observed at the lake. More than 100,000 ducks and 66,000 Canada geese are usually in residence here, and during the year approximately 254 kinds of birds visit the lake.

## Reelfoot Lake State Park (all ages) 🏕️ 🍴 ♿

**Highway 21; (731) 253–7756 or (800) 250-8617. Open year-round. Free.**

The area around most of the lake is now the Reelfoot Lake State Park. Many activities are offered, including official eagle and birding tours, daily pontoon cruises, and the National Wildlife Refuge Visitor Center and Museum, where you can learn about the diverse flora and fauna of the area. The park's visitor center and interpretive center offer exhibits that explore the formation, history, natural diversity, and future of Reelfoot Lake. Outside the visitor center is a scenic boardwalk where you can take a walk out over the lake and through the cypress trees.

On the north side of the park is the Airpark Inn and Restaurant. Built out over the lake, the inn's twenty rooms all provide magnificent views of the lake, especially in the morning at sunrise. The pier outside the restaurant provides a great place to watch eagles in the winter. Behind the inn there's a lighted, 3,500-foot-long landing strip. There are campsites, boat ramps, and picnic facilities throughout the area. About 16 miles away, Samburg, the oldest community on the lake, has a large offering of motels, restaurants, and shops.

The best place to start your visit at Reelfoot Lake is at the visitor center off Highway 21 on the lake's south shore, east of Tiptonville. There you can get a list of trails, local accommodations, events, and activities.

## The Reelfoot Lake Arts and Crafts Festival (all ages) 🔒

**Reelfoot Lake State Park; (731) 253–7276. First weekend in October. Free.**

This festival features more than 400 indoor and outdoor exhibits, most near the visitor center at the state park. Food is provided by local churches and civic organizations.

## Reelfoot Lake Waterfowl Festival (all ages)

**Kirby Pocket area of Reelfoot Lake, 1 mile north of Samburg; (731) 538–2126. Third weekend of August. Free.**

Presented by a chapter of the Duck Call Maker and Collector Association of America, this festival features arts and crafts and the sanctioned Reelfoot Lake Grand American Duck and Goose Calling Contest. The champion caller goes to the world-champion competition in November.

## Where to Eat

**Blue Bank Fish House & Grill,** Highway 22, Tiptonville; (731) 253–6878. Good catfish and country ham. $ (lunch), $$ (dinner)

**Lakeview Dining Room,** Highway 22; (731) 253–7516. Fish, chicken, ham, and specialty dishes. $–$$

## Where to Stay

**Boyette's Resort,** Highway 21; (731) 253–6523. Furnished cottage with screen porches. Restaurant, pool. $–$$$

**Cypress Point Resort,** 3535 State Route 21 East; (800) 394–1886 or (731) 253–6659. Rooms, kitchen, cabins, houses, RV sites, marina, boat rentals, lighted pier fishing, a bait and tackle shop, outdoor pool, game room. Fishing and guided floating eagle-sighting packages available. Rooms $; cabins and houses $$–$$$$

## For More Information

**Reelfoot Lake Chamber of Commerce,** 130 South Court Street, Tiptonville, TN 38079; (731) 253–8144; www.reelfootarea chamber.com. Open 10:00 A.M. to 4:00 P.M. Monday through Friday.

**Reelfoot Lake Tourism Council,** 4575 State Route 21 East, Tiptonville, TN 38079; (731) 253–2007. Open 8:00 A.M. to 5:00 P.M. Monday, Tuesday, Friday, and Saturday; 1:00 to 5:00 P.M. Sunday.

## Amazing
# Tennessee Facts

Tennessee's state gem is the Tennessee river pearl.

# Union City/Hornbeak

## Dixie Gun Works/Old Car Museum (ages 8 and up)
**On the Highway 51S bypass of Union City; (731) 885–0561. Open Monday through Saturday. Museum admission: $.**

Unless you're a gun collector or live in Union City, chances are you have never heard of the Dixie Gun Works. Since its beginnings in the 1950s, the business has probably become the best-known antique gun dealership in the world, with a long list of international clients. At any given time, the store has around 1,500 antique revolvers and rifles on hand

and sells an average of 80,000 guns a year, mostly through mail-order sales generated from three different catalogs. Most of the guns sold here were made before 1898. The shop carries all types of original guns dating back to the early 1700s and also deals in replica guns.

A museum houses antique automobiles, a passion of the late founder, Turner Kirland. Now operated by his stepson, Lee Fry, the Old Car Museum features thirty-six antique autos, all in running condition; 2,000 antique auto accessories and mechanical items; and a collection of farm engines, steam engines, and steam whistles. There is also a small log cabin gun shop that was moved onto the property. Inside are two rifling machines and more than 1,000 old hand tools that were used in the manufacture of guns.

## Obion County Fall Festival (all ages)

Obion County Fairgrounds, Union City; (731) 885–8330. Third week in September. Admission is **free.**

Obion County residents usher in the harvest season with their annual festival, which includes a parade, tennis tournament, golf scramble, magic shows, and all kinds of food, including a barbecue cook-off.

## Flippen's Hillbilly Barn (all ages) 🍴

Shawtown Road, 8 miles off Highway 22; (731) 538–2933. Open daily.

South of Union City, near the little community of Hornbeak, three generations of the Jack Flippen family have built their reputation on fruit. Flippen's Hillbilly Barn was created originally as an orchard but has expanded through the years to include a restaurant featuring the country-cooking skills of Mrs. Flippen and her talented staff. The catfish and the country ham dinners are two of the most requested meals, but prime rib and steaks are also offered.

There is outside deck seating overlooking two ponds. Peach trees surround the ponds and the decks, and in the spring, when the trees are in full bloom, usually in mid- to late-March, the color is fantastic. It's a popular local eatery, and many of those who frequent it say it's the Flippens' fried fruit pies that keep them coming back.

The orchard produces more than twenty-seven varieties of apples and peaches, which are available in the farm's market, as are the restaurant's popular homemade jams and jellies.

# The State **Flag**

Tennessee's flag was adopted in 1905. The three white stars represent the three divisions of the state: east, middle, and west.

## Other Things to See and Do

**Obion County Museum** (all ages), 1004 Edwards Street; (731) 885–6774. Open Saturday and Sunday 1:00 to 4:00 P.M.; open by appointment during the week. **Free**

## Where to Eat

**Flippen's Hillbilly Barn,** Shawton Road, off Highway 22, Hornbeak; (731) 538–2933. $

**Penny Hill Shoppe,** 131 East Jackson Street, Union City; (731) 884–2184. Subs, pitas, gyros, and salads. People come from all over the state to eat here. $

## Where to Stay

**Hospitality House,** 1221 West Reelfoot Avenue; (731) 885–6610. $$

**Union City Hampton Inn,** 2201 West Reelfoot Avenue; (731) 885–8850 or (800) HAMPTON. $$

## For More Information

**Obion County Chamber of Commerce,** P.O. Box 70, 214 Church Street, Union City, TN 38281; (731) 885–0211; www.obion countytennessee.com. Open 8:00 A.M. to 4:30 P.M. Monday through Friday.

# Paris

## World's Biggest Fish Fry (all ages)

**Henry County Fairgrounds, Fairgrounds Road; (731) 644–1143. Last full week of April. Free. Admission charged to rodeo.**

The World's Biggest Fish Fry attracts people from all over the South. For more than forty years, the local Jaycees have held this event at the Henry County Fairgrounds, and as the name implies, it has turned into an enormous event.

The shopping list is huge. Officials say that annually they use nearly 1,500 pounds of cornmeal, more than 200 pounds of salt, and approximately 10,000 pounds of fresh catfish taken from the waters of Kentucky Lake. Once the fish are prepared, they are dropped into old-fashioned black kettles and cooked over oil burners in more than 250 gallons of vegetable oil. Add a generous serving of cole slaw, white beans, and hush puppies, and you have a family feast that will be hard to beat. These folk know how to cook fish.

In addition to the fish, there are tons of fun activities, including amusement rides, an arts-and-crafts show, a junior fishing tournament, a square dance, a car show, a three-hour parade on Friday, and a three-night Professional Rodeo Cowboys Association rodeo.

## Eiffel Tower (all ages)

**Memorial Park on Volunteer Drive; (731) 642–3431. Open year-round. Free.**

What would Paris be without the Eiffel Tower? There's a 65-foot scale model version of the famous structure standing at the entrance of Memorial Park.

## Historic Downtown (all ages)

**Information at Paris/Henry County Heritage Center, 614 Poplar Street North; (731) 642–1030. Year-round. Free.**

Andrew Jackson bought the land upon which Paris stands from the Chickasaw Indians in 1818. Paris became the first incorporated town in western Tennessee in 1823. Today most of the buildings along the city square date to 1900 or before, and the district is one of the most vibrant downtown areas in the state. A walking tour features most of the century-old buildings. Several of the structures now house antiques stores. Walking-tour cassette players, tapes, and maps are available at the Heritage Center office and the W. G. Rhea Library.

## Paris Landing State Park (all ages)

**16 miles northeast of Paris, on Highway 79; Buchanan; (731) 644–7359 or (800) 250–8614 (park information), (731) 642–4311 (inn and dining reservations). Open year-round. Free. Fees charged for various activities.**

Kentucky Lake, created in 1944, is the largest in the Tennessee Valley Authority's chain of lakes and the largest man-made lake in the United States. It's 184 miles long with more than 2,300 miles of shoreline. Paris Landing is the widest area of the lake, and that's where you'll find the magnificent Paris Landing State Park.

The Paris Landing Inn offers 130 rooms, many of them overlooking the lake. The inn has a day-use dock complex, tennis courts, an Olympic-size swimming pool, a conference center, and a 385-seat restaurant, known for its huge buffet featuring southern cuisine.

For those who prefer alternative lodging, the park has ten lakeside villas. Each has three bedrooms and two baths and contains five double beds. All have central heat and air, a stone fireplace, and a deck or porch with a lake view. Linens and kitchen utensils are also included. Reservations are taken well in advance, so call ahead.

There are unsupervised swimming beaches along an area of the lake, and the park's marina offers fishing supplies, groceries, a **free** launch ramp for your boat, and a fuel pump. A reminder if you plan to fish: Unless specified differently, a fishing license is required of all persons over thirteen years of age in Tennessee. Licenses are available here at the marina.

The park has full-service and primitive campsites along the lake, as well as a championship eighteen-hole golf course and pro shop. Numerous picnic facilities dot the 841-acre park, and an outdoor amphitheater offers **free** entertainment every Saturday night during the summer.

## Mansard Island Resort (all ages)

**3 miles west of Paris Landing State Park, off Highway 79 on East Antioch Road, Springville; (731) 642–5590 or (800) 533–5590.**

The Mansard Island Resort, on the shores of Kentucky Lake, offers a convenient place to stay while exploring the area. Overnight facilities range from primitive and full-service campsites to town-house apartments, economy cabins, and modern cabins. Prices range from $30 to $175. There is also a grocery, a Laundromat, a swimming pool, a playground, and two tennis courts. The covered, full-service marina has a bait store, pontoon boat rentals, and fishing and paddleboat rentals.

### Tennessee National Wildlife Refuge (all ages)

**Northern Benton County, 15 miles north of Big Sandy, off Highway 69A; (731) 642–2091 or (800) 372–3928. Open year-round during daylight hours, but certain areas may be closed to boat and vehicle traffic during winter months.**

The Tennessee National Wildlife Refuge combines 25,000 acres of water, 19,000 acres of woodland, and 5,000 acres of farmland and pasture to offer irresistible resting and feeding opportunities for migrating waterfowl on one of the nation's major flyways. Stretching along 80 river miles, the refuge is administered by the U.S. Fish and Wildlife Service in cooperation with the TVA. There is a multitude of waterfowl viewing areas where more than thirty species may be spotted.

The Big Sandy unit is the northernmost spot of the refuge. You may also enter near Parsons or in New Johnsonville, both of which are farther south along the river.

## Amazing
# Tennessee Facts

John W. Crockett, son of Davy Crockett, is buried in Paris's cemetery.

## Other Things to See and Do

**Market Street Antique Mall** (all ages), 414 North Market Street (Highway 641); (731) 642–6996. **Free.** 60,000 square feet of shopping under one roof.

## Where to Eat

**Knott's Landing Restaurant,** 209 North Poplar Street; (731) 642–4718. Specializing in catfish. $

**Paris Landing Inn,** Paris Landing State Park; (731) 642–4311. Three daily buffets. $

**Tom's Pizza and Steakhouse,** 2501 East Wood Street; (731) 642–8842. The locals frequent this eatery, which serves a variety of pizzas and grilled steaks. $

**The Kitchen Table,** 2613 East Wood Street; (731) 642–0274. Offers a daily buffet and down-home country cooking. $

## Where to Stay

**Paris Travelers Inn,** 1297 East Wood Street; (731) 642–8881. $

**Mansard Island Resort,** 3 miles west of Paris Landing State Park off Highway 79, Springville; (731) 642–5590 or (800) 533–5590. $–$$$$

**Paris Area Resorts and Marinas** There are several resort and marina complexes in the Paris area. For a complete listing call the Paris Chamber of Commerce at (800) 345–1103.

**Paris Landing State Park,** 16 miles northeast of Paris, on Highway 79, Buchanan; (731) 644–7359 or (800) 250–8614 (park information), (731) 642–4311 (inn and dining reservations). Variety of accommodations, including Paris Landing Inn, campsites, and ten large cabins. $–$$$$

**Terrace Woods Travel Lodge,** 1190 North Market Street; (731) 642–2642. This inn is located in the historic downtown district. $–$$

## For More Information

**Paris/Henry County Chamber of Commerce,** P.O. Box 8, 2508 East Wood Street, Paris TN 38242; (731) 642–3431 or (800) 345–1103; www.paris.tn.org. Open 8:00 A.M. to 4:30 P.M. Monday through Friday.

# Camden

### Nathan Bedford Forrest State Park (all ages)
**At the end of Highway 191, about 10 miles outside of Camden; (731) 584-6356. Open year-round. Free.**

This is the site of the Civil War Battle of Johnsonville and home of the Tennessee River Folklife Center. The park has cabins, a group lodge, campsites, a museum, a gift shop, a picnic area, fishing areas, boat-launch ramps, swimming areas, playgrounds, and hiking trails.

### Tennessee River Folklife Center (all ages)
**Nathan Bedford Forrest State Historic Park; (731) 584–6356. Open daily April through December. Free.**

On the highest point in the western part of the state, inside the Nathan Bedford Forrest State Park, you'll find the Tennessee River Folklife Center, a fabulous tribute to the people who lived, loved, and labored on the Tennessee River. The interpretive center is located on Pilot Knob, a longtime landmark for pilots and for anglers who worked the river far below. The view of the river from up here is magnificent.

Most of the exhibits incorporate segments of oral histories taken from the locals who lived the river life. The audio segments recall the early industries, music, religion, and community events of the area. *Old Betsy*, a retired workboat from the early musseling industry along the river, is the centerpiece of the exhibit. The boat belonged to T. J. Whitfield, whose family had farmed the fertile river bottomlands until the TVA condemned the land for the construction of the Kentucky Lake reservoir. When the land was flooded, Whitfield had nowhere to turn for a living but to commercial fishing. His story is told in detail and is quite moving.

Maggie Sayre lived on a houseboat on the river for more than fifty years. She captured her life on film, using a Brownie camera. The center has her collection on display, and what a heartwarming story her photos portray!

## Amazing
# Tennessee Facts

Tennessee's official sport fish is the largemouth bass. The state commercial fish is the channel catfish.

### A Pearl of a Tour (all ages)

**Birdsong Marina on Kentucky Lake, 255 Marina Road, 9 miles north of I–40, off exit 133; (731) 584–7880 or (800) 225–7469. Tours available May through October by appointment, $$$$. Museum, pearl farm, and jewelry showroom are free and open daily year-round.**

Believe it or not, there's an active freshwater pearl farm on Kentucky Lake, and it's the only freshwater pearl farm in the United States. Back in the 1960s, John Latendresse developed a technique for creating freshwater pearls in mollusks, and in 1985 he harvested his first crop of Tennessee-produced pearls. It all has to do with implanting a small piece of shell nucleus and live tissue inside the mollusk. In response, the mollusk will continuously excrete a protective coating around the foreign substance to relieve the irritation. That coating is what turns into the pearl.

You can take a tour of the farm where these mollusks are "planted" while the pearls grow inside them. Tours last three to five hours and are priced at $45.00, including lunch. You climb aboard a pontoon boat that takes you out to where you will be able to see divers working the mollusk fields. An on-site jewelry store and museum feature the local pearls.

## Other Things to See and Do

**Patsy Cline Memorial,** Mount Carmel Road; (731) 584–8395. **Free.** Country-music legend Patsy Cline died in a plane crash in Camden in 1963. A memorial stone and information booth are located at the site of the crash.

## Where to Eat

**The Catfish Place,** 201 Highway 641 North; (731) 584–3504. $

**Country & Western Steakhouse,** 189 Extension Street; (731) 584–3026. $

**The 1850s Log House Restaurant,** 2635 Highway 641 North; (731) 584–7814. $

## Where to Stay

**Birdsong Resort, Marina and Family Campground,** 255 Marina Road, 9 miles north of I–140, off exit 133; (731) 584–7880 or (800) 225–7649. Cottages and campsites. $–$$$$

**Days Inn,** Highway 70 East; (731) 584–3111 or (800) DAYSINN. $

**Guest House Inn,** 170 Highway 641 North; (731) 584–2222 or (800) 21–GUEST. Outdoor pool, and free Belgian waffle breakfast; rooms available with whirlpool tubs and microwaves. $–$$

## Miles of **Bargains**

Each September, on Labor Day weekend, Benton County hosts a huge yard sale. And I mean huge. It's the Benton County Bargain Highway, and it stretches for 30 miles, the entire length of Benton County. From daylight until dark, you can shop until you drop. It begins at exit 126 off I–40 and goes north through the county. For more information call (731) 584–8395.

## For More Information

**Benton County/Camden Chamber of Commerce,** 202 West Main Street, Camden, TN 38320; (731) 584–8395 or (877) 584–8395; www.bentoncountycamden.com. Open 8:00 A.M. to 4:00 P.M. Monday through Friday.

# Trenton/Milan/Humboldt

### Trenton Teapot Museum (all ages)
**City Hall, 309 South College; (731) 855–2013. Open year-round. Free.**

You'd never guess it, but Trenton is the home of the world's largest collection of a rare type of eighteenth- and nineteenth-century porcelain teapot, the veilleuse. A New York doctor, originally from Trenton, was going to donate his extensive teapot collection, valued at more than $5 million, to the Metropolitan Museum of Art in New York City, but he ended up donating the 500 pieces to his hometown instead. The colorful collection is quite fun to view. Many teapots are in the shape of buildings and have a whimsical sense to them.

The teapots are now in showcases in the Trenton City Hall and can be viewed during regular office hours. If you get there after-hours, you can ask someone at the fire station or police department, located in the City Hall building, to let you in.

### Teapot Festival
**Downtown Trenton the last week of April; (731) 855-0973. Free.**

To celebrate their teapot collection, "Trentonians" hold an annual festival complete with fireworks, a parade, a concert in the park downtown, 5K and 10K races, and all kinds of food.

## West Tennessee Agricultural Museum (ages 8 and up)
**University of Tennessee Agricultural Experimental Station, 3 Ledbetter Gate Road at High-way 70A/79N, Milan; (731) 686–8067. Open 8:00 A.M. to 4:00 P.M. Monday through Friday and noon to 4:00 P.M. Saturday. Free.**

The West Tennessee Agricultural Museum is a treasure trove of memories of a lifestyle that has all but disappeared. It houses an extensive collection of farming tools spanning two centuries of agricultural development in this part of the state. The two-story museum is housed in a massive barnlike structure. But this place is much more than a barn filled with old tools.

The designers of the museum made excellent use of large dioramas, life-size man-nequins, and full-size props. Beautifully painted murals form the backdrop to several of the exhibits. The layout presents a chronological account of the region's agricultural his-tory, beginning with Native Americans. Specific areas and corresponding exhibits include a Cherokee settlement along the river, early white settlers clearing the land, Civil War–era cotton farmers, and the 1920s and 1930s, when iron-wheeled tractors began replacing horses and mules.

One special exhibit is a tribute to the farmwife, put together by the women of the Farm Bureau. It's a reproduction of a typical farm kitchen from the early twentieth century, complete with all the modern conveniences of the time, including old boiler cookers, peel-ers, presses, scrub boards, and a wooden washing machine.

## West Tennessee Strawberry Festival (all ages)
**Downtown Humboldt; (731) 784–1842. First full week in May. Admission varies, depending on events. Some activities are free.**

The strawberry is the fruit of choice in Humboldt. Every year in May, the sweet little berry is saluted during the West Tennessee Strawberry Festival, held on the streets of down-town Humboldt. There are two big parades—one promoted as the longest nonmotorized parade in the nation, a street dance, a checkers tournament, a strawberry recipe contest, a pet parade, a bike show, a car show, a motocross, 5K and 10K races, and a carnival with all sorts of family and kiddie amusement rides.

Amazing
# Tennessee Facts

Among the early settlers in Gibson County was the famous pioneer Davy Crockett.

**Humboldt Strawberry Festival Historical Museum** (all ages)
1200 Main Street; (731) 784–1842. Open 9:00 A.M. to 4:00 P.M. Monday, Wednesday, and Friday.

This museum includes memorabilia of past festivals dating back to 1934, displays from early city governments, exhibits of local culture, and other items and artifacts collected through the years.

**West Tennessee Regional Arts Center** (ages 8 and up)

1200 Main Street; (731) 784–1787. Open Monday through Friday 9:00 A.M. to 4:00 P.M. $

A truly outstanding collection of art is located here. The center is the home of the Caldwell Collection, which consists of more than 175 pieces of eighteenth-, nineteenth-, and twentieth-century art donated by a local physician and patron of the arts. Items include oil paintings, sculptures, watercolors, prints, lithographs, pastels, and silk screenings.

## Where to Eat

**Hig's,** 109 Oakwood Drive; (731) 686–9901 Fish, country ham, and a daily buffet. $

**Kappis Steakhouse,** Highway 45 Bypass, Humboldt; (731) 784–2077. $

**Majestic,** 2050 Highway 45 Bypass, Trenton; (731) 855–4808. Steaks, food bar, and salad bar. $

**Wall Street Grill,** 2120 North Central Avenue, Humboldt; (731) 784–1214. $

## Where to Stay

**Heritage Inn,** 3350 East End Drive, Humboldt; (731) 784–2278. $

**Executive Inns and Suites,** 3022 South First Street, Milan; (731) 686–3345. $

## For More Information

**Greater Gibson County Area Chamber of Commerce,** 103 South Court Square, Trenton, TN 38382; (731) 855–0973; www.gibsoncountytn.com. Open 8:00 A.M. to 4:30 P.M. Monday through Friday.

**Humboldt Chamber of Commerce,** 1200 Main Street, Humboldt, TN 38343; (731) 784–1842; www.humboldttnchamber.org. Open 8:00 A.M. to 4:30 P.M. Monday through Friday.

**Milan Chamber of Commerce,** 1061 South Main Street, Milan, TN 38358; (731) 686–7494; www.cityofmilantn.com. Open 8:00 A.M. to 4:30 P.M. Monday through Thursday, to 3:00 P.M. on Friday.

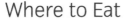

# Dyersburg

### Lenox Bridge (all ages)
State Route 182; (731) 285–8188. Open daily. Free.

This bridge, constructed in 1917, is a hand-operated, swing-span footbridge in Lakewood Subdivision, spanning two scenic man-made lakes (Lake Luana and Lakewood) and surrounded by 600 acres of water and trees.

### Dr. Walter E. David Wildlife Museum (ages 8 and up)
Dyersburg State Community College campus, Glover Building; (731) 286–3200. Open Monday through Friday, 8:00 A.M. to 5:00 P.M. Free.

This building houses an amazing collection of African and North American big game trophies as well as waterfowl trophies, donated to the college by Dr. David.

### Dyersburg Walking Tour (all ages)
Information at Dyersburg Chamber office, 2000 Commerce Avenue; (731) 285–3433. Free.

Downtown Dyersburg has more than eighty historical homes and artifacts, ranging from the Dyer County Courthouse to the statue they call Soldier in Grey on the courthouse lawn. While you're in the area, check out General Strahl's Cannon in the nearby Old City Cemetery.

### McIver's Bluff Celebration (all ages)
Last weekend in September, downtown Dyersburg; (731) 285–3433. Free.

McIver's Bluff is what the area used to be called before it was renamed Dyersburg, and the people come together to celebrate their shared heritage and culture.

Delicious food, handmade crafts, face painting, music, balloon animals, and games of all kinds are sure to keep the kids happy.

## Where To Eat

**Abe's Ribeye Barn,** 500 Henry Street; (731) 285–4648. Open for dinner only. As the name implies, this eatery specializes in steaks, but it also serves seafood and salads. $

**Neil's,** 470 Mall Boulevard, Suite A; (731) 285–2628. For years, Neil's has served some of the best barbecue to be found in this part of the world. They pack family-sized barbecue picnics for those who want to take their dining experience in the out of doors. $

## Where To Stay

**Hampton Inn,** 2750 Mall Loop Road; (731) 285-4778. This hotel has an outdoor pool and accepts pets. Free continental breakfast every morning. $-$$

## For More Information

**Dyersburg/Dyer County Chamber of Commerce,** 2000 Commerce Avenue, Dyersburg, TN 38025; (731) 285–3433; www.dyercountynet.com. Open 8:00 A.M. to 5:00 P.M. Monday through Friday.

# Jackson

### Casey Jones Home and Railroad Museum (all ages)

**At exit 80A off I–40; (731) 668–1222. Open daily 9:00 A.M. to 8:00 P.M. (until 9:00 P.M. in the summer). $, free for children under 6.**

The legendary train engineer Casey Jones was living in Jackson when he took the throttle of "Old 382" on the night of April 30, 1900. Just outside Vaughn, Mississippi, Casey and his fireman came upon a stalled train on the same tracks. Knowing that it was too late to come to a complete stop, he told the fireman to jump, but Casey remained aboard, fighting the brakes and valiantly trying to stop the train. The crash occurred, but Casey had slowed down the train enough so that he was the only casualty of the wreck. Casey immediately became a folk hero, and his experience has been recounted for a century in story and song.

The house he was living in at the time of his death is now the Casey Jones Home and Railroad Museum. It is located within the Casey Jones Village complex in Jackson. Visitors get a chance to learn about the man through exhibits and a fifteen-minute video. There is also a model train exhibit in an 1890s railcar, as well as a full-size steam locomotive outside.

### Brooks Shaw and Son's Old Country Store Restaurant
(all ages) 🛍️ 🍴

**56 Casey Jones Lane; (731) 668–1223 or (800) 748–9588. Open daily.**

In addition to the museum, the Casey Jones Village offers the 500-seat Brooks Shaw and Son's Old Country Store Restaurant, which features three family-style buffets each day. Children ten and under pay 30 cents times their age for their meal. If you like hearty country breakfasts, you've come to the right place. You can enjoy the buffet or order from a menu that features everything from Tennessee country ham to homemade biscuits. Breakfast ordered from the menu is always available, even if the breakfast buffet has already closed down.

Inside the Old Country Store Restaurant, there are more than 15,000 century-old antiques; a 6,000-square-foot gift, confectionery, and souvenir shop; and an 1890s ice cream parlor.

### Cypress Grove Nature Park (all ages)

**Highway 70 West, west of Jackson; (731) 425–8364. Open year-round. Free.**

A wonderful outdoor family adventure is a trip to the Cypress Grove Nature Park, owned by the city of Jackson. It's a great place to get a close-up view of the flora and fauna of this part of the state. You can walk through the 165-acre cypress forest on a

2-mile-long, elevated boardwalk. Along the path you'll walk among bald cypress and water tupelo trees and acres of colorful wildflowers. There's also a good chance you'll see hawks, the barred owl, muskrats, great egrets, white-tailed deer, and many other creatures that call the park home. In the spring this is a great place to view migratory wetland songbirds.

There's a visitor center, where guided tours begin, and the Raptor Center, which has six large enclosures full of birds of prey. This is a great place, known mostly to the locals.

### N.C. & St. L. Depot and Railroad Museum (all ages)
582 South Royal Street; (731) 425–8223. Open 10:00 A.M. to 3:00 P.M. Monday through Saturday and by appointment. **Free.**

In 1886 Tennesseans received a charter to build a railroad from Memphis to Knoxville through Jackson and Nashville. The first train arrived in Jackson on June 1, 1888. The present depot building was completed about 1910. Now restored, the building features a museum and a model-railroad display.

## Other Things to See and Do

**Britton Lane Battlefield** (ages 6 and up), 280 Britton Lane; (731) 935–2209. **Free.** A restored Civil War–era cabin, this building was used during the war as a hospital by both armies.

**Lake Graham** (all ages), 300 Hurts Chapel Road; (731) 423 4937. **Free.** A great fishing lake. You'll find everything you need here, including bait, tackle, rental boats, boat ramps, and a picnic area.

**Pinson Mounds State Archaeological Area** (all ages), 460 Ozier Road; (731) 988–5614. Open Monday through Saturday 8:30 A.M. to 4:30 P.M. and Sunday 1:00 to 5:00 P.M. This is the site of a dozen historic ceremonial mounds, built by ancient native peoples. One in particular, Saul's Mound, is the second largest such mound in the United States. In the third week of September, Pinson Mounds has a celebration, ArcheoFest, during which time there is dancing and singing by Native Americans, booths featuring Native American food and jewelry, storytelling, nature walks, and wildlife demonstrations. Admission: $, per car, **free** on Tuesday.

**Wildlife in Wood Studio** (ages 10 and up), Casey Jones Village; (731) 668–2782. **Free.** This shop, in the gazebo in front of the country store, features a life-size carved eagle that took more than 23,000 hours to create. The resident artist is there most days.

## Where to Eat

**Carl Perkins' "Suedes" Restaurant,** 2263 North Highland Avenue; (731) 664–1956. This restaurant has the feel of a museum, as your family dines surrounded by memorabilia of the late famous rockabilly and blues singer and songwriter, best known for his song "Blue Suede Shoes." His family still runs the place, and they have a wide variety of fare from which to choose, all with some connection to a song. Check out their "Whole Lotta Steakin' Goin' On." $–$$

**Old Town Spaghetti Store,** 550 Carriage House Drive; (731) 668–4937. $

## Where to Stay

**Casey Jones Station Inn,** Casey Jones Village, I–40 at Highway 45 Bypass; (731) 668–3636 or (800) 628–2812. Families can sleep in one of the two original red cabooses or an 1890s railcar suite. Additional rooms and a pool are also available. $$

**Comfort Inn,** 1963 Highway 45 Bypass; (731) 668–4100 or (800) 228–5150. $$–$$$

**Holiday Inn,** 541 Carriage House Drive; (731) 668–6000 or (800) HOLIDAY. $$$

## For More Information

**Jackson/Madison County Convention and Visitors Bureau,** 314 East Main Street, Jackson, TN 38301; (731) 425–8333 or (800) 498–4748; www.jacksontncvb.com. Open 8:30 A.M. to 4:30 P.M. Monday through Thursday and 8:30 A.M. to 4:00 P.M. Friday.

## Amazing
# Tennessee Facts

The official Tennessee wild animal is the raccoon.

# Henderson

### Chickasaw State Park (all ages)
**Highway 100, 8 miles west of Henderson; (731) 989–5141 or (800) 458–1752. Open year-round. Free. Fees charged for various activities.**

Before Andrew Jackson purchased it in 1818, the area that makes up this 14,400-acre state park was part of the vast land holdings of the Chickasaw Nation. Many miles of fire roads and trails wind through the scenic timberlands.

The park's Lake Placid offers paddleboating, fishing, and swimming. The park also has a restaurant open for dinner Wednesday through Sunday and for breakfast and lunch on Saturday and Sunday. In-park accommodations include cabins and tent, RV, and wrangler campsites.

## For More Information

**Henderson/Chester County Chamber of Commerce,** P.O. Box 1976, Main Street, Henderson, TN 38340; (731) 989–5222. Open 8:30 A.M. to 4:00 P.M. Monday through Friday.

# Adamsville/Shiloh

### Buford Pusser Home and Museum (ages 6 and up)

342 Pusser Street; (731) 632–4080. Open 11:00 A.M. to 5:00 P.M. Monday through Friday, Saturday 9:00 A.M. to 5:00 P.M., and Sunday 1:00 to 5:00 P.M. May through October. November through April the site closes at 4:00 P.M. Admission: $.

Proclaiming their community as the "Biggest Little Town in Tennessee," the residents of Adamsville are proud that their town was once home to one of America's most celebrated lawmen, Buford Pusser. The home in which he was living in 1974 when he died is now the Buford Pusser Home and Museum. Pusser was sheriff of this county from 1964 to 1970 and had a widespread reputation as a no-nonsense, hard-nosed lawman. His exploits were the basis of the three Walking Tall movies.

His years as a lawman were not easy ones. He was shot eight times, knifed seven times, and gunned down in an ambush that killed his wife. Many still believe that the flaming auto crash that took his life was no accident. The house is much as he left it on the day he died, and the museum exhibits include everything from his credit cards to his toothbrush. The famous walking stick he used in the movies is also on display.

### Shiloh National Military Park (all ages)

1055 Pittsburgh Landing Road, off Highway 22, south of Adamsville; (731) 689–5696 (visitor center), (731) 689–5275 (headquarters). Open daily 8:00 A.M. to 5:00 P.M. $.

Shiloh was the first major battle in the western theater of the Civil War, and when the last wisp of cannon smoke cleared on April 7, 1862, the casualty count for the two-day battle numbered more than 23,000. Today the Shiloh National Military Park is located on the site of the battle and offers an in-depth look at what took place. There are approximately 500 markers explaining the battle. They are color-coded so you can tell

## Tracking Civil War **Soldiers**

The National Park Service's Web site, www.nps.gov, contains information on Civil War soldiers. Log onto the site, then click on Links to the Past. That will take you to the Civil War Soldiers and Sailors System, where you can find basic information about servicemen who served on both sides during the war, as well as related information. Currently about 90 percent of the names of the 4.5 million servicemen known to have been in the war are in the system.

which army each refers to, and the shape of the marker tells you whether the event happened on the first or second day of the battle. The battle was very complex, but the markers make it easy to follow.

In the visitor center a film, *Shiloh—Portrait of a Battle,* is shown every thirty minutes, and you can pick up a map for a 9½-mile self-guided auto tour as well. The park also has a bookstore, picnic area, national cemetery, and the Shiloh Indian Mounds National Historic Landmark.

## Where to Eat

**Hagy's Catfish Hotel,** North Highway 22, Shiloh; (731) 689–3327. Named one of the top ten catfish restaurants in the United States by the Catfish Institute in 1997. On the banks of the Tennessee River just north of the battlefield. Children's menu. $

**Pusser's,** 142 Main Street; (731) 632–1199. The late Buford Pusser's daughter operates this casual restaurant. $

## Where to Stay

**Deerfield Inn,** 414 East Main Street (High way 64), Adamsville; (731) 632–2100. $$

## For More Information

**Hardin County Convention and Visitors Bureau,** 507 Main Street, Savannah, 38372; (731) 925–8181 or (800) 552–FUNN; www .tourhardincounty.org. Open 9:00 A.M. to 5:00 P.M. Monday through Saturday and 1:00 to 5:00 P.M. Sunday.

**McNairy County Chamber of Commerce,** 144 Cypress Street, P.O. Box 7, Selmer, TN 38375; (731) 645–6360; www .mcnairy.com. Open 8:30 A.M. to 5:00 P.M. Monday through Friday.

# Savannah/Pickwick Dam

**Tennessee River Museum** (all ages)
507 Main Street (in the old post office building), Savannah; (731) 925–2364 or (800) 552–FUNN. Open 9:00 A.M. to 5:00 P.M. Monday through Saturday and 1:00 to 5:00 P.M. Sunday. $, **free** for children under 17.

The Tennessee River Museum in Savannah is a tribute to the Tennessee River—from Paducah, Kentucky, to Muscle Shoals, Alabama—and the influences it has had on the people who lived and worked along it. Exhibit areas include displays on the early steamboats that plied the river, paleontology, archaeology, and the Civil War.

### Pickwick Landing State Park (all ages)
**Highway 57; (731) 689–3135 or (800) 250–8615. Open year-round. Free. Fees charged for various activities.**

A water sportsman's paradise awaits at the Pickwick Dam, close to where Highway 57 and Highway 128 cross south of Savannah. The Pickwick Landing State Park, on the shores of the Pickwick Reservoir, offers a full-service marina, boat rentals, overnight docking slips, three public launching ramps, a new 125-room inn, cabins, a rustic restaurant specializing in southern cooking, an eighteen-hole championship golf course, campsites, a Laundro-mat, and miles of hiking trails within the park's 1,400 acres. The headwaters near the dam offer some of the best smallmouth bass fishing you'll find anywhere, thus earning the lake the reputation as the "smallmouth bass capital of the world." They also have many catfish tournaments.

From the park it is possible to take a boat through the Pickwick Dam lock system for a 150-mile scenic cruise up the Tennessee River that passes Shiloh National Military Park, the historic downtown section of Savannah, and the Tennessee National Wildlife Refuge.

### National Catfish Derby (ages 6 and up)
**Pickwick Landing State Park, call Chamber of Commerce for more information at (731) 925–8181.**

Every summer for more than fifty years, Pickwick Landing State Park has been the site of this six-week-long catfish tournament. People of all ages are encouraged to try their luck at catching the bewhiskered fish not only at Pickwick but anywhere along the Tennessee River. The culmination of the event is a catfish cook-off, a hush puppy cook-off, a Biggest Catfish contest, and the World Championship of Catfishing, where the results of the six weeks of fishing are compared and celebrated. The world champion catfisher gets a cash prize. Admission to compete in the Catfish Derby depends on the particular competition; kids get to participate for **free.**

## Other Things to See and Do

**Savannah Historic Trail and District** (all ages), downtown; (731) 925–2364 or (800) 552–FUNN. **Free.** Historic markers, scenic river overlooks, walkways, and other areas focusing on Savannah's Civil War history, Alex Haley, Native Americans, and the Trail of Tears.

## Where to Eat

**Christie's,** Highway 1285, Savannah; (731) 925–5566. Breakfast and lunch buffet, cat-fish, steaks, seafood, and chicken. $

**Pickwick Inn,** Pickwick Landing State Park, Highway 57; (731) 689–3135 or (800) 250–8615. Breakfast, lunch, and dinner menu, plus daily buffet. $

**Pickwick Inn,** Pickwick Landing State Park, Highway 57; (731) 689–3135 or (800) 250–8615. Offers 125 rooms, ten cabins, and campsites. $–$$$

## Where to Stay

**Days Inn,** 1318 Pickwick Road, Savannah; (731) 925–5505. $–$$

**Hampton Inn,** 90 Old South Road, Highway 57, Pickwick; (731) 689–3031 or (800) HAMP-TON. $$

## For More Information

**Hardin County Convention and Visitors Bureau,** 507 Main Street, Savannah, TN 38372; (731) 925–8181 or (800) 552–FUNN; www.tourhardincounty.org. Open 9:00 A.M. to 5:00 P.M. Monday through Saturday and 1:00 to 5:00 P.M. Sunday.

# LaGrange/Grand Junction

### Historic District (all ages)
Highway 57; (901) 878–1246. Free.

The quaint village of LaGrange is located just a few miles north of Mississippi. We should all be thankful the residents of the area have been able to shun most aspects of modern commercialization through the years. LaGrange was the antebellum center of wealth, education, and culture, having had two colleges, four academies, two newspapers, and 3,000 residents in 1862. Today about 160 people call LaGrange home.

A smattering of antiques and crafts shops are located in several restored buildings. Among them is the LaGrange General Store. Built in 1892, the store is a town landmark. Less than a block away is the Trading Post Antiques shop, located in an 1880s building. Shops are usually open on weekends but not always during the week.

### National Bird Dog Museum and Field Trial Hall of Fame and Wildlife Heritage Center (all ages)
505 West Highway 57, Grand Junction; (901) 764–2058 or (901) 764–3396. Open 10:00 A.M. to 4:00 P.M. Tuesday through Saturday and 1:00 to 4:00 P.M. Sunday. Free.

Each February the National Field Trial Championships, the Super Bowl of bird-dogging, is held on the 18,600-acre Ames Plantation (4275 Buford Ellington Road, off Highway 18, north of Highway 57), but bird-dog owners and aficionados gather in the small town of Grand Junction a few miles away on Highway 57.

At the National Bird Dog Museum and Field Trial Hall of Fame, the dedication plaque for the facility, which opened in 1991, tells it all: DEDICATED TO PRESERVING THE PAST, PROTECTING THE FUTURE FOR SPORTING DOG FANCIERS THE WORLD OVER.

Even if the kids don't understand bird-dogging, they'll enjoy their visit here. There are several interesting displays, including many species of stuffed game birds and animals. A gallery displays paintings, photographs, and other dog-related artifacts and memorabilia. The volunteers who run this place love their canines and are more than willing to spend as much time with you as possible, pointing out things and telling you some great dog tales.

## Home for the **Holidays Festival**

The architecture in this part of the state is magnificent. Stately homes, churches, and plantations dot the landscape. Although you can view many of the structures from a distance throughout the year, an organized historic building tour is held during the Christmas season in Somerville. The tour is done by candlelight and in carriages, to add to the ambience of the event. The tour consists of at least four historic homes and one church. After the tour, there is caroling in the courthouse, apple cider, and arts and crafts vendors selling their wares. Tours cost $10.00 for adults, and $5.00 for children under twelve. Contact the Fayette County Chamber at (901) 465–8690 for more information.

## For More Information

**Fayette County Chamber of Commerce,** P.O. Box 411, 107 West Court Square, Somerville, TN 38068; (901) 465–8690; www.fayettecountychamber.com. Open 9:00 A.M. to 5:00 P.M. Monday through Friday.

**Hardeman County Chamber of Commerce,** 500 West Market Street, Bolivar, TN 38008; (731) 658–6554; www.hardeman countytn.org. Open 9:00 A.M. to 4:00 P.M. Monday through Friday.

# Brownsville

### West Tennessee Delta Heritage Center (all ages)
121 Sunnyhill Cove, off I–40 at exit 56; (731) 779–9000. Open 9:00 A.M. to 5:00 P.M. Monday through Saturday and 1:00 to 5:00 P.M. Sunday (closes early during winter). Free.

This welcome center has a variety of visual displays and information on western Tennessee. There's a music room, Hatchie River room, and cotton museum room, all filled with interesting objects and educational information.

### Sleepy John Estes House (all ages)
**West Tennessee Delta Heritage Center, 121 Sunnyhill Cove, off I–40 at exit 56; (731) 779–9000. Open 9:00 A.M. to 5:00 P.M. Monday through Saturday and 1:00 to 5:00 P.M. Sunday. Free.**

Blues music legend Sleepy John Estes was born in Nutbush and lived in the area most of his life. This house, where he was living when he died in 1977, was relocated from Brownsville's Main Street in 1999. Inside are photographs and biographies, and you can listen to tapes of his music. Other Brownsville-area legends, such as Yank Rachell, Hammie Nixon, Tina Turner, and Alex Harvey, are highlighted as well.

### College Hill Center (ages 5 and up)
**129 North Grand Avenue, Brownsville; (731) 772–4883. Open 10:00 A.M. to 4:00 P.M. Monday and Wednesday through Friday and 1:00 to 5:00 P.M. Sunday. Free.**

Nestled among the old structures in the Brownsville historic district, this building includes the Felsenthal Lincoln Collection, a large private collection of Abraham Lincoln books and memorabilia, as well as the Haywood County Museum.

# Talented Tennesseans

From east to west, Tennessee has produced some of the world's best-known musical entertainers.

Bristol, in the northeast part of the state, is known as the birthplace of country music and was home to such industry pioneers as the Carter family and Jimmie Rodgers as well as Ernie Ford. Other East Tennessee towns have given us the likes of Chet Atkins (Luttrell), Kenny Chesney (Luttrell), Dolly Parton (Sevierville), and Roy Acuff (Maynardville).

Chattanooga, in the southeastern part of the state, was the birthplace of Bessie Smith, known as the Empress of the Blues. In the northwestern corner of the state there's Tiptonville, where rockabilly's Carl Perkins was born. The tiny southwestern Tennessee town of Nutbush is the hometown of rock and soul singer Tina Turner and of legendary bluesman "Sleepy" John Estes. Then there's Memphis, known for its blues and, of course, as home to the King of Rock and Roll, Elvis Presley.

## Other Things to See and Do

**Hatchie National Wildlife Refuge** (all ages), 4172 Highway 76 South; (731) 772–0501. **Free.**

## Where to Eat

**Back Yard Bar-Be-Cue,** 703 East Main Street, Brownsville; (731) 772–1121. $

**Olympic Steakhouse,** 326 West Main Street, Brownsville; (731) 772–5555. Casual family restaurant. $$

**ZZ's Kream Kastle,** 16 South Grand Avenue, Brownsville; (731) 772–3132. Sandwiches, steaks, ice cream, and doughnuts. $

## Where to Stay

**Best Western,** 110 Sunnyhill Cove, off I–40 at exit 56; (731) 779–2389 or (800) 528–1234. $

**Holiday Inn Express,** 120 Sunnyhill Cove, off I–40 at exit 56; (731) 772–4030 or (800) HOLIDAY. $$

## For More Information

**Brownsville/Haywood County Chamber of Commerce,** 121 West Main Street, Brownsville, TN 38012; (731) 772–2193; www.brownsville-haywoodtn.com. Open 8:30 A.M. to 4:30 P.M. Monday through Friday.

# Nutbush

Just up Highway 19 from Brownsville, in the small community of Nutbush, Anna Mae Bullock was born on November 26, 1939, to sharecropper parents. She was a young girl surrounded by cotton fields and dreams. With a few lucky breaks and an immense amount of talent, she moved away, got married, and became Tina Turner, the queen of rock and roll.

The sharecropper's shack in which she was born has long since disappeared, but the farm where that shack stood still stands, as does the elementary school where she was educated. The Nutbush Grocery Store, which she visited quite often, is still standing and is now a soul food restaurant. The churches she sang in on Sundays are still there. The high school she attended in Brownsville still stands, as does the junior high school she attended in nearby Ripley.

### Nutbush Tina Turner Heritage Center (ages 8 and up) 
255 Cottondale Drive, Brownsville; (731) 772–4265. Tours by appointment only. $$$$.

Sharon Norris, another Nutbush native and a relative of Tina Turner, has created a small business centered on the entertainer. If you give Sharon a call, she'll invite you over, show you a small exhibit she has at the Nutbush Tina Turner Heritage Center, then load you up in her car and take you on a trip through the area, telling you fascinating stories about the superstar.

She also organizes the Tina Turner Day Celebration, which takes place each year in June. The tours include as many people as she can squeeze into her car, and last as long as you want.

## Amazing Tennessee Facts

Nutbush is named for the area's beautiful nut-bearing trees planted among the acres of cotton fields.

## Where to Eat

**Nutbush Grocery Store,** Highway 19 West, Nutbush; (731) 772–4544. Soul food. $

## For More Information

**Brownsville/Haywood County Chamber of Commerce,** 121 West Main Street, Brownsville, TN 38012; (731) 772–2193; www.brownsville-haywoodtn.com. Open 8:30 A.M. to 4:30 P.M. Monday through Friday.

# Henning

### The Alex Haley House Museum (ages 6 and up)
**200 South Church Street; (731) 738–2240. Open 10:00 A.M. to 5:00 P.M. Tuesday through Saturday and 1:00 to 5:00 P.M. Sunday. Admission: $.**

The Alex Haley House Museum honors the author whose novel *Roots* won him the 1976 Pulitzer Prize as well as international acclaim. Haley's boyhood home is the first state-owned historic site devoted to the African American in Tennessee.

It was on the front porch of this small house that Haley soaked up the stories of his family's history as told to him by his grandmother and her sisters. The stories began with Kunta Kinte, brought to America in 1767 from West Africa and sold into slavery, and continued through five generations of African Americans struggling to gain independence and freedom. They were stories Haley never forgot, and he was subsequently led by them to tell the story he wrote in *Roots*.

The entire house has been restored and is furnished as it would have been when Haley lived there. The museum is a splendid interpretation of rural small-town life in the 1900s in western Tennessee, and each room tells a different story about Haley's life. There are many family portraits on the walls and mementos and furnishings from the family. Haley died on February 10, 1992. He is buried in the front yard of the house.

### Fort Pillow State Historic Park (all ages)
**Highway 207 just off Highway 87 (18 miles west of Henning); (731) 738–5581. Open 8:00 A.M. to 10:00 P.M. daily (visitor center open 8:00 A.M. to 4:30 P.M. Monday through Friday). Free.**

Fort Pillow State Historic Park was the site of a Civil War skirmish on April 12, 1864. Gen. Nathan Bedford Forrest led his 1,500 Confederate cavalrymen into the fort and overwhelmed the 500 soldiers who were stationed there. After a few minutes of fighting, the Union troops broke rank, ran down the bluffs to the Mississippi River, and became trapped between the Confederates and the muddy river. When the smoke had cleared, more than 250 Union soldiers had been killed, with the South losing 14. The northern newspapers were soon calling it the Fort Pillow Massacre, prompting an investigation by the Committee on the Conduct of War.

Today a replica of the original fort has been built, and the still-extant earthworks can be seen. An interpretive center has an audiovisual presentation explaining the battle and an exhibit of artifacts recovered from the fort's remains. A study by the state's division of archaeology has uncovered a wealth of information, including clothes, tools, utensils, and skull fragments.

The site includes a campground, picnic areas, and 15 miles of hiking trails.

## For More Information

**Lauderdale County Chamber of Commerce,** 123 South Jefferson Street, Ripley, TN

38063; (731) 635–9541; www.laudcc.com. Open 8:30 A.M. to 4:30 P.M. Monday through Friday.

# Memphis

The muddy Mississippi serves as the western boundary of both the state of Tennessee and Memphis, the state's most populated city. Through the years several residents of the city have had tremendous influence on both the blues and rock and roll.

## Beale Street Historic District (all ages)
**Downtown Memphis; (901) 526–0110.**

Beale Street, in downtown Memphis, is considered the spiritual home of the blues. During its heyday in the 1920s and '30s, Beale Street was probably the best-known street in America. The zoot suit originated here, and Machine Gun Kelly peddled bootleg liquor on the streets. Today the area is still a mecca for musicians and, as part of a major entertainment district in Memphis, a haven for tourists and blues aficionados.

A convenient way to start a tour of Beale Street and of Memphis is to stop by the police museum at 159 Beale Street. You can pick up maps and brochures there. On Friday, Saturday, and Sunday, there are visitor-information staffers on hand to provide more information. An official Memphis Visitor Information Center has recently opened in East Memphis. It is located at 12036 Arlington Trail, off I–40. The telephone number is (901) 543–5375.

Beale Street's claim to fame all began in 1909 when a young bandleader and trumpet player named William Christopher Handy wrote a campaign song for Memphis mayoral candidate E. H. Crump. The song and the candidate turned out to be winners, and the song, "Memphis Blues," became the first blues number to be published. Handy followed up that hit with "St. Louis Blues." These classics established Handy, a native of Muscle Shoals, Alabama, as the father of the blues and Beale Street as its home. Today Handy's statue overlooks the street from a shady park named in his honor.

The Beale Street Historic District stretches several blocks east of the river bluffs and has a huge selection of restaurants, blues and rock clubs featuring live music, boutiques, and historic structures.

## Classic **Blues**

Often referred to as the Father of the Blues, W. C. Handy penned such classic blues songs as "St. Louis Blues," "Beale Street Blues," and "Yellow Dog Blues."

### A. Schwab's Dry Goods Store (all ages)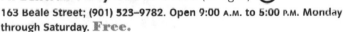

163 Beale Street; (901) 523-9782. Open 9:00 A.M. to 5:00 P.M. Monday through Saturday. **Free.**

You may not feel comfortable taking the kids into the clubs, but there is a lot for families to do on Beale Street, including a fun trip to A. Schwab's Dry Goods Store, operating on Beale Street since 1876. The shelves are stocked with all sorts of "life's little necessities," including clerical collars, 99-cent neckties, men's pants to size 74, and the largest selection of hats and caps in Memphis.

Management's philosophy is reflected in the official slogan of the family-run operation: "If you can't find it at A. Schwab's, you are better off without it!" The store also has its own Beale Street Museum and offers **free** guided tours of the store and the museum. Each visitor gets a **free** souvenir.

### Graceland (ages 6 and up)

3734 Elvis Presley Boulevard; (800) 238-2000; www.elvis.com. Open 9:00 A.M. to 5:00 P.M. daily year-round (the mansion is closed Tuesday, November through February). Admission: $-$$, Platinum tour $$$-$$$$.

Elvis Presley, the undisputed king of rock and roll, called Memphis his home. Although he died in 1977, Elvis is more popular today than ever, especially in Memphis. His heirs have done well with what he left. His estate was worth $4.9 million when he died. Today it's worth more than $100 million. The complex that surrounds Graceland Mansion, where Elvis lived for twenty years, is alive with shops, restaurants, and Elvis attractions.

Graceland is probably one of the most famous private homes in America. The huge gates at the entrance to the mansion could be called the threshold to the rock and roll mecca. Fans visit regularly, and when they don't go inside, they stand outside the gates and gaze at the mansion.

A tour through the mansion takes you inside the world in which Elvis lived during the periods when he was escaping the pressures of performing. This was his home, his refuge. On the tour you'll visit the all-white living room; his famed jungle-room den; his business office; his trophy building, which houses an enormous collection of gold records, awards, clothing, jewelry, and photographs; and his racquetball building. The tour ends with a visit to the Meditation Garden, where Elvis and members of his family have been laid to rest.

The tour begins at the Graceland Plaza, located at 3675 Elvis Presley Boulevard across the street from the mansion. That's where you'll also find the Elvis Presley Automobile Museum, the Sincerely Elvis Museum, and the Airplanes Tour, (all included in Platinum Tour; separate admission, $). The tour of the mansion includes a twenty-two-minute film that traces the highlights of Elvis's career. Mansion tours last about ninety minutes.

## Elvis Week

Each year in mid-August, Memphis hosts Elvis Week, an action-packed, citywide celebration that includes trivia contests, candlelight vigils, and special tours that include Humes Junior High School, where Elvis graduated in 1953.

### Sun Studios (ages 6 and up)
**706 Union Avenue; (901) 521–0664 or (800) 441–6249; www.sunstudio.com. Open 10:00 A.M. to 6:00 P.M. daily. $$, free for children under 12.**

Sun Studios, often referred to as the "most famous recording studio in the world," is thought of as the birthplace of rock and roll. Before he hit the big time, Elvis Presley recorded a song for his mother at Sun Studios. He was charged $4.00 for studio time. Founded by the legendary Sam Phillips, Sun was the first studio to record such musicians as Presley, Jerry Lee Lewis, Carl Perkins, and Johnny Cash.

Sun Studios is still a working recording studio and is open to the public. On the guided tour you'll hear quite a few inside stories about Elvis and his various recording sessions, and you'll get a chance to listen to tapes of many of those early sessions. There's a gallery upstairs full of memories, photos, and musical instruments. Sun Studios is located just a few blocks from Baptist Hospital, where Elvis was pronounced dead on August 16, 1977.

# African American Visitors Guide

The Tennessee Department of Tourist Development (615–741–2159) puts out a splendid publication called *The African-American Guide to Cultural and Historic Sites*, which highlights interesting attractions throughout Tennessee. Several Memphis locations are included.

Memphis has the ninth-largest black population in the nation, and 43.5 percent of all blacks in Tennessee live in Memphis. It's also the site of the country's largest African American parade, the Memphis Kemet Jubilee, formerly known as the Cotton Maker's Jubilee. The jubilee has been held since 1936. Each May more than 100,000 people join in this tribute to King Cotton. Call (901) 774–1118 for more information.

### National Civil Rights Museum (all ages)
450 Mulberry Street; (901) 521–9699; www.civilrightsmuseum.org. Open September through May, 9:00 A.M. to 5:00 P.M. Monday through Saturday and 1:00 to 5:00 P.M. Sunday. $$, free for children under 4. Free admission each Monday from 3:00 to 5:00 P.M.

The National Civil Rights Museum is the nation's first museum dedicated to documenting the complete history of the American civil rights movement. Constructed on the site of the Lorraine Motel, where Martin Luther King Jr. was assassinated on April 4, 1968, the center features an interpretive education center, audiovisual displays, interactive exhibits, and civil rights memorabilia. The center brings to life the most significant epoch of modern American history as it chronicles the sights, sounds, and tensions of the civil rights movement.

### LeMoyne-Owen College (ages 8 and up)
807 Walker; (901) 774–9090.

LeMoyne-Owen College is one of America's oldest African American colleges. Steele Hall, the private school's first building, served as Memphis's only high school for blacks from 1919 to 1925.

### Slavehaven/Burkle Estate (all ages)
826 North Second Street; (901) 527–3427. Open 10:00 A.M. to 4:00 P.M. Monday through Saturday (closed Tuesday and Wednesday during the winter). $.

This was a station on the Underground Railroad. Built in 1849 by a German immigrant, it appears the house was used to hide and ferry African Americans to the North from the day it was constructed. Recent discoveries have revealed Trails that led to outside rail and river routes.

## Memphis Zoo (all ages)

**200 Prentiss Place, in Overton Park; (901) 276–WILD; www.memphiszoo.org. Open 9:00 A.M. to 5:00 P.M. daily (until 6:00 P.M. March through October). $$, free for children under 2. Tennessee residents with an ID are admitted free from 4:00 P.M. to closing on Tuesday. Several children's amusement rides are available for $1.00 per ride.**

Zoos are always a fun outing for families, and the Memphis Zoo is no exception. Housing more than 3,000 animals representing 400 species from around the world, the Memphis Zoo is located on more than seventy wooded acres. You'll find the zoo a calm, laid-back place to visit. The Cat Country exhibit, which houses 13 species of cats, is a great way to view some beautiful animals. There's also an African veldt, an aquarium building, a Primate Canyon exhibit, and a new panda exhibit.

Memphis takes its name from a city in ancient Egypt, and the zoo carries that association along in its Egyptian entrance gates, complete with colorful hieroglyphics.

## The Pyramid (ages 4 and up)
**1 Auction Avenue; (901) 521–9675.**

When the time came for a new arena in Memphis, it was only natural, some say, that it should also be a tribute to the city's Egyptian connection and be built in the shape of a pyramid. That's the thinking behind the thirty-two-story stainless-steel structure known as the Pyramid, set along the Mississippi River in downtown Memphis. Rising out of the delta like a shining diamond, the base of the 321-foot-tall building is longer than six football fields. Inside, the multipurpose facility features a 22,500-seat venue for sporting events, family shows, exhibits, and concerts.

## Memphis **in May**

For the entire month of May, Memphis hosts the Memphis in May International Festival. There are concerts, plays, specialty foods, amusement rides, and all kinds of other activities going on throughout the city.

## Libertyland (all ages)

**940 Early Maxwell Boulevard, at the Mid-South Fairgrounds; (901) 274–1776; www.libertyland.com. Open Saturday and Sunday April through mid-June, Wednesday through Sunday from June 16 through September. Closed Monday and Tuesday. Hours: noon to 9:00 P.M. weekdays, 10:00 A.M. to 9:00 P.M. Saturday, and noon to 9:00 P.M. Sunday. $–$$, free for children under 4.**

If the name Libertyland sounds patriotic, that's because the amusement park opened on July 4, 1976, during America's bicentennial. The park has loads of exciting thrill rides, as well as musical stage shows and one of the most beautiful antique carousels still in existence. The park's Zippin' Pippin wooden roller coaster—moved here from another park nearby—not only is the oldest operating coaster in the country but was also Elvis's favorite. He would rent out the entire park so he, his family, and friends could enjoy the coaster, as well as the rest of the rides, without being bothered by fans.

In front of the coaster's loading station, there's a restored coaster car and a big sign proclaiming that it was Elvis's favorite. Put the kids in the car, have them throw their hands up in the air as if they were going down a hill, and take a picture of them with the sign in the background.

In all, there are twenty-five rides, including eight for the younger members of the family.

### The Children's Museum of Memphis (all ages)
**2525 Central Avenue, on the Mid-South Fairgrounds; (901) 458–2678. Open 9:00 A.M. to 5:00 P.M. Tuesday through Saturday and noon to 5:00 P.M. Sunday. $, free for children under 1.**

Parents and kids both will discover a fun new world at the newly renovated Children's Museum of Memphis. Of course, parents don't have to play and learn along with the kids, but you'll probably want to. This place is a real hoot. You can crawl through a tree house, climb an eight-story skyscraper, help the little ones shop for their own groceries, watch them cash a check at the bank, and join with them as they command a 911 center.

They'll be able to "drive" a real car, sit in a wheelchair, or see what it's like being blind. Through the special exhibits, performances, and programs everyone learns something.

### Chucalissa Archaeological Museum (ages 4 and up)
**1987 Indian Village Drive; (901) 785–3160. Open May through November, 9:00 A.M. to 5:00 P.M. Tuesday through Saturday and 1:00 to 4:30 P.M. Sunday. Usually open for group bookings only during the winter. $, free for children under 4.**

Under the auspices of the University of Memphis, Chucalissa Archaeological Museum is a reconstruction of a prehistoric Native American village dating to the fifteenth century. Chucalissa, a Choctaw word meaning "abandoned house," features an archaeological park, a museum, earthworks, and a village on the site of an actual Mississippian-period community. Choctaw staff members provide guided tours and demonstrate traditional crafts. Inside the museum there are exhibits on the prehistory of the mid-South, stone tools and pottery, southeastern Native American culture, and a preserved archaeological excavation trench.

### Mud Island (all ages)
**125 North Front Street; (901) 576–7241 or (800) 507–6507. Open mid-April through October. $$, free for children under 4.**

Perhaps the most unusual educational experience in the state takes place on Mud Island, a fifty-two-acre park and entertainment complex dedicated to life on the Mississippi River. That's where you'll find the Mississippi River Museum, an eighteen-gallery facility that re-creates 10,000 years of history and folklore of the mighty Mississippi. There's a three-story reconstruction of an 1870s steamboat, intricate models of river craft, and a working steam engine with a paddle wheel. Via film you'll be able to relive the fires, floods, and epidemics that have caused heartbreaks to thousands along the river.

Outside, a leisurely stroll down 900 miles of the river, from Illinois to the Gulf of Mexico on the River Walk attraction, is both fun and educational. The twists and turns of the river are in miniature, complete with bridges, levees, and the streets of twenty river cities in mosaic. The 5-block-long flowing scale model includes ninety panels of fascinating information. You can learn a lot by taking the walk by yourselves, but if time permits, take a **free** guided tour. You'll have a lot more fun.

The model river dumps into the Gulf of Mexico, which also happens to be the state's largest chlorinated swimming pool, with 1.3 million gallons of water and 20,000 square feet of sand for beach play.

There are two ways to get out to the island. You can pay extra for parking in the lot at the end of the Auction Street Bridge, or you can take a monorail across as part of your admission charge. The monorail departs from 125 North Front Street.

### Memphis Queen Line Riverboats (all ages)

**Docks are at the foot of Monroe Avenue; (901) 527–5694. $$–$$$, free for children under 4. Special luncheon or dinner cruises cost extra.**

If you feel like experiencing the river firsthand after your visit to Mud Island, the folks at the Memphis Queen Line Riverboats can fulfill that wish. Their cruises down the mighty and majestic river take about an hour and a half, and you'll get a great view of the Pyramid and the rest of the Memphis skyline. You'll also get to see the huge floodplains along the river and the historic lineup of old cotton warehouses along Front Street. Cruises leave at various times, so call before you make your plans. There's a snack bar on board.

### Fire Museum of Memphis (all ages)

**118 Adams Avenue; (901) 320–5650. Open 9:00 A.M. to 5:00 P.M. Tuesday through Saturday and 1:00 to 5:00 P.M. Sunday. $, free for children under 3. Group rates.**

This interactive museum is housed in Fire Engine House No. 1, built in 1910. The museum contains artifacts dating back to the early 1900s and features a number of interesting and fun attractions, such as the Fire Room, which shows you what it feels like to be trapped inside a burning building.

### Memphis Pink Palace Museum and Planetarium (ages 3 and up)

**3050 Central Avenue; (901) 320–6320. Open 9:00 A.M. to 4:00 P.M. Monday through Thursday, 9:00 A.M. to 9:00 P.M. Friday and Saturday, and noon to 6:00 P.M. Sunday. Summer hours are extended one hour in the evenings Monday through Thursday. There are separate admission charges for the exhibits, the planetarium, and the IMAX theater. A combination ticket for all three is the best deal: $$–$$$.**

The Pink Palace Museum features the cultural and natural history of the mid-South region. Permanent exhibits include dinosaur fossils, seventy-million-year-old specimens of sea life, and a huge mineral collection. One exhibit you'll find especially interesting is a full-scale replica of America's first self-serve grocery store. The museum also offers an audiovisual journey through space and time in the Pink Palace Planetarium. Laser concerts are offered throughout the year, with a special Elvis laser show in August.

### Union Planters IMAX Theater (all ages)

**3050 Central Avenue; (901) 763–IMAX, (901) 320–6362 (reservations). $–$$.**

And finally, to get the *big picture* in Memphis, be sure to drop by Union Planters IMAX theater at the Pink Palace Museum. If you've never been to an IMAX theater, here's your chance to enjoy a totally new cinematic experience. The clarity of the high-tech images combined with the sensational stereo sound immerses the viewer in the film itself. It's awe-inspiring, even for the kids. The film is projected onto a screen four stories high by five stories wide.

## Other Things to See and Do

**Al's Tee Time Golf Practice Center** (all ages), 1884 East Raines Road; (901) 332–9481. Open 8:00 A.M. to dusk Monday through Saturday, with extended hours in summer. Pay per attraction. Two miniature golf courses, go-carts, a sixty-tee driving range, and baseball and softball batting cages.

**Dixon Gallery and Gardens** (ages 3 and up), 4339 Park Avenue; (901) 761–5250. Open 10:00 A.M. to 5:00 P.M. Tuesday through Saturday and 1:00 to 5:00 P.M. Sunday. Galleries closed but gardens open Monday. Art museum focusing on nineteenth-century French paintings, surrounded by seventeen acres of gardens and woodlands. $

**Main Street Trolley** (all ages), 547 North Main Street; (901) 274–6282. Check the change in your pocket—exact fare required. Open 6:00 A.M. to midnight Monday through Thursday, 6:00 A.M. to 1:00 A.M. Friday, 9:30 A.M. to 1:00 A.M. Saturday, and 10:00 A.M. to 6:00 P.M. Sunday. Antique trolleys serve several downtown attractions, including the Pyramid, the Pinch District, Memphis Cook Convention Center, Beale Street, Orpheum Theater, and the National Civil Rights Museum. It's fun to leave your car parked in the garage and take the trolley—your kids will love it. $

**Peabody Place Museum and Gallery**
(ages 8 and up), 119 South Main Street; (901)
532–ARTS. Open 10:00 A.M. to 5:30 P.M. Tuesday through Friday and noon to 5:00 P.M. Saturday and Sunday. This museum features one of the country's most extensive and rare collections of Chinese art. $

**Putt-Putt Golf and Games** (all ages), 5484 Summer Avenue; (901) 386–2992. Go-carts, a lighted golf driving range, bumper boats, a game room, three miniature golf courses, a swimming pool, batting cages, and more. Pay per attraction.

## Where to Eat

**Dyer's Burgers,** 205 Beale Street; (901) 527–3937. Burgers, shakes, and atmosphere that have been a part of Memphis since 1912. $

**Hard Rock Cafe,** 315 Beale Street; (901) 529–0007. $$

**Huey's,** 77 South Second Street; (901) 527–2700. There are several other locations around town. Winner of the best burger in town for more than a decade. They let you write on the walls here. $

**Rendezvous,** 52 South Second Street, rear; (901) 523–2746. This long-established restaurant specializes in charbroiled and dry-rub barbecue that has become world famous. It's part of the Memphis experience! $

## Where to Stay

**Elvis Presley's Heartbreak Hotel,** 3677 Elvis Presley Boulevard; (901) 332–1000 or (877) 777–0606  Elvis Presley Enterprises purchased an existing hotel across from Graceland, renovated it, and themed it to Elvis. **Free** in-room Elvis movies. $$$

**Madison Hotel,** 79 Madison Avenue; (901) 333–1200 or (866) 446–3674. Located in an old renovated bank building, the hotel is decorated in fifties-era Art Deco. The vault is now used as—get this—the exercise room! $$$$

**Marriott Hotel-Memphis,** 2625 Thousand Oaks Boulevard; (901) 362–6200 or (800) 627–3587. $$$$

**Park Place Hotel,** 5877 Poplar Avenue (I–240/Poplar Avenue); (901) 767–6300 or (800) 424–6423. $$–$$$

**Peabody Hotel,** 149 Union Avenue; (901) 529–4000 or (800) PEABODY. This historic hotel features world-famous ducks. Rates start at about $220 per night. $$$$

**Radisson Hotel,** 185 Union Avenue; (901) 528–1800 or (800) 333–3333. Full breakfast included. $$$$

**Sleep Inn at Court Square,** 40 North Front Street; (901) 522–9700. $$$

## For More Information

**Memphis Convention and Visitors Bureau,** 47 Union Avenue, Memphis, TN 38103; (901) 543–5300 or (800) 873–6282. Open 8:30 A.M. to 5:00 P.M. Monday through Friday.

**Visitor Information Center,** 119 North Riverside Drive, Memphis, TN 38103; (901) 543–5333 or (888) 633–9099; www.memphis travel.com. Open 9:00 A.M. to 6:00 P.M. daily.

# Annual Events

## JANUARY

**Elvis Presley Birthday Celebration**
Memphis
(800) 238–2000

**Reelfoot Eagle Watch Tours**
Reelfoot Lake State Park, Tiptonville
(731) 253–7756

**Wilderness Wildlife Week of Nature**
Pigeon Forge
(865) 429–7350

## FEBRUARY

**Annual Americana Sampler**
Nashville
(615) 227–2080

**Antiques and Garden Show of Nashville**
Nashville
(615) 352–1282

**Cherokee Indian Heritage and Sandhill Crane Viewing Days**
Birchwood
(423) 334–5496 or (423) 499–3584

**House and Garden Show**
Knoxville
(865) 637–4561

**Kroger St. Jude Tennis Championships**
Memphis
(901) 765–4400

**Smoky Mountain Storytelling Festival**
Pigeon Forge
(865) 429–7350

**West Tennessee Boat, Sport, and RV Show**
Jackson
(901) 584–7880 or (800) 225–7469

## MARCH

**Annual Heart of Country Antiques Show**
Nashville
(800) 862–1090

**A Mountain Quiltfest Pigeon Forge**
Pigeon Forge
(865) 429–7350

**NASCAR Busch and Winston Cup Series**
Bristol
(423) 764–1161

**Nashville Lawn and Garden Show**
Nashville
(615) 352–3863

**Wearin' o' the Green Irish Celebration**
Erin
(931) 289–5100

## APRIL

**Blount County Dogwood Arts Festival**
Maryville
(865) 983–2241

**Charlie Daniels Rodeo**
Murfreesboro
(615) 217–1855

**Dogwood Arts Festival**
Knoxville
(800) DOG–WOOD

**Dolly's Spring Parade**
Pigeon Forge
(865) 429–7350

**Main Street Festival**
Franklin
(615) 791–9924

**Mule Day**
Columbia
(931) 381–9557

**National Cornbread Festival**
South Pittsburg
(423) 837–0022

**Old Timers Day Festival**
Dickson
(615) 446–2393

**Spring Festival**
Townsend
(865) 448–6134

**Spring Wildflower Pilgrimage**
Gatlinburg
(865) 436–7318

**Teapot Festival**
Trenton
(731) 855–0973

**Tennessee Iris Festival**
Dresden
(731) 364–3787

**World's Biggest Fish Fry**
Paris
(731) 642–3431

# MAY

**Annual Tennessee Strawberry Festival**
Dayton
(423) 775–0361

**Casey Jones Train Fest**
Jackson
(731) 427–1565

**Colonial Fair**
Goodlettsville
(615) 859–7979

**Cosby Ramp Festival**
Cosby
(423) 625–9675

**Festival of British and Appalachian Culture**
Rugby
(423) 628–2441

**Forked Deer River Festival**
Jackson
(731) 427–1565

**Gatlinburg Scottish Festival and Games**
Gatlinburg
(865) 436–5346

**Iris Festival**
Greeneville
(423) 638–4111

**Iroquois Memorial Steeplechase**
Nashville
(615) 322–7450

**Mayfest Party in the Park**
Oak Ridge
(800) 887–3429

**Memphis in May International Festival**
Memphis
(901) 525–4611

**Middle Tennessee Strawberry Festival**
Portland
(615) 325–9032

**Nashville RiverStages**
Nashville
(615) 346–9000

**Poke Sallet Festival**
Gainesboro
(931) 268–0971

**Tennessee Crafts Fair**
Nashville
(615) 385–1904

**West Tennessee Strawberry Festival**
Humboldt
(731) 784–1842

## JUNE

**Chet Atkins' Musicians Days**
Nashville
(615) 256–9596

**Covered Bridge Celebration**
Elizabethton
(423) 547–3850

**Golden Fleece Festival**
Gallatin
(615) 451–3738

**International Country Music Fan Fair**
Nashville
(615) 889–7503

**Lester Flatt Birthday Celebration**
Sparta
(931) 738–3225

**National Catfish Derby**
Somerville
(731) 925–8181

**RC & Moon Pie Festival**
Bell Buckle
(931) 389–6574

**Rhododendron Festival**
Roan Mountain
(423) 772–0190

**Riverbend Festival**
Chattanooga
(423) 756–2212

**Shannon Street Blues and Heritage Festival**
Jackson
(901) 427–7573

**Tennessee Quarter Horse Association Hillbilly Classic**
Harriman
(800) 386–4686

**Tina Turner Day Celebration**
Nutbush
(731) 772–4265

**"Trash & Treasures"**
Cross Plains
(615) 654–2256

## JULY

**Annual Gatlinburg Craftsmen Fair**
Gatlinburg
(865) 436–7479

**Folk Medicine Festival**
Red Boiling Springs
(615) 699–2180

**Historic Jonesborough Days**
Jonesborough
(423) 753–5281

**July Fourth Celebration and**
**Anvil Shoot**
Norris
(865) 494–7680 or (865) 494–0514

**Lauderdale County Tomato Festival**
Ripley
(731) 635–9541

**The Official State and National**
**Championship Smithville Fiddlers'**
**Jamboree and Crafts Festival**
Smithville
(615) 597–8500

**St. Patrick's Irish Picnic**
McEwen
(931) 582–3417 or (931) 582–3986

**Scopes Trial Play and Festival**
Dayton
(423) 775–0361

**Tennessee/Kentucky Threshermen's**
**Association Show**
Adams
(615) 696–8179

**Uncle Dave Macon Days**
Murfreesboro
(615) 893–2369

***The Wataugans* Outdoor Drama**
Elizabethton
(423) 543–5808

**Watertown Jazz Festival**
Watertown
(615) 237–3318

# AUGUST

**Air Show**
Halls
(731) 836–7448

**Bell Witch Bluegrass Festival and Arts**
**and Crafts Show**
Adams
(615) 696–2589

**Cherokee Days of Recognition**
Red Clay State Historic Park, Cleveland
(423) 478–0339

**David Crockett Days**
Lawrenceburg
(931) 762–4911

**Elvis Week**
Memphis
(901) 332–3322

**450-Mile Highway 127 Corridor Sale**
From Covington, Kentucky, to Gadsden,
Alabama
(931) 879–9948

**NASCAR Busch and Winston Cup**
**Series**
Bristol
(423) 764–1161

**Reelfoot Lake Waterfowl Festival**
Tiptonville
(731) 538–2323

**Smoky Mountain Fiddlers Convention**
Loudon
(865) 458–9380

**Tennessee Walking Horse National**
**Celebration**
Shelbyville
(931) 684–5915

# SEPTEMBER

**ArcheoFest**
Pinson Mounds
(731) 988–5614

**Brownsville Bluesfest**
Brownsville
(731) 772–1831

**Clarksville RiverFest**
Clarksville
(931) 645–7476

**Coffee County Crafts Festival**
Manchester
(931) 728–7635

**Franklin Jazz Festival**
Franklin
(615) 794–1225 or (800) 356–3445

**Germantown Festival**
Germantown
(901) 757–9212

**Goodyear Car Show**
Union City
(731) 884–2255

**Harriman Labor Day Festival**
Harriman
(854) 882–5432

**Italian Street Fair**
Nashville
(615) 255–5600

**McIver's Bluff Celebration**
Dyersburg
(731) 285–3433

**Middle Tennessee Antique Tractor Show**
Cookeville
(931) 372–6967

**Middle Tennessee Pow Pow**
Lebanon
(615) 444–4899

**Mid-South Fair**
Memphis
(901) 274–8800

**Obion County Fall Festival**
Union City
(731) 885–8330

**Scott County Sorghum Festival**
Oneida
(423) 569–6900 or (800) 645–6905

**Smoky Mountain Harvest Festival**
Gatlinburg, Pigeon Forge, Sevierville
(800) 267–7088, (800) 251–9100, or
(800) 255–6411

**TACA Fall Crafts Fair**
Nashville
(615) 665–0502

**Tennessee River Folklife and Music Festival**
Camden
(731) 584–8395

**Tennessee State Fair**
Nashville
(615) 862–8980

**Upper Cumberland Quilt Festival**
Algood
(931) 537–3447

**Watts Bar Arts and Crafts Festival**
Ten Mile
(423) 334–5850

## OCTOBER

**Annual Candlelight Cemetery Tour**
Gallatin
(615) 451–3738

**Autumn Gold Festival**
Coker Creek
(423) 261–2242

**Celebration of Fine Crafts**
Chattanooga
(615) 385–1904

**Del Rio Days**
Del Rio
(423) 487–5863

**Fall Color Cruise and Folk Festival**
Chattanooga
(800) 766–2784

**The Great Casey Jones Balloon Classic**
Jackson
(901) 427–4431, ext. 10

**Harvest Festival and Southern Gospel Jubilee**
Pigeon Forge
(865) 428–9488

**Jack Daniel's World Championship Invitational Barbecue Cookoff**
Lynchburg
(931) 759–6180

**National Storytelling Festival**
Jonesborough
(423) 753–2171 or (800) 952–8392

**Newport Harvest Street Festival**
Newport
(423) 623–7201

**Nillie Bipper Arts and Crafts Festival**
Cleveland
(423) 478–3114

**Ocoee River Days and Whitewater Rodeo**
Ocoee Whitewater Center/Cherokee National Forest, Ducktown
(423) 496–5197

**Oktoberfest**
Chattanooga
(423) 265–5033, ext. 4

**Old Fashion Fall Fest**
Jellico
(423) 784–3275

**Old Hickory Antique and Classic Car Show**
Old Hickory
(615) 847–3780

**Pioneer Day on the Mountain**
Crossville
(931) 484–8444

**Reelfoot Lake Arts and Crafts Festival**
Tiptonville
(731) 885–0211

**Tennessee Fall Homecoming**
Norris
(865) 494–7680 or (865) 494–0514

**Webb School Arts and Crafts Festivals**
Bell Buckle
(931) 684–3482

# NOVEMBER

**Cheekwood's "Trees of Christmas"**
Nashville
(615) 353–6978

**Christmas at Graceland**
Memphis
(901) 332–3322 or (800) 238–2000

**"A Country Christmas" at Opryland USA**
Nashville
(615) 889–1000

**Deck the Falls**
Ruby Falls
(423) 821–2594

**Dollywood's "Smoky Mountain Christmas"**
Pigeon Forge
(423) 428–9488

**Rock City's Annual Enchanted Garden of Lights: A Holiday Spectacular**
Chattanooga
(706) 820–2531

**Smoky Mountain Winterfest**
Gatlinburg, Pigeon Forge, Sevierville
(800) 568–4748, (800) 251–9100 or (800) 255–6411

**Smoky Mountain Winterfest Kickoff**
Pigeon Forge
(865) 429–7350

# DECEMBER

**Christmas at Historic Rugby**
Rugby
(423) 628–2441

**Christmas in Old Appalachia**
Norris
(865) 494–7680 or (865) 494–0514

**Christmas in Olde Jonesborough**
Jonesborough
(800) 952–8392

**Country Christmas**
Kingsport
(423) 288–6071

**Dickens of a Christmas**
Franklin
(615) 595–1239

**Dickens on the Square**
Collierville
(901) 853–1666

**First Night Kingsport**
Kingsport
(423) 246–2017

**Home for the Holidays Festival**
Somervile
(901) 465–8690

**The Liberty Bowl Football Classic**
Memphis
(901) 795–7700

**Plantation Christmas Tour**
Maury County
(931) 381–7176 or (888) 852–1860

**A Victorian Christmas**
Savannah
(800) 552–3866

# Index

# About the Author

T. Jensen Lacey is the author of more than 600 newspaper and magazine articles and a contributor to the *Chicken Soup for the Soul* books. She has published five books including *Amazing Tennessee*. She lives in Clarksville, Tennessee. Visit Theresa's Web site at www.tjensenlacey.com.